RUNNING WITH THE BALL

RUNNING WITH THE BALL

Football's Foster Father

being the autobiography of H.C.A. Harrison
originally published under the title of

The Story of an Athlete: A Picture of the Past

with a Preface on Harrison's family origins
and his role in the start of Australian Rules football

edited by A. Mancini and G.M. Hibbins

LYNEDOCH PUBLICATIONS
MELBOURNE

© A. Mancini and G.M. Hibbins

First published in this edition 1987
Lynedoch Publications,
40 Brighton Street,
Melbourne, Victoria

National Library of Australia
Cataloguing-in-Publication entry:

Running with the ball
Includes index.
ISBN 0 7316 0481 4

1. Harrison, H.C.A. (Henry Colden Antill), 1836-1929.
2. Australian football — History. 3. Football
players — Australia — Biography. I. Mancini,
Anne, 1935- . II. Hibbins, G.M. (Gillian Mary),
1936- . III. Harrison, H.C.A. (Henry Colden
Antill), 1836-1929. The story of an athlete.
IV. Title : Story of an athlete.
796.33'6'0924

Typeset in 11/13 Garamond by Meredith Typesetters
Printed by The Book Printer

Contents

H.C.A HARRISON'S FAMILY TREE
(abridged to show only those members mentioned in the text)

>Sarah Wills
}m. (1)Dr W. Redfern
}m. (2)James Alexander

>Thomas Wills
Sarah }M.(1)Celia Reibey
Harding }m.(2)Marie Anne >Catherine [Cousin Kate]
Barry }m. Lewis C. Conran
m.(1) }d.f.m.(3) Mary Ann
Mellard >Arthur &
Edward >>>3 other children
Wills

> Horatio Spencer Wills > Thomas Wentworth
}m. Eliz. McGuire > **Emily**
}*m. H.C.A. Harrison*
> Cedric
> Horace
> Egbert &
>>>>> 4 other children

>Frances [Fanny]
Capt. John Harrison }m. Dr. H. Budd

}m. >Adela [Addie]
>Jane Howe }m. Henry Norcott
> **Henry Colden Antill** > Kate
Sarah }m. Emily Wills > Rosalie
Harding [Rose]
> Henry
m.(2) Norman
> Ruby
George > Alma &
Howe >>>>> 5 other ch.

> George
> Kate
}m. Ohlfsen Bagge
> Florence
> Alice
> Horace
> Ernest

ACKNOWLEDGEMENTS

The production of *Running with the Ball* has been underwritten by the Victorian Football League, without whose assistance it would not have been possible to make the book so readily accessible to the sporting public. Originally written by Harrison in 1923, *The Story of an Athlete* has too long been only available as a 'rare' volume in a few Victorian libraries. Its reprint has provoked some detailed research on the origin of Australian Rules Football, generally the victim of much misleading assertion and myth. The Victorian Football League has generously seen fit to make a substantial contribution to Australian sporting history and Victorian social history by its support of this book.

The editors are grateful for help given by many people, and wish to acknowledge the special role played by the descendants of the Harrison family, Mrs A.M. Smith, Ms Sue Smith, and Dr T.W. Smith, and those of the Wills family, Dr G. Buckwell, Mr D. Cooke, Mr L. Cooke, and Mr T. Wills Cooke, in providing material from their family files.

Among others who gave valued help was the Melbourne Cricket Club honorary librarian, Rex Harcourt. Norman Sowden with his encyclopedic knowledge of football and the 'MCC Monday men' made MCC library research particularly profitable and enjoyable. Thank you also to the honorary curator of the MCC Cricket Museum, Bill Gray, and the Director of the Australian Gallery of Sport, Tom McCullough and his staff, for timely assistance.

We would like to thank Scotch College and Melbourne Grammar School and their staffs for locating and providing access to material we needed. Lex Hibbins, Ralph Biddington and Frank Cusack replied to queries with much helpful information.

In addition to family sources, we gratefully acknowledge the contribution of the following people and institutions in providing illustrations: The Melbourne Cricket Club, the Mitchell Library in Sydney, the La Trobe Library Melbourne, the National Library of Australia, the Geelong Historical Society, Melbourne Grammar School, Stan Bird, Dr J.A. Daly, David Condell and Ron Greenway. Jan Schmoeger of Designpoint Pty Ltd photographed the cover and designed the book. Sporting artefacts on the cover were provided by the Melbourne Cricket Club and the Fitzroy Football Club.

H.C.A. Harrison, a sketch by Ruby Harrison. T. Wills Cooke collection

PREFACE

In 1923 Henry Colden Antill Harrison[1] wrote his autobiography and, in its title, *The Story of an Athlete: a Picture of the Past*, declared his intention: his 'story' is that of an athlete, a man who spent his life in pursuit of 'strength, endurance, courage and self-control'. Harrison's considerable athletic abilities inclined him to the ready acceptance of the values and assumptions of muscular Christianity. This late nineteenth century creed, originating in England and embraced in Melbourne as elsewhere, was characterised primarily by a belief in 'the duty of patriotism, the moral and physical beauty of athleticism, the salutary effects of spartan habits and discipline, the cultivation of all that is masculine, and the expulsion of all that is effeminate, unEnglish and excessively intellectual'.[2]

Such teachings reached the colonies in various forms: during Colden Harrison's lifetime the new literary form of the boy's adventure story presented these ideals in a particularly persuasive manner, the stereotype heroes projecting physical vigour, personal fortitude, and honest sentiment. As Harrison's account of his childhood and adolescence shows, the experiences of colonial youth both rivalled and provided the factual basis for boys' tales of the time. Possibly Harrison recalled William Howitt's *A Boy's Adventure in the Wilds of Australia* which parallelled Harrison's reminiscences in several respects and was first published in 1854 when Harrison himself was 18 years old. In addition to spreading the values of muscular Christianity throughout the Empire, popular adventure stories provided ready-made models for colonial autobiographers, presenting murderous conquests of the native inhabitants as tales of pioneering courage and manliness in a landscape

1

of exotic flora and fauna. The childhood that Harrison wrote about was the pioneering one of pastoral expansion with its hardships and danger of Aboriginal attack, and his adolescence that of the rigours and excitement of the goldfields. His mundane life as a public servant was given short shrift except as it related to the romance of the tall-masted sailing ships.

The creed of muscular Christianity was institutionalised in the English public schools and Colden Harrison attended Melbourne's equivalent in 1850. However Harrison's stay was brief, and athletics sparse, at the fore-runner of Melbourne Grammar School which was administered by Dr. R.H. Budd who had been educated at Rugby under the famed Dr. Arnold. Nevertheless Harrison, in later life, took great pride in attending old boys' dinners and in claiming to be the oldest public schoolboy alive in Victoria.

That Colden Harrison's life was dominated by sport, his auto-biography makes quite clear. Apart from his fame as a runner, and his long involvement with football, he also played cricket and tennis. In later life he explored the Yarra by canoe and, when he was sixty-two, rode a bicycle to Sydney. The emphasis in his life, as he related it, is placed on the male sporting ethos of manliness, pluck and endurance. Although he was successful in the Victorian civil service, rising to be Registrar of the Titles Office, and widely praised for his administrative work in the sporting world, it is apparent that he felt more at ease with the physical side of life. So when Colden Harrison realised that 'of those who travelled overland from N.S.W. to Port Phillip [he] was the only survivor', and was persuaded by his daughter to write his reminiscences, his selection of material owed more to the conventions of the world of the adventure story than to any comprehensive historical search for truth, and he relied greatly on the use of a scrapbook of clippings of his sporting successes as a source. In particular, his reticence about his family background and his role in the early days of football blurs Harrison's 'picture of the past'. This preface attempts to redress those omissions.

1   FAMILY ORIGINS

For a man of Colden Harrison's morality, there was much in his family circumstances to cause embarrassment; his family was not as readily socially acceptable as he infers. Through his mother Jane Howe, he was directly descended from an extensive network of convict emancipist families. Growing up in the close family relationships he describes, he could not have been ignorant of this past. Yet, though it was an ancestry which included some of the most enterprising and intellectually productive achievers of the colony, he omitted altogether any mention of the family's early days in NSW. In what is claimed to be a natural response for his time, Harrison took little pride in the entrepreneurial success of convict ancestors and instead sought to concentrate on their respectability,[3] for instance, to emphasise his mother's connections with Captain Antill, (the husband of her stepsister who was aide-de-camp to Governor Macquarie in 1818,) and visits to the Harrison sheep station at Swanwater by impeccable notables such as Bishop Perry.

Colden's Harrison's grand-mother was Sarah Harding who accompanied her first husband to NSW on the notorious convict death ship, Hillsborough. Edward Wills had been convicted at Kingston-on-Thames Surrey, of highway robbery but within nine days his death sentence was commuted to transportation for life. In Sydney Sarah and Edward Wills prospered, first as store-keepers and then as traders in seal skins and as tavern keepers. Their children did well. Their eldest daughter, Sarah, married Dr. William Redfern when she was fourteen. Harrison notes that the cattle overlanded by his father bore the Quadrant R, renowned brand of the Redfern cattle, but not that Redfern was his uncle. The convict surgeon was, according to the *Dictionary of Australian Biography*, 'one of the greatest of the early medical practitioners of the colony, the first to receive an Australian qualification, the first teacher of Australian medical students, and the author of important reforms in the convict transports'.[4]

After Edward's death, Sarah married George Howe. They had a daughter called Jane who married Captain John Harrison and became Colden's mother. George Howe was thus Colden Harrison's maternal grandfather. He was another convict ancestor who, though he made a substantial contribution to the intellectual life of Australia, remained unacknowledged by his grandson in *The Story of an Athlete*.

George Howe was born in St. Kitts in the West Indies in 1769 where his father and brother were engaged on the Government Press. He was convicted at the Warwick assizes on 25 March 1799, sentenced to seven years' transportation,[5] and was about 31 when he reached Sydney in 1800. Howe became government printer two years later. He printed the first book, and published the first newspaper in Australia.[6] He published a book of poetry entitled *First Fruits of Australian Poetry* and the first natural history book printed in the colony, *Birds of New South Wales with their Natural History*. Howe has been described as 'the Caxton of Australia ... For more than twenty years, his role in the dissemination of ideas was substantial. He was an active Wesleyan, devoted to evangelism, philanthropic causes, and colonial education. He combined printing and publishing with retailing and speculation in trade, livestock and real estate. He fathered three families, married money, and died a rich man'.[7]

Colden Harrison's Uncles

From Colden Harrison's point of view his two most admired relatives were his mother's step-brothers, Thomas Wills and Horatio Spencer Wills, whom he presents as vigorous overlanders and pioneering land-owners, 'the highest type of adventurous Briton'. They were both wealthy gentlemen of some standing in the community.

Thomas was the eldest son of Sarah's first marriage to Edward Wills. He bought Port Phillip land at the first sales held in Sydney in 1838 before coming overland and buying more land on the Darebin Creek at Port Phillip in 1840. There he set himself up as a gentleman and built one of the most elegant houses of colonial Melbourne — Lucerne Farm. Typically, Harrison recalls social functions there, at which Tom's second wife presided. An evocative description of Lucerne Farm in the forties is given by Thomas Wills' neighbour:

> the house with its pillared and balconied front is of graceful architecture, delightfully situated on pleasant knolls and slopes, seen from the south of the river, with the garden, like an English one with the windings of the Yarra at a distance before it, and the gleam of natural ponds near it, partly hidden in trees too, the landscape is picturesque enough. Walking in the garden, amongst the sedges and reeds, for a natural lake encircles it, you see nearly tame, so well are they protected by their tasteful owner, ducks divers and widgeons not native of the country, and added to these, what is very rare, the Australian coot, with its sky blue body, crimson bill and legs, a most beautiful bird. To see all these creatures so nicely located and to find the garden in its character so very English, inspired you with regard for the owner.[8]

However Thomas Wills, even with all these trappings of the landed gentry, was never admitted to the Melbourne Club. A contemporary claimed 'colonial society is divided by a well defined line which marks off the criminal from the unconvicted population, and is particularly adhered to on the part of the upper classes'.[9] Wills did become the first President of the Port Phillip Club, described recently as ' having the character of a second eleven'.[10]

Not only was Thomas descended from a convict, but so was his first wife, the mother of 'cousin Kate'. Celia Reibey was the daughter of Mary Reibey 'legendary in the colony [of New South Wales] as the successful business woman'.[11] Harrison completely ignored this connection in his biography, concentrating on Wills's second marriage, after Celia's early death, to Marie Anne Barry, 'a true "grande dame" and a splendid hostess'. It is perhaps more understandable that he neglected to add that the latter marriage was not successful: Thomas built himself another house across the Yarra called Willsmere and his

Willsmere, Kew 1877, a sketch by Arthur Wills. Dr G. Buckwell collection

four youngest children were the result of a relationship which he established in England. The eldest, Arthur, returned to Melbourne and lived with Colden and his wife between 1876 and 1886, before claiming Willsmere.[12]

Colden Harrison was also close to his other uncle, Horatio Spencer Wills, who was Sarah Wills' youngest son, but born after her husband Edward's death and before her second marriage to George Howe. When George Howe died in 1821, his son Robert took over the printing business and Horatio Spencer Wills became his apprentice. Relationships between the Wills side of the family and the Howe descendants deteriorated. Horatio ran away twice and sided with brother-in-law Dr.William Redfern in a public dispute with Robert Howe.[13] Sarah, Howe's widow (and Colden Harrison's grandmother), fought a lengthy case in the courts over ownership of property which she had brought into the family on her marriage to George Howe. Horatio led an adventurous life as a youth — he may well have worked on a whaler — and, when Robert Howe died, Horatio took over the printing business and published a newspaper called *Currency Lad*.

However Horatio, when Colden Harrison knew him, had become a pious God-fearing patriarch claiming in his diary[14] to have been reformed by his wife. The diary which Horatio wrote as a guide to his sons[15] affords some glimpses of the extended family life of the Harrisons and of the Wills. The heights of Colden and his brother George are included with the measurements of Horatio's children[16] at Lexington, Horatio's Ararat property, and Colden Harrison's step-sister, Fanny, is elsewhere mentioned as caring for baby Emily in the nursery.[17] Harrison later married Emily and Horatio became his father-in-law.

Colden Harrison's Cousin — Thomas Wentworth Wills

A most important friend of Colden Harrison's youth was undoubtedly his cousin, Tommy Wills, Horatio's son and Harrison's eventual brother-in-law. It was natural that Harrison, as an an old man in his eighties in 1923, chose to recall for his readers the young Tommy Wills of the 1850s whom he admired, and not the alcoholic Wills of the 1870s. For Colden Harrison and many of his contemporaries, Wills was the 'beau ideal' of an athlete, a 'public favourite', especially remembered for his 'good nature' and 'kind heart'.[18] Harrison specifically acknowledged the crucial role played by his cousin in the start of Australian Rules football.[19]

Thomas Wentworth Wills was born at Parramatta, New South Wales, on 19 August, 1835 and, aged four, came overland to Port Phillip in 1839-1840, the family settling near what is now Ararat. Horatio wanted Tom, his eldest boy, to be a lawyer and proudly records his son's scholastic progress in his diary, sending Tom to Brickwood's 'seminary' in Melbourne when he was 11 and where he probably learnt to play cricket.[20] In 1850 Tom had a long and dangerous voyage to England at the age of 14 to attend Rugby. He struggled to cope with the expectations of his father, in one letter home copying out sermons he had heard and then recounting his sporting success with detailed cricket scores.[21] His aunt, Sarah Alexander, who kept an eye on his progress from London and took him for holidays, wrote: 'I paid Rugby a visit and am most happy to confirm that Tom is a fine youth — sensible, well-looking, and gentlemanly, but rather backward in his aspirations for a start in the great struggle of life'.[22]

Horatio's response to Tom was pointed:

> Your letter containing the account of games at Rugby came to hand yesterday; and, as with all letters from you, gave considerable satisfaction. You still however continue to write with a scrawl that would make a writing master eat his nails, and there are occasional errors in spelling and in grammatical construction of your sentences at which I am much surprised. If you cannot write correctly now I am afraid you never will, and if you should after all my trouble turn out a dunce! You should at 18, with all the means at your disposal, be able to write in English correctly and well, to write and talk French, and have a pretty fair knowledge of Latin. You must strive to accomplish this as soon as possible for you must shortly commence your studies for a profession. The law is the most honourable — the merchant also has a fair time of it. If you have brains take the law. Come out here 5 or 6 years hence a barrister. Remember that everything you do is for yourself, and if you do not succeeed in life and obtain the reputation of a clever gentlemanly fellow, no one will be to blame but yourself.[23]

Thomas Wentworth Wills. D. Wills Cooke collection

A year later however Tom's aunt was urging that Tom not be taken away from school for some time: 'You are aware that he was very backward when he arrived in England, and he has much yet to learn, which could not be acquired with so much ease and advantage as at present when no other occupation interferes to disturb his attention.' She may have been underestimating the distraction of Tom's sporting achievements as captain of cricket and football player at Rugby.[24] At least Tom seems to have taken some of his father's homilies to heart, as she continued: 'Thomas appears to like the notion of becoming a merchant, and as I think he is naturally industrious, I have no doubt he will be a prosperous one. His general conduct is so good, that I indulge the hope that he will be a blessing to you and his mother'. Prefacing this conclusion with remarks which make it quite clear that Tom needed a few more years 'to fit him to to undertake concerns with safety and advantage to himself', she doubted that Tom's nature was assertive enough for the entrepreneurial commercial world.[25] In fact, her husband was reluctant to take Tom into the office.[26] Her instincts were more accurate than her hopeful words: Tom did remain in England — playing cricket — and, on his return to Victoria, worked briefly for a lawyer in Collingwood until his father decided he would be better off on the land.

The Cullinlaringo Massacre

Horatio Wills took up the Cullinlaringo run on the Nogoa River in Queensland and in 1861 father and son, servants and shepherds travelled towards their family tragedy. On the 17 October, nineteen of the party, including Horatio Wills, were killed by Aboriginals in what is regarded as the biggest massacre of white men in Australia by Aboriginals. Tom was away from the run at the time, and it was to his cousin Colden, 'my dear Coley', that Tom Wills appealed for help. His incoherent letter provides a moving insight into the impact the tragedy had on him.

> I have not had time to go into particulars I can only say that all our party except I have been slaughtered by the blacks . . . I am in a great fix no men if we had used common precaution all would have been well my poor Father and Baker were most brutally murdered I want a good man up here that thoroughly understands sheep please to let Mr Roope[27] know it I have given him particulars but urge him to send me a good overseer. Do all that can possibly be done as soon as possible in the shape of shepherds good resolute men that will shoot every black they see Cullinlaringo is a fine station the best in the land 17th Oct. just 9 months from the time we left Melbourne 19 killed I can scarce

even now believe it Tell Elliott that poor George was killed close to the tents and had a small switch in his hand that he used to drive the sheep with I have his pouch now All Clothes of all sorts gone—Flour sugar and tea not touched but blankets zigari shirts and beds all gone What a dreadful end after such trouble as we have had, the climate is splendid but without men I can do nothing. So get us help I have nearly all the sheep all right thank God . . .[28]

Horatio and Tom Wills, it seems, had led their party into what was a guerilla war being waged between the local blacks and the Native Mounted Police Force consisting of white officers and Aboriginal troopers.[29] However Horatio had been reassured by the previous owner of the station, Peter MacDonald, that the neighbouring Aboriginals were a 'fine set of fellows and very kind to him and his party' and Horatio had replied "We'll try to keep friends with them".'[30] Neighbouring squatters were apprehensive about the degree to which Wills allowed the Queensland aboriginals access to the camp and spoke later of Wills' 'trusting genuine benevolence'.[31] Wills had learnt to develop a peaceful relationship with the Aboriginals at Ararat after some early confrontations and possibly expected a similar resolution.[32] By all accounts Tom had also been on good terms with the Aboriginals of Ararat[33] but he was evidently more wary of the local Queensland blacks than his father. Emily retailed her brother's account of the massacre: 'Tom says he always told Pa the blacks meant something because they would come so close to them to look at their women and picannines (sic), but Pa would not believe him for they used to surround them and take off their hats and put them on their heads as a mark of friendship.' She noted also: 'Before Tom left the station, he loaded all the guns, [and?] gave his revolver to Pa as Pa's was damaged. He offered firearms to the men but they would not take them because the blacks were so friendly'.[34]

The attack could not have failed to shock Tom Wills and his natural rage was only a prelude to the white raid which followed. A number of settlers and police hunted down the Aboriginals and 'administered severe punishment, by way of a lesson for the benefit of the other settlers', declared Colden Harrison in his euphemistic way. A letter from Horatio's widow two months after the deaths was more forthright: 'the horrible wretches have payed (sic) dearly for it for the settlers said they had shot 300 and some seventy more were killed by the black police [that is, the Native Mounted Police] which the Sydney papers chose to make a noise about for they said the innocent should not have suffered with the guilty. It is my belief they were all guilty for one called out (as you will see by the paper I post with this) ["]me no kill white fellows["] was shot'.[35] A friend of Tom's, wrote in

Natives attacking a Queensland Outstation, N. Chevalier, *Illustrated Australian News* 1865. La Trobe collection, State Library of Victoria

1883 of the 'fearful slaughter of the blacks [which] took place after this massacre'; he added 'the particulars as related to me are too sickening for recital'.[36]

Later Tom's young brother Cedric recalled Tom Wills' own account of the cause of the massacre.[37] An Aboriginal stock man had told Tom the Aboriginals had found some sheep which they believed to be strays, 'thrown away' by white men. So they killed some of them for a feast and when the Native Police and Gregson, the owner of the sheep, came to their camp they made no attempt to defend themselves. In the affray which followed some of the Aboriginals were injured (the number is disputed) and later died. It was then that the tribe decided to revenge the murders. Runners were sent to neighbouring groups and a large meeting was held at Separation Creek on the boundary of Cullinlaringo and Gregson's run. They made no distinction between Gregson and Horatio Spencer Wills, considering them to be 'brothers' because they rode together and looked alike.[38]

Colden Harrison makes passing unsourced reference to Cedric's account in *The Story of an Athlete* but at the same time finds the 'cupidity' of the blacks to be the motive for the attack. Consequently Harrison finds it strange that goods such as tea, flour and tobacco were not stolen but scattered around the site, offering the explanation that the 'blacks had not learned to appreciate them'. His assessment has been uncritically repeated, until more recent research which provides strong evidence that the Gregson attack was but the last straw for the Aboriginals who had, in fact, been the victims of many such assaults in the area.[39]

Soon after the tragedy, Tom made a vow over his father's grave to 'stick to Cullinlaringo and the station will be the pride of Queensland yet'.[40] Horatio, having himself 'never known a father's care', had been assiduous in the care of his 'dear boys' but his constant admonitions to work hard, as he had done for them, left a heavy burden of gratitude upon his sons.[41] Tom Wills stayed to establish the new settlement and a letter home recounts some of the difficulties he faced: one of his eyes was blinded by sandy blight and his clothes all needed repair. He felt 'overwhelmed' by work and had fallen out with his uncle who had come to help and had left. He was very lonely, weary, and needing 'a bonny little wife.' He was feeling his isolation and yet was living in the shadow of his dead father: 'I only act now as if he were himself present or could approve of what I do.'[42]

He endured it for just over 2 years until leaving for New Zealand to play against the English cricket team in the summer of 1863-64. A family conference in March 1864 agreed that he should not return to manage Cullingaringo; there is a strong suggestion that Horatio's trustees were not satisfied with Tom's financial handling of the property and its management was left to Cedric Wills, Tom's brother, who had returned from schooling in Germany some time in 1863 to help Tom with the station.[43]

Cullinlaringo, a sketch by Arthur Wills. Dr G. Buckwell collection

It is possible that the white retribution preyed upon Tom's mind. Although there is no evidence that he took part in it, his family certainly expected him to revenge his father's death and the initial retaliatory tone of his letters may have fuelled this expectation.[44] Yet in 1866 he was putting considerable effort into helping an Aboriginals' cricket team in Victoria. He then became a professional cricketer and coach of the Melbourne Cricket Club, not really a 'gentlemanly' occupation. The whole tragedy may well have had its effects on him which were to surface at a later date: he became alcoholic, had to be kept restrained at home and committed suicide by stabbing himself with a pair of scisssors when briefly left unattended.[45] He was only forty-four. By that time only his young brother Egbert, Colden Harrison and E.[Emily Harrison?] went to see him and it was they who arranged the burial.[46] Just over a year later Cullinlaringo was auctioned.

Colden Harrison's Father — Captain John Harrison

If Colden Harrison saw fit to exclude an account of his maternal family, his father's life also provided him with editorial problems. John Harrison was born in Cumberland in 1802 and allegedly trained as a midshipman in the British navy before becoming a captain in his father's merchant fleet which traded with South American countries. Colden Harrison did not mention that Captain Harrison spent two years imprisoned in Monte Video after he attempted to run a Uruguayn blockade against British ships.[47] This was but the first instance of what Colden Harrison described as 'the bad luck which seemed to dog my father's footsteps through life'. The Captain lost his own father overboard, wrecked a boat, failed at squatting, neglected his son and an auctioneering business on the gold diggings, and accidentally shot himself in the arm.

But such ineptness on the part of Captain Harrison was the least of his son's embarrassments. For a muscular Christian such as Colden Harrison, patriotism was a necessity, and one's readiness to defend queen and country part of the rationalization for keeping healthy and fit. Captain John Harrison made a career from being 'agin the government' in an outspoken way. Acknowledging that his father was a rousing speaker, Colden Harrison did not add that what the speeches usually aroused was a public outcry. Captain John described himself as a democrat but his more frequently expressed republican sentiments advocated the cutting of ties with the British monarchy. His public protests about the cost of maintaining the royal children and the immorality of a British government which paid large sums for 'new kennels for Prince Albert's dogs' while thousands of British people were starving,[48] earned the Captain the reputation of a dangerous man amongst the more conservative elements of society.

The first evidence of Captain Harrison's interest in the organisation of public opinion is found in the campaigns against the tax policies of Governor Gipps. His objections were that the taxes were unjust because they fell heavily on the small squatters of whom he was one.[49] In addition, he believed that Port Phillipians received very little for the taxes they paid. It was typical of him that he should see his own difficulties as aspects of the broader scene, pointing out that although a rate was levied on his district for police protection, there were 'still only two constables' employed for the whole country of Bourke.[50] He had had first-hand experience of lawlessness when his family was attacked by bush-rangers in 1842.[51]

The Captain had a talent for display and a capacity to appeal to an audience. When Gipps announced plans for taxing settlers in 1844 to pay for a district council, angry local squatters announced a public meeting. They mustered on Batman's Hill at noon on 1 June 1844. Captain Harrison acted as 'Master of Ceremonies, the horsemen formed three deep on the brow of the hill, and the musicians and the banner bearers having taken their positions, the procession started for the place of the meeting' — the Mechanics' Institute.[52] It was Captain Harrison who moved the ninth amendment: 'that a Society of Stock holders be formed for the protection of pastoral interest, to be called the Pastoral Society of Australia Felix. The Captain dealt with the issue of Gipps' proposals by exhibiting a cartoon he'd received showing Gipps 'dressed up as a sour old dame, in tattered habilment and Phillipine, as a buxom damsel held fast to her mother with a pair of handcuffs, holding in her hand her surplus revenue'. His speech referred to the hostility he had aroused earlier when he had expressed his anti-monarchist sentiments, and he claimed he had been unjustly 'stigmatised both as a rebel and a traitor, epithets which he by no means deserved'.

Captain John campaigned for separation for Port Phillip, alleging that to be taxed without the intervention of the Colonial Parliament was to be 'at once reduced to the state of serfdom . . . .' He urged, 'Port Phillipians, with all your gettings, get separation'.[53] It was during the separation campaign that he designed his red flag with a white star that was to rise later above the gold-field meetings.[54]

Following the accidental shooting of his arm which restricted physical work, Captain John began campaigning professionally. In July 1851 he was employed by an organisation against the transportation of convicts called the Australasian League. Harrison spoke at Brighton, Geelong, Darebin, Heidelberg, Plenty, Williamstown, Keilor and Bacchus Marsh. His speeches were published in the press.[55] Was it because of his wife's background that on many occasions although he advocated banning 'felons', meaning 'someone who from child-hood had been taught to steal, whose education has led to nothing but degradation', he distinguished 'felons' from emancipists who had succeeded in Australia despite being transported 'for their country's good'? Harrison also used these opportunities to speak on other matters close to his heart, for instance, his ideas on constitutional reform and his preference for the Napoleonic code of laws rather than those of Britain.[56]

The news of the gold discoveries in Victoria made the anti-trans-portation campaign unnecessary and Captain John, 'not the man to resist the call of such an adventure',[57] took his sons and joined the rushes, first to Ballarat and then to Castlemaine. When the Captain's friend, squatter Frederick Fenton, sent word that gold had been found on his run Ravenswood, (Bendigo) the Harrisons headed for the new field, making quite an impression on another digger as they arrived: 'They came up with red shirts and knee boots and we thought they were commissioners or troopers, and would take the gold from us — [we] having no licences'.[58] According to Colden Harrison, they did find some gold but his father's attempts to set up as an auctioneer failed because the Captain neglected the business for his agitations on behalf of the diggers.

The government sought both to discourage people from going to the gold fields and to raise funds for the increasing costs of admin-istration in its attempts to maintain law and order. It doubled the cost of the licence fee from 1 January 1852 and 'the diggers were alienated to a man'.[59] 'Always a man for knocking about',[60] Captain John did little for most of 1852 but travel around organising and protesting on the part of the diggers. A digger later recalled the Captain's methods of campaign:

> headed by our officers we marched, all the red shirt men in the front, and when we got to within 200 yards of the Commissioners's tent, the order was to halt, and Capt. Harrison rode up and down the line telling the men not to be rash, that he would go and interview the commis-sioner. We saw them walking up and down in front of the tent. Many of the men wanted to rush the tents, so excited had they become when they saw four or five police come out, carbines in hand. Capt. Harrison came back in a short time, and said that the commissioner could do nothing himself, as he was only a deputy, but that he would do all he could, and let us know as soon as possible.[61]

Captain Harrison's speech given to the diggers at Mount Alexander on 15 December 1851 was enthusiastically received by the audience. He attacked the Commissioner whom he alleged had pleaded: 'I would

Detail from The Great Meeting of Gold Diggers, Mt. Alexander 1851, drawn by D. Tulloch and engraved by T. Ham, from the *Gold Diggings of Victoria*, Melbourne,1852. La Trobe collection, State Library of Victoria

send you police with pleasure, but the truth is, I have not enough to protect myself'. Harrison protested, 'We give a fee for protecting us, but it is us who are taking care of them'. He objected to the royalty paid to the Queen: 'Has the Queen not enough, or does she want it to buy pinafores for the children?' He reminded all that 'a similar tax lost Charles the First his head', and added that' it was unjust taxation that caused the United States to throw off the burden'. The *Melbourne Morning Herald* reporter did not share the diggers' enthusiasm, writing: 'Next came that furious rebel Captain Harrison who began by declaring his contempt for Queen Victoria and her myrmidons, and poured forth a volley of rant and abuse so utterly beside the point, and so indicative of a diseased imagination, that we in charity hear it as the ravings of a political maniac and dismiss it accordingly'.[62] Harrison was undaunted but the effect on his adolescent son was probably distressing, especially when young Colden was left to cope alone at the diggings while Captain Harrison, a natural choice to be one of the delegates to petition the government, went back to Melbourne.

By September 1852, Harrison was campaigning 'in favour of unlocking the land and extending the franchise to the diggings'. Noted the *Argus*: 'he has been very successful hitherto, and is now visiting every gully obtaining signatures to a petition to the Legislative Council requesting that the present system of land sales be abolished; that small townships be laid out surrounded by agricultural lots of 20, 30, 40, 80 and 100 acres, to be sold at a fixed price, and no person to be allowed to select more than one lot in each parish'. Also, he advocated that the 'elective franchise be granted to diggers in such proportion as is now enjoyed by the population of Melbourne'.[63]

Less impressed by Harrison's oratory than the diggers were the solid citizens of Melbourne. At the Hargreaves testimonial dinner, Harrison in replying to the toast to the Army and Navy, (after the band had played 'See the Conquering Hero Come'), garrulously attacked the British Government's failure to provide any defence for the Colony, alleging that the colonial funding of the part-regiment which had been supplied was 'money taken out of the pockets of colonists for Imperial purposes'. When he moved on to the need to sever connections with Great Britain and Queen Victoria, he was hissed and shouted down.[64]

The Captain's marriage to Jane Howe, who was fourteen years younger than him, was evidently not a successful one[65] and Colden Harrison seems to have found more guidance and support from a family friend, Norman MacLeod, than from his own father. Nearly twenty years older than Colden Harrison, MacLeod had a background untainted by convict associations, and his young days were of the sort Colden admired — the adventurous overlander and unofficial explorer.[66]

Colden Harrison made no mention of his father's radical beliefs, nor did he reflect on any of the major political changes which occurred in his own life-time. Apparently he confined his own political activities to the board-rooms of sports clubs and the Victorian civil service. He remained a dutiful son to his reckless father sending gifts of money when 'the diggers' friend' finally became the station-master at North Williamstown. Local oral history has it that the Captain remained defiant to the end, hanging the governor in effigy at the station on the occasion of some colonial celebration. Captain Harrison died from bronchitis in 1867.

Colden Harrison's Family

Colden Harrison's own marriage to his step-cousin, Emily Wills, does not seem to have been a close one in later years. Bearing in mind that he is writing about his life as an athlete, it is nevertheless notable that his wife is mentioned only in a description of their wedding, and this brief paragraph lacks an endearing adjective. Colden Harrison was what used to be called 'a man's man' and his references to women tend to be of the patronising 'fair sex' variety. It must have been a source of great distress to Colden that of his ten children, his three sons all died, two in infancy. He identifies his daughters simply in relationship to the prowess of their husbands. It is hard to discern how satisfying family life was for him although it is apparent that the company he enjoyed was that of heroic explorers, prominent cricketers, and past football friends and foes.

2   THE START OF AUSTRALIAN RULES FOOTBALL AND COLDEN HARRISON'S ROLE

'The game of football promises . . . to be one of the popular amusements of the ingenuous youth of Victoria', predicted the *Herald* on 23 August 1858, a modest calculation if ever there was one! By 1861 the game was well established and, less than twenty years after its beginning, was attracting more spectators than any other outdoor sport in the colony: 10 000 to Melbourne versus Carlton matches in 1876.[1] Wrote one observer in the early eighteen nineties, 'It is no uncommon thing on a Saturday afternoon in Melbourne when the famous clubs meet in a Cup Tie, to see from 25 000 to 30 000 spectators present. Considering the population as compared with some great English cities, this, I think, is an extraordinary attendance'.[2]

The phenomenal growth of Australian Rules Football in Victoria in the last half of the nineteenth century has surprisingly received little serious attention from historians except for the pioneering work of Ian Turner.[3] In Victoria much attention has focussed on when, and by whom, 'football' was first played but little on why colonial football developed in an entirely different way from Rugby and soccer and why football in Victoria was organized before the other codes were established in England. Harrison's own account of the start of Australian Rules is brief, and, contrary to general belief, his nomination as 'father of Australian Rules football' should rely more on his fostering of the game than on its conception.

Some English Background

From the fourteenth century, English football consisted of loosely-organised contests with simple traditional rules varying from place to place, and with no fixed numbers of players, time or territory — 'folk-games' sports historians called them.[4] From the 1840s to the 1860s newer versions of this chaotic pastime evolved into the two recognised codes of today, Rugby and Association (soccer). This evolution occurred within the growth and reformation of the English public school, and was one aspect of the rising middle class's search for a suitable education for its children.[5]

As a relatively new school with a large percentage of the sons of this increasingly powerful middle class, Rugby was in the forefront of these changes. Headmaster Thomas Arnold, frowning on hunting sports, preferred cricket and football, part of the emerging educational ideology which officially viewed team games as character-building, and pragmatically as useful in reducing the libidinous urges of school-boys.[6] With official recognition of football within the school, came organization: Rugby began to allow carrying the ball under certain conditions and, by setting out these stipulations, had in 1845 the first written rules for organised football in the world — but they were rules followed only at Rugby school.

In 1849 the more aristocratic Eton followed suit but, in an effort, perhaps, to maintain a status distinction between the two schools,[7] Eton's rules differed substantially. Whereas at Rugby the ball could be picked up and carried, at Eton this was forbidden. Soon the pupils and staff at the other five leading English public schools had also laid down a set of football rules: Harrow and Winchester in the 1850s, Shrewsbury about 1855, Westminister about 1860, and Charterhouse in 1862 — so that varieties of football existed, each peculiar to a school.[8] There were spasmodic efforts at conciliation between the differing sets of school rules until 1863. At that time two main codes emerged, the main difference being that in Association football, unlike Rugby, the ball could not be handled except by the goal-keeper.[9]

Melbourne favours Rugby School-style football

Before the emergence of the two main English codes Australian Rules Football, or Melbourne Club Rules Football as it was called at the time, was away and kicking. In three seasons between 1858 and 1860 the game was basically organised and it was then claimed with con-siderable justification: 'football as played in Victoria is now fit to run alone . . . we seem to have agreed on a code of our own', that of 'the Melbourne Football Club . . . whose rules are universally accepted in Victoria'.[10] How was this competition between teams playing to an agreed code of rules achieved so quickly, when in England there was still considerable debate and continual wrangling? How is it that Australia had an organised football code *before* England?

There were several reasons for this, and the first was that the colonists were less divided than the English on what type of football to favour. Decision was therefore easier to reach. Immigrants to Australia doubtless brought with them the English trend to frame rules for the folk-style football games then played in England and occasionally in the Australian colonies.[11] Whereas the English divided in a closely balanced and obstinate disagreement based on class divisons over whether the ball could be handled or not, the colonists were not pressed to adopt rules barring ball-handling in football, as favoured by the English upper class or ancient public schools. The colonists naturally preferred the handling game of the Rugby School type of football, identifying more with the ascendant middle classes than with the aristocracy they had left behind them. Colonial imitations of the English public school had closer links with the new English public schools developed during the nineteenth century for the sons of businessmen rather than with the older schools which had long catered for the aristocracy. Ex-pupils, as colonial parents or teachers, brought with them a bias for the Rugby school, ball-handling style of football to which the more recent English public schools inclined.[12] An early football player claimed (much later) that games 'under Rugby rules were played by the miners on many of the "diggings" and during these exciting times a small coterie of Rugbyites (sic) kept the ball rolling in Melbourne', although he may well have been embellishing in hindsight the rough and tumble of the folk-style game.[13]

The 1845 written Rugby school rules, which left some matters unclear, were also supplemented by word of mouth explanation. When a Rugbeian could not be consulted on Rugby custom, the players filled in as best they could.[14] In that sort of situation, a colonial direct from Rugby itself was mentor indeed, and it was significant that in 1857 Victoria had one in the form of Thomas Wills.

In the hope of having a lawyer in the family, Victorian pastoralist and Legislative Assembly member, Horatio Spencer Wills, had sent his son to Rugby School in 1850 where young Tom very quickly had a lesson in the importance of that school's insistence on rules.

> The first week there he was chosen to play in his "house" [cricket] eleven and was put on to bowl. He tried underhand, no doubt a veritable Sydney grubber but was told that style would not do for Rugby, so at once assumed a roundhand delivery. He bowled his man down the first delivery, and from that moment on, writes Tommy Wills, "I felt I was a bowler." He was quickly chosen in the eleven and in his first innings he got five wickets in five successive balls.[15]

Wills captained Rugby in 1855 in a cricket match against Marlborough College. At the end of 1856 Tom returned to Melbourne, after a very short stint at Cambridge University, with a name as a promising cricketer and was welcomed to Victorian cricket at the prestigious Melbourne Cricket Club, the second oldest club in Melbourne.

Role of the Melbourne Cricket Club

The Melbourne Cricket Club's role in the start of Victorian football was crucial. It provided the early players, an organizing base, and the status — kindling the spark supplied by Tom Wills. Wills was the Secretary of the MCC when, on 10 July 1858, Melbourne's sporting journal, *Bell's Life in Victoria*, published his now-famous letter suggesting that cricketers should keep fit in the summer by playing football, and adding moreover 'it would be of vast benefit to any cricket-ground to be trampled upon, and would make the turf quite firm and durable . . .' It was a letter to provoke thought, for although only a young man of 22, the colourful Wills had already confirmed his cricket reputation in the eighteen months after his return. No apparent obstacles to his suggestion existed: there was plenty of flat space, and the winter weather in Melbourne, although unpredictable, was milder than that of England. A rail link between Melbourne and Geelong had been completed the previous year and shorter suburban lines were beginning to radiate from the vicinity of Flinders Street and Princes Bridge.

Three weeks later on 31 July 1858, James Mark (Jerry) Bryant, the first professional bowler the MCC had ever engaged,[16] supported Wills' call. Believing 'an ounce of practice to be worth a pound of theory', he would provide a ball for those who would like to play football in the Richmond Paddock, the area adjoining the cricket reserve at Jolimont, and most conveniently close to Bryant's Parade Hotel on the nearby road to Richmond. An invitation was published in *Bell's Life*.[17]

The response from the colony's overwhelmingly male and predominantly young population was 'a large and heterogeneous crowd'. An early football player recalled:

> While a large percentage were Rugby players from England, still not a few hailed from Ireland and Scotland, all eager to refresh their memories with the games of their faraway homes. Englishmen of course played Rugby, Scotchmen a nondescript game, . . . while Irishmen contented themselves by yelling and punting the ball as straight as a die heavenwards. Each man played a lone hand or foot, according to his lights, some guided by their particular code of rules, others by no rules at all.[18]

On the same day, some Melbourne Grammar School boys, according to their headmaster, played 'a football match against the St. Kilda Club [which] came to an untimely end; the grown men, irritated that after an hour and a half's struggle they were unable to kick (a goal), began to fisticuff, and it was thought better to close the game'.[19]

(The Grammar School had already played and beaten Mr W.C. North-cott's boys from St. Kilda Grammar in June.[20])

A week afterwards, Melbourne Church of England Grammar School and Scotch College played a football match. Forty-a-side, including six or seven masters, they also played on the Richmond Paddock at Jolimont.[21] The match was played over three days, on 7 and 21 of August, and on 4 September. Then, as neither side had scored the requisite two goals, the contest was declared a draw. The headmaster of the Grammar School considered it 'a great feather in our cap that so young a school (it had begun the previous April) can maintain its ground against the oldest and most numerous in the colony'.[22] It was an epic struggle: on at least one occasion when the game had lasted three hours, the Grammar 'boys were so exhausted, they were obliged to go to bed an hour earlier than usual'. Obviously owing much to the village games of folk football, the match had distinct Rugby school aspirations. Thomas Wills acted as one umpire and Doctor John Macadam, the Scotch College chemistry lecturer with commanding presence and powerful voice, patrolled the other flank. Robert Hervey, a Scotch College classics master who played in it and allegedly had attended Rugby, is said to have imported 6 balls from England and been encouraging the boys to kick them.[23]

These events attracted a lot of attention and as the *Herald* phrased it, 'stimulated by the ardour with which the juveniles went into the sport, a number of the members of the MCC and friends got up an opposition game' and these impromptu events occurred on the last three Saturdays of the same month of August.[24] It would seem that about this time the Melbourne Football Club was informally established as a constituent part of the MCC, as its membership was initially restricted to members of the Cricket Club.[25]

Thus football enthusiasts had an existing club base from which to organise the hotch-potch which had presented itself, and organization was a necessity, as one who played explained:

> Disputes, wrangling, and utter confusion were the inevitable outcome of such a state of affairs, but nevertheless we have to thank this football babel for many of the best points in the game as now, or should I say, formerly, played. Three or four Saturdays of this kind of play sufficed to show that something must be done to reconcile the different codes of rules. A meeting was called and rules unwritten, or more strictly speaking unpublished, were drawn up.[26]

If it occurred, this meeting would then have been in 1858. This could be possible as both Wills' letter and the *Bells'* invitation of 31 July had suggested that a committee would be formed to draw up a short code of rules and there may have been some verbal agreement.

Yet the *Herald* wrote on the 7 August: 'We believe no definite code of rules has yet been drawn up for the guidance of members of the MFB but it is not improbable that the laws of football will shortly be as well known as those of cricket.'[27] Both of the Melbourne papers refer to football being played at this time according to 'a modification of Rugby rules'.[28]

On 25 September the Melbourne Club had its first engagement when 26 players took on 'the like number of South Yarra', (who were alleged to 'bring with them the prestige of old Winchester and Rugby experiences . . .'[29]). On this day, the Grammar School headmaster wrote: 'The game is so fashionable just now, that several grave senators and public characters are always to be seen kicking with all their might'.[30] Presumably the good headmaster was referring to 'a small coterie of Rugbyites (sic) . . . who played in the then wilds of South Yarra near what is now Fawkner Park, and among those who played were [Thomas Howard] Fellows, Reginald Bright, Murray Smith and W.J. Greig'.[31] Fellowes had just become a member of the Legislative Council of Victoria.

During August the MCC had evidently asked its Secretary, Tom Wills, to draw up a set of rules.[32] But spring was approaching; hotter weather and the cricket season with its impending clash with NSW dominated the interests of sports-loving Victorians. Football began again in the May of 1859, with a match between two pick-up sides, and then a meeting definitely was held at the Parade Hotel, 'with the object of forming a "Football Club"'. A list of 51 members was submitted and from amongst them the following were selected as a committee to draw up rules, etc: Messrs. Wills, Hammersley, Bruce, Smith and Wray. Mr. Sewell was appointed treasurer, and Mr. J.B. Thompson, Secretary.'[33] The Club was no longer restricted to MCC members.[34]

Not surprisingly then, the members of the Football Committee were all cricketers, most of them very well known cricketers at the time. Most importantly Wills as Captain, Hammersley as batsman and Thompson as emergency had only four months previously become household words, covering themselves with glory by defeating the NSW eleven in Sydney for the first time. Thomas Wray was also in this team but he was very quickly replaced on the Committee[35] by Thomas Butterworth who, although not a first class player like his brother Benjamin, also played cricket.[36] Hammersley, Thompson and Butterworth were on the Melbourne Cricket Club Committee in one or more of the years between 1857 and 1859. Alex Bruce, despite the loss of his left arm, was a fast round-arm bowler whose 1857 figures had been very profitable for the Melbourne Cricket Club (and whose hook replacement was to prove a fearsome weapon in

FIRST VICTORIAN ELEVEN.

FIRST INTERCOLONIAL MATCH PLAYED AT SYDNEY. 1859.
WON BY VICTORIA, BY 2 WICKETS.

Victoria Cricket Eleven 1859 MCC collection. This is not the first cricket
eleven despite the heading. Note T. Wills, W.J. Hammersley and J.B.
Thompson as well as J. Bryant, G. Marshall, and G. Elliott, also
mentioned in the text

football!)[37] Presumably Sewell and Smith also played cricket because
they both attended annual general meetings of the MCC in 1858-
59.[38] As cricket, apart from horse-racing, was definitely the most
prestigious sport in the Colony which was described as 'cricket-mad',[39]
and as 'the young cricketers of Melbourne [were] mostly engaged in
professional or mercantile pursuits'[40] the associated football club
must have been bathed in reflected glory.

The First Rules

On the Tuesday following this meeting, that of 17 May 1859, the
rules were discussed over a few drinks at the Parade Hotel and decided.
The written document was headed by the names of the Melbourne
Football Club Committee — T.W. Wills, T. Butterworth, W.J. Hammersley, [T.H.] Smith, Alex Bruce, J. Sewell as Treasurer, and J.B.
Thompson as Secretary.[41] But it would seem only four of the committee actually met to decide the rules, for four names are most
commonly mentioned in connection with this Tuesday rules meeting:

Wills, Hammersley, Thompson (all from the victorious Victorian cricket eleven) and Smith.[42]

Perhaps it was just as well there were only four of them as the small number reduced the potential for disagreement found in larger committees, a potential which may well have already existed, arising from the rivalry of the cricket field. Wills was 'the great gun of the colony',[43] the most feted cricketer of the four, and subject to the head-turning glory which accompanied his success. Yet he was the junior by some six or more years, the others being about 30 years of age whereas Wills was only 23 at the time. He had also the status of being the son of a wealthy landowning member of the first Legislative Assembly of Victoria. The other three were very recent arrivals whereas Wills had the best of both worlds, being a third generation Australian with an English public school education. Wills is something of an enigma. Although there are testimonies to his good nature, in his public life he appears as unreliable and pugnacious. He fell out with Thompson at the end of 1859 when Thompson chastised him publicly for not turning up to captain a cricket match, and returned a biting reply.[44] In later years Wills and Hammersley also quarrelled when Hammersley was critical of Wills.[45] They were not the only ones to comment unfavourably in print on the young cricketer.[46]

Nor was Smith known for his amiability, having a 'very peppery temper', and not being afraid to make his views known.[47] He was the outsider: not a Victorian cricketer, and Irish, not English. Apparently he was not so well known as the others, for whoever wrote out the rules omits Smith's initials from the list of Committee members which heads the document. Was it experience at football that won him his place on the committee, or some other quality?

It seems natural that the football background and experience of these four would have an influence on their decisions. Little is known of Thomas Henry Smith who is described as a tall, well-built man of military carriage known as Red Smith presumably for the colour of his hair. He was the son of a baker, grocer and spirit merchant in Carrickmacross, County Monaghan, Ireland, where he was educated by Mr William Hogg, headmaster of the Free Grammar School. He then studied and graduated as a Bachelor of Arts from Trinity College, Dublin between 1846 and 1850.[48] He certainly had played football previously, for he played in the Scotch College-Melbourne Grammar match and captained one of the scratch sides in the game played directly before the inaugural Melbourne Football Club meeting. When Smith had been at Trinity College Dublin, the students probably played some form of Rugby-orientated uncodified football, for five years after Smith left, a club playing Rugby School rules existed at the College and a 'list of early members contains names of many

W. J. Hammersley. MCC collection

Football at Rugby School in the 1840s, Smyth, *Illustrated London News*

students who entered the College five or six years before that date',[49] that is, at the time when Smith attended the College.

Considerably more is known of Wills. His views and knowledge of the game he had played at Rugby School were publicly acknowledged, for instance, as an umpire at the game between Scotch College and Melbourne Grammar.

Probably Hammersley and Thompson had played football of the Rugby School style. They doubtless knew each other from Trinity College, Cambridge University for both were admitted in October 1845, Hammersley matriculating in 1846 and Thompson in 1848.[50] This was the college at Cambridge University to which most Rugbeians went[51] but it is not only the presence of a strong Rugby school undergraduate contingent which is noteworthy but the dates which are even more important.

This was a significant period in the history of football in England because it was at this time that the desire of public school boys to play football at university first made itself felt. 'The style of football played at Rugby school' had been introduced to Cambridge in 1839 but soon other expublic school boys wanted to play. The Old Etonians 'howled at the Rugby men for handling the ball'[52] and complained especially about 'hacking', the practice of kicking an opponent's legs to persuade him to release the ball. In 1846, when both Hammersley and Thompson were at Cambridge, the first attempt to form a club was made and Cambridge began to experiment with framing its own football rules. Moreover it was at Trinity College that a meeting was convened in 1848 which reached a consensus enabling the Cambridge Rules of Football to become a reality.[53]

This precedent, in calling together representatives of different schools and compromising on a uniform code, was to have far-flung ramifications when the Melbourne Football Club found itself faced with a similar situation. For just as the Old Etonians had 'howled at the Rugby men for handling the ball' at Cambridge, in the scratch match which had preceeded the election of the Melbourne Football Club committee some players had followed 'the practice of catching and holding the ball, while others strenuously objected to it, contending that the ball should never be lifted from the ground other than by foot.'[54] The undergraduate experience of Hammersley and Thompson at Trinity College, Cambridge would prove relevant to Melbourne. Changes, Thompson considered, were 'necessary, as exceptions were taken last year to some of the Rugby [School] regulations, which even a perusal of *Tom Brown's Schooldays* has not made altogether palatable to other than old Rugbians' (sic).[55] He had support. According to the *Herald* at the end of 1858 'hitherto a modification of the Rugby rules has been adopted, which, in the opinion of some, might be altered for the better'.[56] So although Rugby had a strong general following in the local community and was known by members of the committee, there were some reservations about the game.

It is clear that the four rule-framers were concerned about the violence which accompanied football as played at Rugby School. Hacking, or kicking an opponent's legs, was seen by many as an integral part of English football. Early colonial football too, was 'a very rough game and no mistake'. Hammersley later ruefully testifed, 'My shins now show honourable scars, and often have I had blood trickling down my legs. No wonder, for hacking was permitted, and no objection was taken to spiked shoes'.[57] As this had previously been an issue at Cambridge and one over which controversy raged in England until the early 1870s,[58] it was not purely a colonial disquiet as some commentators have suggested, theorizing that the colonials could not afford the leisure available to the aristocracy of England to recover from broken bones, or that the dryer and therefore harder grounds in Australia aggravated the risks inherent in the game. Be that as it may, it is quite apparent that rough, and indeed brutal, play had caused and was still causing considerable unease in England at the time the Melbourne cricketers met to decide on their own football rules.

The problem then for the Melbourne committee was to retain the Rugby school style of football which most people favoured and were already playing but to reduce the more damaging features of it. By 1859 Rugby school had itself removed the worst aspects of hacking in that holding and hacking, hacking with the heel, hacking above the knee and dangerous footwear were prohibited but shin-kicking was still allowed. At this time Thompson wrote of excluding the vices and combining the merits of both Rugby and Eton rules,[59] but writing to Tom Wills some eleven years later he widened that frame of reference: 'You may remember when you, Mr Hammersley, Mr T. Smith and myself framed the first code of rules for Victorian use. The Rugby, Eton, Harrow and Winchester rules at that time (I think in 1859) came under our consideration . . .'[60]

The result of this consideration was the formulation of ten rules.[61] Rules 6, 7 and 8 dealt with the crux of the game. Rule 7 tried to moderate the barbarities of the game for hacking was banned completely. The code allowed tripping and pushing when an opposing player had the ball (except in one case[62]) but this leniency was brief — tripping was banned the following month.[63] Compare this with the (slightly later) English situation on which there is information:[64] in 1863 hacking was allowed at Rugby and Eton but not by Harrow and Winchester. Cambridge University had no rules on hacking until

Football maul, *Australasian Sketcher* 1875.

La Trobe collection, State Library of Victoria

1863 when it was banned. In 1864 Rugby had no rules on tripping but the other schools had banned it.

Certainly the outcome of the Melbourne Football Club Committee's consideration of the English public schools' rules was 'that we all but unanimously agreed that regulations which suited schoolboys well enough would not be patiently tolerated by grown men'.[65]

That adults would prefer a less injury-prone game was the contention being raised in support of a less violent game in England. In Victoria there was little, or at least impotent, opposition to the traditional view that football was not football unless it involved a kick in the shins. Such dogma was less tenacious ten thousand miles away from its origin. It has been argued that the desire to develop a skilful but tough sport which would distinguish gentlemen's football from the original rough and brutal variety, was the cause of this concern in England[66] and such English values probably weighed with the young gentlemen Victorian cricketers also. It is difficult to find explicit evidence to this effect, although even today 'legend has it that Melbourne [Football Club] players have such nice manners they apologise when they hit you in the groin'.[67]

If Rugby school rules had no influence on rule 7, this was off set by Rule 6 which favoured the handling game of the Rugby type. Rule 6 allowed that 'any player catching the Ball directly from the foot may call "mark" '[and mark the ground where he caught the ball]. 'He then has a free kick; no player from the opposite side being allowed to come inside the spot marked.' This catching and marking of the ground was part of the Rugby 'try' at goal but not part of the general play in which a player catching a ball simply ran with it. Harrow had a similar rule applicable all over the ground, the player calling 'yards' instead of 'mark' and being allowed a run of three yards without interference. Cambridge University Rules allowed a free kick after a catch but without a run before the kick. At Winchester the player could run with the ball after a catch and dodge until stopped, when he could take a free kick.[68]

Rule 8 became the main point of contention: 'the ball may be taken in hand only when caught from the foot [a mark], or on the hop [bounce]. In no case shall it be lifted from the ground.' Picking up the ball and carrying it was only allowed under Rugby rules and to a minor extent by Winchester. There was no mention of running with the ball in the Melbourne rules.

The unanimity on the part of the colonial rules committee to reduce the violence in football was significant when one compares its attitude to that of its counterpart in England. Four years later, in 1863, the concern of the English committee formulating rules was also over hacking; but division over the retention or abolition of hacking was tied to division over handling or not handling the ball; those who were against hacking were also against handling the ball, and those who favoured the handling style of football also favoured hacking because kicking shins was considered an effective, indeed necessary, way of breaking up the packs which developed. In Melbourne the unanimity on abolishing hacking allowed the handling/not handling division to be considered as a separate issue, and the handling style of football was accepted even though hacking was rejected; possibly, it was a compromise between Wills' insistence on the Rugby handling style of football which had general support in the colonial community, and the anti-hacking arguments on which they all agreed. Despite the unanimity on the subject of hacking, there was a continued battle over handling the ball during the decade of the sixties.

Front page of the 1859 football rules. MCC collection

According to Hammersley, the other thing the committee tried to do was to 'draw up as simple a code of rules, and as few as possible, so that anyone could understand' and that was another reason why the 33 Rugby school rules were rejected.[69] Certainly on the whole the Melbourne rules were regarded as 'short, very simple, easily understood and remembered'.[70] Not for the colonists, six rules needed to clarify offside; it was simply disregarded, making way for a new footballer — the goal sneak! More importantly, although the game for some considerable time began with both sides on opposing ends of the ground, the captains soon learnt the value of deploying man against man.

Diffusion of the Rules

Once these 1859 rules had been decided, they had to be put about and then agreed to by the great mass of players — not an easy achievement. At first 'during the infancy of the game it was kept alive by scratch matches played between the members of the Melbourne Club or any spectators willing to take part. As these matches were played by sides varying from 15 to 30, a large number of young men soon became conversant with the rules'.[71]

However, this in itself would not have been sufficient to publicise the new game, and diffusion of the MFC rules was, in fact, made easier by publication. After the first meeting in May 1859, the *Argus* said, 'This complete code will be printed and distributed amongst the members of the club, of whom there are now about 70 on the list' and, by June, the paper was referring to 'the lately published rules which appear to give general satisfaction'.[72] Indeed some swift work meant the rules were published in the 1858-1859 edition of *The Australian Cricketers's Guide* with its summary of the just past cricket season, as 'The Rules of the Melbourne Football Club as played in Richmond Paddock 1859' along with 'The Rules of Football as played at Rugby School' and 'The Rules of Football as played at Eton School'.[73] The following year J.B. Thompson edited the first number of *The Victorian Cricketers's Guide* for 1859-1860 in which only the Melbourne Football Club Rules were given space.

The role of James Bogne Thompson, a member of the Melbourne Football Club Committee rules quartet, in publicising the game has not been fully recognised. Thompson was the sports reporter for the *Argus* and the de facto publicity officer for the football club. The youngest son in a large family of a Yorkshire solicitor, Thompson had attended Cambridge University before emigrating to the goldfields. Describing football as 'a most manly and amusing game', he hoped that it 'may continue to grow in favour until it becomes as

J. B. Thompson. MCC collection   The Geelong Trainer, *Australasian* 1888

popular as cricket'. To encourage spectators, he maintained that 'a well-contested match is as interesting a sight as can be conceived'.[74] The *Argus* columns promoted 'this excellent game' with vigour, providing its readers with a flourish of a start each season, the whereabouts of matches, the formation of new clubs, and information about rule changes. Nothing succeeds like success, Thompson evidently believed, so much so that the wary historian must take account of Thompson's orchestration[75] and, in the interests of truth, make allowance for the enthusiasm of the *Argus*. Thompson's influence extended beyond Melbourne because the metropolitan and country papers customarily reprinted each other's material.[76] It is noticeable that when Thompson departed for Bendigo in 1861 the interest of the *Argus* declined, and it may not be coincidental that his departure was followed by an apparent loss of support for football during 1862-1864.[77]

Thompson was not the only journalist on the Committee: William Josiah Hammersley was describing football matches for *Bell's Life* in 1862[78] thus filling, to some extent, the gap left by Thompson's departure. Hammersley became sporting editor of the *Australasian* from 1867 to 1882.

And Tom Wills, as already indicated, was no slouch as a letter-writer to the editor, usually acerbic.[79] It is possible that Wills and Thompson engaged in literary hostilities as a way of gaining publicity for their own purposes, just as today sporting commentators argue on television stations to arouse controversy and attract viewers. For example, in 1859 Thompson regretted Wills' imminent departure to Queensland because 'we could have fought a pretty paper war' over the abolition of the free kick.[80] As for the other papers, the *Age* completely ignored the new sport although the *Herald* followed its progress with interest; one wonders whose pen appears here.

Consolidating the Rules

Testing the new rules was easy as there was only the Melbourne Football club playing pick-up matches at the beginning. The written rules had their first use the following Saturday (21 May, 1859) when T. Wills and Butterworth captained a side each. Wrote the *Argus*, 'some little unpleasantness was occasioned owing to the vague wording of the rule which makes tripping an "institution", and after the match a meeting of the committee was held at which most of the existing rules underwent revision, and some new ones [were] added'.[81] Changes could be introduced promptly; on July 4 the *Argus* was full of praise: 'the new rule against tripping and the other alterations in the MFC football code of directions were observed wonderfully well'. Similarly a month later the *Herald* remarked, 'The rule which relates to pushing requires a slight amendment, for now pushing is carried on when the ball is near or far away. Most probably before the next game this rule will be modified, unless the pavilion is to be turned into a football hospital'.[82]

The early dominance of the Melbourne Football Club players, quickly known as the 'invincible whites' from their constant victories and the colour of their long trousers,[83] helped impose the Melbourne Football Club rules on the new clubs which, when they began, could not challenge this strength. The importance of this factor would have been appreciated by some players such as Hammersley and Thompson whose Cambridge University experience would have alerted them to the fragility of consensus agreements. The South Yarra Club, and then the St. Kilda Club, appear in May of 1859 and play a match on 16 June.[84] Thompson through the *Argus* was able to exert some subtle pressure, observing 'the rules under which the South Yarra gentlemen play differ markedly from those of the Melbourne Club, so that unless some concession is made on one side or both, there is not much chance of a match between the two clubs this season'.[85] When South Yarra did play Melbourne on 9 July (on the Melbourne cricket ground no less,) the MFC rules were those used. South Yarra's reward was delivered by Thompson: the *Argus* after a lengthy description of the game, approved that it was 'worthy of note that the game was conducted throughout with the most perfect good feeling on both sides, and that in each case of acknowledged infringement of the Melbourne rules, a "free kick" was conceded without a murmur.' There was a large number of spectators and a repeat match a fortnight later.[86]

In August the *Argus* reported that 'in Geelong football had been taken up enthusiastically and we learn the Geelong Football Club purpose playing by the rules of the Melbourne Club',[87] quite an achievement as ambitious Geelong was some fifty miles away and if there was to be a rival renegade, this town was its likely home. The Geelong Club was formed at a meeting on 18 July 1859, and later reminiscences[88] support the supposition that Tom Wills was involved in getting the game started there. His family had a property at nearby Point Henry and Wills, who had abandoned the attempt to become a lawyer, spent much of 1860 near Geelong learning skills such as blacksmithing which his father decreed would be good training for him.[89] An early player recalled Wills

> was responsible for the introduction of this popular game to Geelong. The first game was played early in the sixties on an open piece of ground near the old Corio cricket-ground. Sides were picked by T.W. Wills and Captain Fraser (who afterwards commanded a company in the Maori war). As nearly all who participated in this scratch game knew little or nothing about rules, it was more remarkable for spills than good football. However we all enjoyed the sport and a meeting was afterwards held in a nearby hotel when it was resolved to form the Geelong football club. If I recollect aright, Mr J. Elkington was appointed secretary.'

Melbourne played Geelong at the end of the 1860 season on a ground situated near the Argyle Hotel.[90]

Possibly the influence of Wills' Rugby background combined with the competitive ambitions of Geelong to be the 'pivot' of Victoria, encouraged the Club to take a more independent approach to the Melbourne Rules than did other clubs, for it allowed running with the ball. Thus 1859 was a year of some experimentation and jostling for status.

It was Thompson who saw the necessity to reassure prospective adult players that the new game was not the brutish, injury-prone football of their youth, writing early in the 1860 season, that this had changed:

> Though still manly, [football] has become a decorous, and to a certain extent tame pastime. Under the humane legislation of the Melbourne

Football Club tripping has been tabooed, and "hacking" renders a member to excommunication. These rare old "bullies" so famous at one time at least, at Winchester, Eton, and Harrow, have no place in Victoria, and in vain do we in these degenerate days anticipate the spectacle of a dozen players rolling on the ground together. But if sore shins and aching shoulders are less common and the excitement be less intense, we make up in some measure by increased good humour and the absence of severe accidents. So that perhaps after all, football under the rules of the "Humane Society" is preferable to the horseplay we so much glorified in as schoolboys, when our hebdomadal bruises were deemed trophies of pluck, and a good limp or black eye a thing to talk about and be proud of. Besides, fully a moiety of the football players here are grown men, and don't take a kick as they would a dozen years ago. Black eyes don't look so well in Collins Street.[91]

Thompson went on to talk about the danger to boys involved in playing with 'children of larger growth' under the old rougher rules, and this was often the case in these early football matches when both clubs and schools occasionally needed to supplement their sides with schoolboys, or alternatively with masters and old boys.[92] The public schools, lacking the individual traditional games of their English forebears, also adopted Melbourne Football Club rules, as did the Melbourne University Football Club. This was significant as they then provided a continuing pool of young footballers which graduated to the local teams. Thomas H. Smith, member of the first rules committee, was a classics master at Scotch College before going on to become headmaster of the Model School in Spring Street from 1860 to 1863,[93] and had played in the first games against the Melbourne Boys Grammar School. Leading footballers whom Colden Harrison mentions such as Bennie, A.E. Clarke, David and James Ogilvy, and George Tait all went to Scotch College as did Tom Power who was later to be a force in the football world with his 1870s publication the *Footballer*. Melbourne Grammar boys, such as the O'Mullanes, tended to go on to the South Yarra Club. Jack Conway was another Melbourne Grammar boy who made his mark early in Victorian football playing in the first match against Scotch and later captaining Carlton. In the seventies it was observed that many of the school players from Geelong Grammar and Geelong College were also members of the Geelong Club.[94] The school involvement also augmented the gentlemen status which football had assumed in its association with the MCC. Skill at football, arguably, suggested that the owner had enjoyed a public school or university education. It was a recruiting procedure which provided ongoing support in the nineteenth century and into the twentieth.

So in three seasons Victorian football had developed from knock-about games to several clubs including at least one in Geelong, and with school sides developing potential players, all playing one agreed code of football. J.B. Thompson this time writing in *The Victorian Cricketer's Guide for 1860-61* prophesied: 'Football in and about Melbourne promises soon to be as much an institution of the wet as cricket is of the dry season', and reviewing the 1860 football season, reported: 'several new clubs sprang into existence — for instance the Richmond, the Collingwood and the University, nor did any of the old ones exhibit any symptoms of decline. The Melbourne Club by whose rules . . . the game in Victoria is now universally played, still retains it supremacy, having suffered but one defeat . . . The Richmond and South Yarra clubs come next in point of strength'. Captained by Wills, Richmond was a spin-off from the Melbourne Club which had become too large.

Encouraged by Pleasure, Ideology, Tom Brown and Defence

Leaving aside local enterprise, some form of football was sure to have been adopted, for football was a game whose time had arrived. First, the pleasure that the participants enjoyed should not be underestimated. After all, football in various forms had been played in England for over five hundred years and defied numerous efforts by ruling authorities to ban it for its damage to person and property. There had to be some inherent attraction for that to have happened! 'Whether it is from a natural love of the game, or admiration of Tom Brown's description of a football match in the inimitable *"Schooldays"*, we certainly have not witnessed for a long time so much enthusiasm and real enjoyment in an outdoor game, as was shown on this occasion'.[95] Such journalistic comments were not uncommon, even allowing for Thompson's promotional expertise.

Not only was it enjoyable, it was soon advocated as an almost religious way of life. Football's appeal to the young men of the day and for many decades to come was amply justified by the Tom Brown syndrome, or, as it was called at the time, 'muscular Christianity', a doctrine for the robust extravert quickly embraced by the male pioneers of the young Victoria.

The appellation, "muscular Christianity", originated some time in 1857 and *The Edinburgh Review*'s comments in January, 1858, are most often cited in explanation. The *Review* advised that it was 'the school of which Mr Kingsley is the ablest doctor,' and, in turn, that the chief characteristics of Kingsley's writings 'are his deep sense of

the sacredness of all the ordinary relations and the common duties
of life and the vigour with which he contends for the merits of a
simple massive unconscious goodness and for the great importance
and value of animal spirits, physical strength, and hearty enjoyment
of all the pursuits and accomplishments which are connected with
them'.

Thomas Hughes was bracketed with Charles Kingsley as the principal exponents of this creed, and his *Tom Brown's Schooldays*, published in 1857, rapidly popularised it. Three years later in *Tom Brown
at Oxford* Hughes tried to emphasise the moral man rather than the
muscle man: 'the true muscular Christian has hold of the old chivalrous
and Christian belief that a man's body is given to him to be trained
and brought into subjection, and then used for the protection of the
weak, the advancement of all righteous causes, and the subduing of
the earth which God has given to the children of men'.[96]

To middle class colonists busy turning forests into pastoral land
and to entrepreneurs running railway lines to all parts of the colony,
the last injunction must have held particular appeal. Muscular Christianity and Tom Brown immigrated quickly. As Tom Wills was writing
to *Bell's Life* suggesting football for cricketers, Melbourne Grammar's
headmaster wept over *Tom Brown's Schooldays*, ('a noble work, and
very pathetic withal'[97]) and the *Argus* (Thompson) was quick to
associate 'that manly and healthy book', with football, suggesting
that it may well have 'produced a love for violent exercise' in the
colony.[98] In April 1858 *Bell's Life in Victoria* reprinted an article on
Muscular Christianity and Public Schools from *The Times*, and another
in July 1859 on *Muscular Christianity* from the *English Weekly Des-
patch*, the latter erroneously referring to Dr. Arnold as the founder.[99]
At the beginning of 1860 the editor of *Bell's Life in Victoria* maintained: 'Within the last five years a different tone has pervaded society.
The advocates of Muscular Christianity have become the majority.
Such books as *Tom Brown's Schooldays* are among the most popular
works of fiction . . . That this gratifying change in public opinion
has taken place in Australia to quite as great an extent as Europe is
evidenced by the events of the last year'.[100]

Morality, however, had not the staying power of muscularity:
spiritual stamina faltered in the philosophy's heathen catch cry of the
last half of the nineteenth century, 'Mens sana in corpore sans' (a
sound mind in a sound body), and its voguish companion, 'manly'.
Both phrases were general enough to bear a variety of blurred inter-
pretations, but one simple attitude dominated: physical robustness
and moral rectitude could both be attained by a dedication to athletic
sports; indeed the former almost certainly indicated the presence of

Tom's first exploit at football, Arthur Hughes' illustration from T.
Hughes, *Tom Brown's Schooldays*, Macmillan, 1889

the latter. It was a philosophy heavily promoted in the colonial public schools modelling themselves on their English counterparts.[101] The authorities approved of the importance placed on the social values of co-operation, loyalty, courage, obedience to rules, and the rewards of dedication and persistence. A capitalist society approved the emphasis on competition and striving for success. This was social control in the classical sense of the members of a society voluntarily embracing a code of ethics and regulations rather than having such moral dictates imposed upon them.

The particular attribute which football was considered most likely to develop was 'pluck — downright bulldog pluck', and, as such, excellent training for soldiers. The benefit of the 'mimic-battle' basis of football was enhanced by the war scares of the eighteen fifties which inspired the volunteer defence artillery associations of that decade in Melbourne (and which incidentally comprised Wills' second suggestion for cricketers' off-season training!) 'The boy who would charge one bigger than himself without a moment's hesitation, who would kick his hardest at close quarters without showing the white feather, although his shins were streaming with blood — that boy, when a few years older, would probably stand a bayonet charge, or head a forlorn hope, with almost certain death staring him in the face'.[102] In 1879 a verse published on the Geelong versus Carlton match concluded:

> 'One thing we rely on, if foes should e'er try on
> A game that is sterner than football to view;
> When bullets are flying, and comrades are dying,
> Our boys to the bright "Southern Cross" will be true.'[103]

Such sentiments culminated in preparedness for the first world war. At the Jubilee dinner of Victorian football in 1908, Prime Minister Deakin spoke of the increased emphasis on sport in life during the last 30 or 40 years, repeating the familiar creed: 'not merely the physical training but the discipline of sport, its effect upon character and courage, its prominence as an educational process, were valuable. It has been found that the true sportsman, pitted at his best against his opponents under the rules of fair play, is the manliest man who walks this planet today. We can say that, and a great deal more, for the football player . . .' He contended: 'We are laying the foundations of a physical stamina and capacity, which is not only exercise and sport, but which in the hour of need will respond to the nation's call . . . may mean a nation's very safety, its name and its existence'.[104]

The Club Shoemaker, *Australasian* 1888

A comparison with NSW and South Australia

It would be instructive to compare the emergence of the different forms of football in the separate colonies of Australia, all subject to the trend to codify football, enjoyment in kicking a ball around, and the approved philosophy of muscular Christianity. It is claimed that New South Wales was the first place outside Britain where Rugby School football was played and that the Sydney University Club is the world's sixth oldest Rugby club, dating from 1863. The Club played against teams from the Sydney garrison and visiting naval ships until the Sydney Club began in 1865. The game survived pressures to outlaw it for brutality.[105] Victorians attributed resistance to adopting the Victorian variety of football to inter-state jealousy. The sooner the name was altered to the Australian Rules of Football, the editor of the *Footballer* declared in 1881, the better.[106] That seems a rather glib supposition which only some detailed research into the events and people of the time will test.

Perhaps the difference had something to do with the greater age of the colony of New South Wales, for the history of South Australia's football more nearly approaches that of Victoria. In South Australia the upper class cricketers were once again instrumental in promoting football and they were supported by the public schools, in this case, particularly by St. Peters College whose headmaster George Farr was a muscular christian par excellence. The rules tended to that of Harrow.[107] The *Argus* claimed that football [in the sense of being unattached to any distinctive adjective] had spread to South Australia and that the Adelaide Club numbered 100 members in July, 1860. The code under which the South Australians played was later described as 'a mixture of the Rugby and Association rules'. The main features were a round ball and no 'off-side' rule. The goal posts were 10 feet high and 18 feet apart with a bar eight feet high and a rope between the tops; a goal could only be scored between bar and rope. Pushing and holding were not allowed but shoulder to shoulder charging was. The ball could only be picked up 'on the hop and bounced'.[108] However, as had occurred in England and briefly in Victoria, there was more than one code played but it took longer before, 'the inconvenience of this being felt', a meeting was organised. In Adelaide a 'code of rules [was] drawn up almost exactly similar to that in use in Melbourne . . .'[109] The possibility of playing inter-colonial football was, arguably, a major factor in the decision to adopt Victorian Rules.[110] Victoria's particular success in establishing its game could be ascribed to the widespread early agreement on the rules, which then survived initial attack and resulted in everybody playing the one code.

The 'Father of Football'?

For one commonly referred to as the 'father of football', Colden Harrison appears very little in this initial period. The first use of this sobriquet is apparently in the *Reminiscences of an Old 'Un* who wrote in 1876 that Harrison may 'justly be called the Father of Victorian Football' and added 'there never was a harder worker than H.C.A. Harrison; a little vicious in his play perhaps but still an undeniably good 'un'.[111] Early documentation of Harrison's participation appears in the *Argus* when he captained a scratch 10-a-side for the Melbourne Club late in 1859.[112] What had he done in the time before 1876, then, to earn this title?

Harrison was a Richmond Cricket Club member and his first football club was also that of Richmond. He was not involved in the formation of the Melbourne Football Club or the establishment of the first rules.[113] In 1859 he was only 22 years of age and had not the status, reputation or football background of the committee members. Harrison himself only claims to have captained Richmond 'in the first year of football' and he points out that it was not the custom to elect a captain for a season but at the beginning of each match. The rules he does claim to have drafted were those for a meeting in 1866, often asserted to be the first rules by those unaware of the existence of the very early written rules of 1859. There were, in fact, at least two other meetings between 1859 and 1866 to consider changes in the rules.

In 1860 'a meeting of the members of the various clubs, was held . . . for the purpose of considering the propriety of altering the present rules, as drawn up by the Melbourne club'. The existing ban on tripping was ratified, free kicks for infringements introduced, and goals forced from scrimmages allowed. The Rugby and Eton Rules were read to the assembled footballers and Rule 8 of the MFC Rules, carrying the ball, was still a matter of controversy. Indeed Victoria's dryer grounds, compared to the muddier and slower grounds of England, possibly aggravated the problem by allowing sprinters to show a clean pair of heels to the rest of the players. On this occasion the non-handlers and non-runners had the numbers and the result was a more explicit rule on not handling the ball except after a catch or on the first hop (bounce) and a specific addition: 'it (the ball) shall not be run with in any case'.[114] Thompson supported this approach and this was quickly reflected in the claims of the *Argus* that the new rule which 'prohibits the lifting of or running with the ball worked admirably.'[115]

Thompson's wishful assertion however was not reflected in reality; the impracticality of deciding when a ball had been picked up on the *first* bounce caused constant disputes and eventually meant that the rule was soon disregarded, the players being allowed to pick up the ball on any bounce. This in turn encouraged the already prevalent Rugby habit of running with the ball, as presumably it was difficult to stop on the spot having chased and gathered in a bouncing ball. Moreover it seems logical that Rugby play should accompany Rugby balls, by then roughly oval in shape, and they were available at the time. Marshall, Melbourne's sporting goods entrepreneur, advertised for sale to the young man about town (concerned no doubt to be up with the latest in English fashion), 'famous Rugby Footballs which took the Prize Medal at the [London] Exhibition . . . being a new description of ball, made on a scientific principle, and that will fly many yards further than the old-fashioned sort'. Old Rugbeian, Tom Wills, was soon insisting on their use in the matches which he captained and the oval ball was being used by Melbourne and Geelong, certainly by 1862.[116]

Flying shot for Goal, *Australasian* 1888

When Geelong did first defeat the Melbourne Club in 1861, a supporter dared to query the Melbourne rules, citing the 'Geelong Rules' which allowed much more freedom in running and handling. Despite the riposte of 'Free Kick' for Melbourne, 'Why should the parent club play by the rules of an off-shoot?',[117] it says much for the confident supremacy of the Melbourne Football Club that it was prepared to compromise. After a dispute broke out in a Geelong-Melbourne match in 1862, running with the ball was allowed, but the fleet of foot, such as Harrison, were brought back to the rest of the field as it was required to bounce the ball *occasionally* while running.[118] It is difficult to determine when this practice developed but 1863 is the most likely year; the careers of Thompson and Smith, stalwart opponents of running, had removed them to Bendigo.

It took some time for this to be clarified and approved. A prominent player later recalled: 'The [bouncing] rule (sic) was the medium of a great deal of wrangling and, as it was more frequently honoured in the breach than in the observance, it became an endless source of trouble. Some players bounced the ball every 10 or 12 yards while others would run 40 or 50 yards and even further without bouncing it'.[119] That running was a tolerated practice, but not yet a rule, seems to be confirmed by the view of the football writer of *Bell's Life* who complained in 1864, 'The rule as to taking up and carrying the ball [that is, against doing this] was very much infringed, and frequently a player would run 20 yards with ball in hand. This may be in accordance with Rugby rules but certainly is not with those of Melbourne . . . The best players, it was noticed, were very often those to set the worst example in this particular'.[120]

Although the 1865 meeting of the MFC did not address itself to the problem,[121] this year saw the resolution of the conflict. In a match between the MFC and Royal Park, a goal was 'run' — clearly a breach of the rules but allowed by the umpire. Theodore Marshall later explained how the situation arose:

> At this time Royal Park played Melbourne. I was captain of the Royal Park [side], and in the team was J.E. Clarke, second only in fleetness on the football field at that time to Harrison. Before the game was commenced, I determined to test the running with the ball question, and it was arranged that if Clarke got the ball, he was to tuck it under his arm and run as far as possible without bouncing it. Clarke, seizing a favourable opportunity, bolted with the ball along the wing, dodging several Melbourne players on the way and, without once bouncing it, flew towards the goal and kicked it. When Clarke had overrun the orthodox 40 or 50 yards, the Melbourne men stood wondering at his audacity, and ceased to interfere with him. Harrison who was nearly a 40 yard man himself, asked me what it meant! I answered that I simply wanted to settle once and for all how far a man should be allowed to run with the ball without bouncing it. After consultation it was agreed that the ball should be bounced at least once in every ten yards, and so this important point in our game was brought about.[122]

To his credit, Harrison incorporated the agreement in the 1866 Victorian Football Rules which he drafted. These 1866 rules differed only in minor details from the earlier rules except for Rule 8 which required the ball to be bounced every five or six yards. It is these rules which have been commonly regarded as the first rules. They are not the first rules but they are very important in that they do specify this distinguishing element of Australian Rules Football as it is known today. The Athletics Sports Committee had large numbers of the code printed and sold them for 11 shillings per 1000 through Colden Harrison.[123] By 1870 such ball handling was fully accepted and considered 'inseparable from our mode of play'.[124]

Colden Harrison played cricket for the Richmond Cricket Club and was probably drawn into football by Tom Wills, his much admired friend and famous cousin. Harrison's speed with a football under his arm meant he quickly became a figure to be respected. He began foot-running in 1859 and, when Wills left Melbourne for Geelong in 1860 and departed for the ill-fated establishment of the family Queensland property in 1861,[125] Colden Harrison was making his own reputation as an athlete and was able to step into the breach left by Wills' absence on the football scene. In 1862 Colden was transferred to the Geelong customs and his ability gave a fillip to the Geelong side. In the same year he used his Easter holidays to travel to Ballarat to demonstrate kicking at an athletics meeting. The Ballarat Club was established in the same year.[126]

Only Wills and Hammersley were still on the Melbourne Football Club committee in 1865. T. Butterworth had set up a general store in Castlemaine.[127] James Thompson was in Bendigo and as an oarsman, it seems he may have become more concerned with the advancement of acquatic sports.[128] Thomas Smith, too, was away from Melbourne as the Inspector of Schools for the Sandhurst district from 1863 to the end of 1864 when he was dismissed from this post for 'official negligence and improper conduct'.[129] Whatever Smith may have done to deserve this, it was not sufficiently disgraceful to prevent him from watching a football match in Melbourne in July 1865[130] but almost certainly he would no longer have been able to teach in Victoria and it seems he moved to South Australia.

As a sporting writer, Hammersley was interested in all sports, particularly racing, and he admitted that football was of less interest once he stopped playing.[131] He turned much of his attention to athletics, forming with Harrison the Melbourne Athletics Committee. The Committee promoted the Athletics Sports Challenge Cup in 1865 and, with its potential for generating excitement, rescued football from temporary doldrums, attracting partisan spectator crowds identifying with their own communities, a slightly more civilised version of the old English folk-games in which most of the men in rival towns could diffuse their tensions by actually joining in the contest![132]

Wills did not return to Victoria permanently until 1864 and cricket was always his first love. He became involved with inter-colonial cricket, coaching the MCC and the Aboriginal cricketers,[133] but gave good-heartedly of his time and advice to footballers, particularly in the Geelong area. By the early seventies he was drinking heavily enough to attract some public comment.[134] In any case, Wills was no administrator. 'He was secretary for the Melbourne Cricket club for one season [1857-58,] and when he left office everything was in a muddle — club papers, cricket-balls, cricket guides, Zingari flannels, cigars, "spiked" boots, — everything one can conceive, stuffed together in the large tin box of the club.'[135] Nor had the others inspired confidence: at the 1860 annual meeting of the Melbourne Cricket Club the financial situation of the Club had been described as impecunious, and an almost clean sweep of the committee had occurred, taking Thompson, Hammersley, Bryant and Butterworth with it.[136]

In contrast, Harrison's strength evidently lay in administration, which his profession as a public servant no doubt assisted. His work was quiet, but effective enough not to go unnoticed by his contemporaries who praised his efforts without saying what those actually consisted of, and who consistently nominated him to positions of

Intercolonial Cricketers *Vic. v. NSW*, *Illustrated Post* 1866. National Library of Australia. Tom Wills is the balding cricketer holding the ball

responsibility as the administration developed. Thus it was that Colden Harrison (and R.W. Wardill) represented the Melbourne Football Club at the 1866 Rules conference and that Harrison was asked to draft the latest set of rules. The new game, after its initial spurt, needed a period of consolidation and continued, consistent supervision to succeed, and this Harrison appears to have provided.

Controversy over rules and violence continued throughout the sixties and the concurrent debate in England included a discussion of the football rules of the leading English public schools from the English sporting paper the *Field* reprinted in *Bell's Life in Victoria*.[137] With the teams from British regiments returning from the Maori wars and stationed in Melbourne in 1867-69, violence and the Rugby habit of running with the ball without bouncing it returned, reminding spectators of the earlier frays in the Richmond paddock,[138] and tested the determination of the locals to forego the 'scrimmage from which half-a dozen men emerge in a semi-nude state' for the more subtle pleasures of 'good kicking and dexterity in dodging'.[139] These matches against the 14th (Buckinghamshire) Regiment of Foot (2nd battalion) and the 40th (2nd Somersetshire) Regiment of Foot under the Rugby player Captain Noyes and cricketer C.S. Gordon became legendary for their violent style of play; Harrison at the end of one 'brutally rough game' made 'a jocular allusion' to the soldiers having treated his side as 'the enemy'.[140] Having made allowances in the first match for the soldiers' ignorance of the rules, he then insisted that the games be played under the Victorian Rules. Harrison never ducked the physical clashes, declaring football was 'not suitable for menpoodles and milksops', and only retired in 1872, after a particularly strenuous game, on his doctor's advice.[141]

Such a reputation for fearlessness stood him in good stead during the early 1870s when 'a noticeable feature in the play at this time was the prevalence of a great deal of roughness in the form of slinging, hacking and other rowdy elements quite foreign to the game and these brought it into a very unpleasant odour. Scribes began to write it down, stigmatising it as brutal and unmanly; particularly condemning the common fashion of holding the ball when collared running with it — the great cause of scrimmages.'[142] In 1872 the rules were again modified, including changing ends at half-time, referring disputes to an umpire instead of to the captains, and decreeing that goals must be kicked not 'forced'. In 1874 a rule was introduced requiring a player, running with the ball and collared, to drop it immediately without handling the ball again before it was kicked, under penalty of a free kick. This allegedly reduced the scrimmages and it was claimed 'the game was consequently contested in a much more friendly

Half Time, *Australasian* 1888

spirit, being of a superior order, and victory was now the result of skill and judgment, and not of mere animal vigour'.[143] In other words, (gentle)manly.

In the 1876 issue of *The Footballer* can be found a celebratory parody which begins:

> 'Muscular Christians, Hurrah! Hurrah!
> Football, the vicious, has passed away;
> Its draws and squabbles nigh made me sick,
> Come, let's give it a passing kick.[144]

In 1877 the Victorian Football Association was formed with William Clarke, the largest landowner in the colony, as its prestigious figure head, and Colden Harrison as vice president, a tribute to his play, physical courage and consistent involvement with administration and rule-making. At football's 'coming of age' in 1879 it was Colden Harrison who organised the party — a light-hearted match of past and present players with the proceeds for the Children's Hospital. Although he may not have conceived the child, he had given it fatherly care and fostered it through a precocious childhood and a turbulent adolescence to maturity. He had played an important role in evoking and laying down the basis for the current ten metre bouncing rule which is a vital feature of the game. He continued to exercise a paternal influence, trying with little success, to persuade other states and countries to take up the game.

With the introduction of enclosed grounds in the late seventies, football was on its way to gate money, betting, veiled professionalism and the secession from the Football Association of a number of clubs to form the League in 1896 — but that is another story. In 1889 Colden Harrison was honoured with life membership of the Football Association, the then governing body. By that time Wills, Thompson, and Hammersley had all died relatively young, Wills and Thompson in their forties and Hammersley at the age of 59. 'Father' also has the meaning of 'oldest member, doyen, member with the longest continuous service': certainly this sense was well and truly justified when the stalwarts of 1908 formally bestowed on Henry Colden Antill Harrison the accolade of Father of Australian Rules Football, as they celebrated the jubilee of the days when enthusiasts first kicked a ball in the 'Richmond paddock'.

Harrison was a familiar figure around wintery sporting grounds, warmed by the affection and sentiment of the football world. Near his ninetieth birthday in 1926, Colden Harrison was seen early at the M.C.G. A journalist wrote: 'Every groundsman and official and member is a friend of his. He loves to loiter in the dressingrooms, where there is the reek of training oil and perspiration. It is the smell of powder to a war horse. Before the game starts, he has some advice to give both sides. It is to tell them to play the game, and to remember that football is a game.'[145] With such prose, a legend was made.

THE STORY OF AN ATHLETE: A PICTURE OF THE PAST

Colden Harrison in his garden. L. Cooke collection

AUTHOR'S INTRODUCTION

I am as old as Melbourne. For, although it was in June, 1835, that Batman took his boat up the Yarra to the first falls, and wrote in his diary those memorable and historic words, 'This will be the place for a Village,' it was not until October 1st, 1836, the year and month of my birth, that his choice received official recognition.

The mere fact of my being the same age as Melbourne is not in itself of particular interest, there being many others in the same category; but my case is, I imagine, unique in that I have also been constantly associated with the growth of the town in its various phases to the present day.

In addition, it has been suggested that, of those who travelled overland from New South Wales to Port Phillip in the thirties, I am probably the only survivor.

Considering these circumstances and being urged thereto by many friends, I have made an effort to record my recollections–those of an Australian born–even at this late hour. Naturally they will contain descriptions of life in the early days only as it came under my own observation and experience.

With regard to athletics, with the early history of which I may truthfully lay claim to close and continued association, I have not, for obvious reasons, altogether depended on my own unaided memory for facts, but have had considerable recourse to the newspapers of the time. In this, as in other cases, where I have been indebted for assistance, the sources of my information are acknowledged in the text.

I hope it will not be considered that I have given undue space or prominence to the contests in running with my famous rival, L. L. Mount; but as they were regarded as the outstanding athletic events of the day, and were indeed, important incidents in my athletic career, I could hardly avoid doing so, especially as I consider that I was fortunate in finding, when just in my prime, so worthy a foeman among the ranks of the amateurs.

As for football, I should have liked to write a more detailed account of its history to recall the doughty deeds of various brilliant players up to the present day, but must be content to leave that congenial task to some younger and abler writer.

Indeed, brief as this effort is, I must confess I should never have attempted it but for the encouragement and assistance of one of my daughters; and I can only hope that the story will prove of some interest to the indulgent reader.

H. C. A. Harrison

Molonglo, Kew
September, 1923

CHAPTER 1

WITH THE OVERLANDERS

As I have once or twice seen it stated in a newspaper that my birthplace was Parramatta, I shall take this opportunity to correct the mistake, and so, to begin at the beginning–I was born on the 16th October, 1836, at Jarvisfield, Picton, one of the old homesteads of New South Wales. My mother was on a visit, at the time, to her half-sister, the wife of Major H. C. Antill, after whom, as he stood god-father to me, I was named.[1] He had come out to Sydney in December, 1809, with his regiment (the 73rd) and as aide-de-camp to Major General Macquarie, Governor of New South Wales, 1810-1821. When General Macquarie returned to England, Major Antill retired from the army, and remained in the Colony. Picton, which was a military grant, was so named by him, in memory of his former General, under whom both he and Macquarie had served in the Peninsular war. I should say that the township, with its surrounding hills, is one of the most prettily situated of any on the railway line between Albury and Sydney.

When my father decided to join in the rush to take up land in the newly opened up district of Port Phillip, I was about one year old, so that, although born in New South Wales, my earliest recollections are of Victoria.

My father, John Harrison, was a sea-captain. He had begun his career as a midshipman in the British Navy, and was a lieutenant on H.M.S. *Ganges* when he retired at the age of nineteen or twenty, to take command of one of a fleet of trading vessels owned by his father, and engaged in the trade with South America. Later on, he came to Sydney, where he met and married my mother, in 1832.[2] On his return to England, about 1833, he persuaded his father to sell off everything and return to New South Wales with him. They fitted out a small cutter of about 40 tons, and sailed for Sydney. The *Rose*, as she was called, was one of the smallest vessels that had ever made that voyage, and it was considered a great feat of seamanship to bring her out safely.[3] On arriving at Capetown, where she was beached to have the barnacles scraped off her, the wondering inhabitants refused to believe that she had come so far.

It speaks well for my mother's courage, that she should have faced so perilous a voyage. One of my father's sisters had started with them, but they had got no farther than the Bay of Biscay, when she became frightened, and insisted so strongly that she could not continue the journey in so small a boat, that my father was obliged to put back and land her in England again. But a fatal accident, which occurred before the completion of the voyage, demonstrated that her fears were not without foundation. One night, during a violent storm, my grandfather was washed overboard, and, as it was pitch dark, and the waves mountains high, it was impossible to rescue him, and so, he was lost. This incident cast a gloom over the small party on board for the remainder of the voyage, and quite spoilt the memory of what might otherwise have been an enjoyable and interesting experience. The redoubtable little vessel afterwards did good service in the New South Wales coastal trade, and among the islands, but was ultimately wrecked on the coast between Newcastle and Port Jackson.

Apropos of the wreck, a curious incident happened, a relation of which may be of interest to those who make a study of telepathy. One day, during the absence of the vessel, my mother remarked to my father, 'I see the *Rose* is back.' 'Why Jane, what makes you think that? She is not due yet,' he replied. But my mother explained that she had just seen the little cabin boy, carrying his bundle (in the usual bandana handkerchief, slung over his shoulder, on a stick), walk up the front path and go round to the back of the house. But, on enquiry being made, no sign of the boy could be found. My mother, who took a kindly interest in the lad, became very anxious, and said she was sure some accident must have happened to him. As the *Rose* was soon overdue, my father began to worry, in his turn, and he had a dream, in which he saw quite clearly the wreck, somewhere on the coast. And so he determined, in company with a friend, to explore the coast in search of the ship–or its wreckage. They had not travelled many miles when he recognised the spot he had seen in his dream. After vainly hunting about for some time for traces of a wreck, they, at last came upon the body of the boy, which had been washed ashore, still grasping in his hand his pathetic bundle. That was all there ever was to show that the *Rose* had made her last voyage.

Jane Harrison nee Howe. A.M. Smith collection

Another ship of my father's was wrecked on the inhospitable coast of Norfolk Island, while he was engaged in carrying Government stores from Sydney.[4]

As everyone knows, though the island itself is very beautiful, the coast is extremely rough, and affords no safe anchorage for ships.

Consequently, the work of landing stores or passengers has always been attended with great difficulty. In this case, the government moorings gave way, and the vessel was dashed to pieces on the rocks. Before this happened, however, rather an amusing incident occurred. The convicts were helping with the work of unloading, when suddently a most curious looking object presented itself to my father on deck, and asked politely whether he could be of any assistance. It was one of the convicts, who, though loaded with chains, had miraculously worked his way along one of the ropes attached to the ship, where he arrived half drowned, with the water flowing from his hair and beard.

After this loss, for which he never received any compensation–though caused by the weakness of the government moorings–my father determined to give up the sea, and engage in pastoral pursuits.

Thus it happened that, towards the end of 1837 (I being then one year old, as I have before stated) we joined the ever increasing band of overlanders for Port Phillip, now Victoria. My father had previously formed a temporary station on the Molonglo River, probably on the very site on which the Federal Capital is now being built, on which to collect his stock. We had the Quadrant R brand of cattle, from the well-known Redfern estate, and the sheep were bought from William Wentworth, the great Australian patriot. I mention this fact because even the stock, in such connection, had a historic interest![5]

In common with the other overlanders of 1837, we followed what was called Mitchell's track, namely, that made by Major (afterwards Sir Thomas) Mitchell, on his return journey from Port Phillip in 1836, after his discovery of what he designated Australia Felix.[6] The squatters generally travelled in groups, in order to be able to give assistance to one another in difficult situations, and also for the purpose of mutual protection against the blacks. Just about the time our party crossed the Murray, then called the Hume, after the explorer, Mr. George Faithful's party had been attacked and several of his men killed.[7] So that every precaution was necessary. On one occasion–just before reaching the camp on the Murray bank–my father had let the stock get some way ahead before coming on with his family, and he found, much to his disquietude, as we drove along, that the blacks had been laying logs across the track to impede our way; so that he was obliged to alight continually and, at the expenditure of great exertion, clear a way. During this operation he was careful to keep his double-barrelled gun in evidence for the benefit of concealed observers, who were evidently acquainted with its mysterious power, as they refrained from attacking us, and we arrived safely in camp just as night was falling.

Crossing the Murray was one of the difficult problems of the route. The covered-in cart, in which we travelled, was floated across, ferry fashion, by the aid of a rope stretched from bank to bank, on empty barrels made into a sort of raft. The cattle and sheep, of course, swam across. If a few could be induced to take to the water and swim to the opposite bank, the others would soon follow. It was sometimes difficult to keep the cattle from 'ringing', that is, following each other round in circles, when they would gradually be carried down stream and some of them probably drowned. But the trouble was generally overcome by the expedient of forming a barrier across the river by a number of horsemen, just below the crossing, and so forcing them to head for the bank.

Among those who travelled at the same time with us, and who also were the first to cross the Goulburn with sheep, were Captain Hepburn, another sea captain, and an old friend of my father's, the Messrs. Hamilton, Mollison, Bowman, and others whose names I cannot now recall.[8] Naturally, my recollections of the journey were formed from hearing the various episodes of the way discussed by my parents and their friends later on. But there is one of my *very* own which I carry in my mind's eye to this day. I remember, distinctly, sitting on my mother's lap (I suppose we were in the cart) and seeing a fierce looking blackfellow standing near, balancing a spear in his hand as if about to throw it. Of course I do not pretend I had sufficient intelligence at the time to realize the danger of the situation, but I suppose it was rather an unaccustomed sight for my childish eyes, and so it attracted and impressed itself on my wandering attention.

The journey lasted about three months, and, when I consider it, I cannot but be struck with the romance of that phase in the settlement of the country. What a remarkable journey was that! And, what a wonderful invasion of a new land was that–extending over a period of about four years–made to the continual accompaniment of the bleating of sheep, the bellowing of cattle and cracking of stockwhips! And the poor, bewildered native population? What must their sensations have been, looking on, for the most part silently and helplessly, while their hunting grounds were being overrun by a race of hitherto unknown beings and thousands of absolutely strange animals. And, when I come to think of it, what a varied collection of flockmasters was there! Most of them, men of good education and possessing a fair amount of capital–all brave, sturdy, self-reliant, and resourceful. In fact, the highest type of adventurous Briton was to be found among them. A few of them, like my father and Captain Hepburn, were accompanied by their wives and families, who faced the journey cheerfully, and undaunted by the risks attending it. I like to think

I took even a small part in an event, worthy of an epic which, I hope, may be written some day.

My mother was very young then and, I dare say, rather enjoyed the experience, as a somewhat prolonged picnic. In some respects, it was not unlike the modern caravanning, which was so popular in England, till motoring superseded it, as a mode of seeing the country.

Of course, sheep travel very slowly, and we used probably to rest occasionally for a day or so in propitious spots. My father would generally drive on ahead with us, thus avoiding the dust produced by the travelling stock, and fix on a site for the next camp, where tents would be soon pitched, and everything arranged for the night. No one, who has not experienced it, can understand the charm of camping out. What is more restful or enjoyable than sitting, or lying round the camp-fire on still, starry nights, after a strenuous day, swapping yarns, or joining in some well-known song or chorus? I defy even the most saturnine person not to succumb to the general geniality and camaraderie of an evening in camp. And so, with plenty of books to read, and an occasional visit to an adjacent camp, except under bad weather conditions, one can imagine the time being passed quite pleasantly.

Most of the men who travelled in our particular group, remained in the Goulburn Valley. But my father notwithstanding the advice of Captain Hepburn to pitch his camp there, unfortunately elected to travel further on, and finally settled on the river Plenty.[9] This was good country, but being within no more than twenty-two miles of Melbourne, somewhere in the vicinity of the present Yan Yean reservoir, in about six years' time we were squeezed out, and obliged to wander again in search of unoccupied country, at a time when it was not so easy to find.[10] However, we had some happy times there. We children led glorious out-of-door lives, and found a never failing interest in the clear, ever-running water of the pretty little river, near which the house was situated. At a very early age, I became initiated into the pensive delights of fishing, and have retained an ardent love of the sport all my life. Never shall I forget the delicious flavour of the blackfish which, in my childish pride in catching them, I thought the finest fish in the world, and still think very hard to beat! Dr. Ronald, who was a near and dear neighbour of ours on the Plenty,[11] and, who remained in the district till his death, used to say of blackfish, that they could not be beaten as a food for invalids, not only on account of their delicacy of flavour, but also for their nutritive properties.

Opposite: Yarra above Studley Park, Grosse, *Illustrated Australasian News* 1865. La Trobe collection, State Library of Victoria

CHAPTER 2

ON THE PLENTY

Our house, like all those of the early settlers, was built of strong slabs, with a bark roof, and formed three sides of a quadrangle at the back. The kitchen had a large open fireplace with a spit for cooking the joint. We children used sometimes to vary our play by running into the kitchen and relieving the cook of the business of turning the spit, so that we could make ourselves 'sop-in-the-pan', considered by us a great bonne bouche. One day, while my eldest sister, Addie [Adela] and I were thus engaged, my mother called me to another room. Addie had already disposed of her piece and remained hungrily watching mine, which was just turning to the right shade of gold; so that I went very reluctantly, and returned as quickly as possible. But, though I had been expeditious, she had been still more so,–the pan was empty and Addie's mouth was full! Taking into consideration my extreme youth and the bitterness of my disappointment, I am sure I shall have the sympathy of all fair-minded readers when I confess that I rushed at the delinquent and fastened my thwarted teeth in her arm. We often enjoyed a good laugh over that episode in later years.

To return to the subject of slab houses. It is wonderful how comfortable most of them were, and how picturesque and suitable to their surroundings of open forest, consisting principally of the various kinds of gums and wattles. I remember that one of our neighbours, Mr. John Pinney Bear,[1] built his house with special defences in case of attack by the blacks, and it was always spoken of as the Castle![2] The blacks in that district belonged to the Yarra Yarra tribe,[3] and

Bear's Castle. La Trobe collection, State Library of Victoria

were considered rather dangerous at first. But only on two occasions do I remember our having an alarm through the blacks. The first time, hundreds of them surrounded the house–the quadrangle was full of them–and, as all the station-hands were away for the day, my father was the only man about. At first it was thought best for the household to keep perfectly quiet, and we all assembled in the nursery, as it was the largest room in the house. The blacks evidently thought there were only women and children at home, for they presently became very cheeky, knocking on the doors with their waddies and sticks. My father, who was rather hot-tempered, could not stand that, and suddenly rushed out on them with his gun in his hand; and they were evidently so surprised at the sight of him that they all disappeared in the most miraculous manner. In two or three minutes there was not one to be seen. But we could hear a great jabbering going on down at the potato patch, a short distance from the house, and there, we could see some of the lubras digging up potatoes with their yam sticks. These were always carried about by them, and were six or seven feet long, about as thick as a man's wrist, with a sharp point at one end.

The second alarm we had was once during the absence of our parents in town. There were only the women servants in the house, but, as soon as the blacks were seen approaching, they shut all the windows and doors, and we all collected in one room, keeping absolutely quiet. The strain on the nerves of everyone there can be easily understood. Addie, evidently to relieve the tension, tried to look through a small hole in one of the slabs to see what was going on, and received a great shock on finding herself eye to eye with a black woman engaged on the same business from the outside. At this she gave voice to a yell which shook the already sorely tried nerves of everyone in the room. Evidently it was too much for the blacks–perhaps they mistook it for a war-whoop!–for they melted away, in their usual silent manner, immediately. But our parents, who returned soon after, had been very alarmed by a report they heard on the way, to the effect that a large number of blacks had been seen on Bende-meer,[4] the name of our home, so that their relief and thankfulness on finding us all safe and sound can be imagined.

After that, I do not think we had any more trouble with the blacks. They seemed to realize that they must keep away from the house–in large numbers, at any rate. Whenever they camped on the station, it was always near the river, about two hundred yards or so from the house. As a matter of fact, we children visited their camp pretty often, and they became a great source of amusement to us. They were very quick in picking up enough English to make themselves understood, but as they found it very hard to ennunciate the letter 's', our great delight used to be to make them practise the phrase, 'A ship in full sail'. But they never could get nearer than 'Jibber a bull jail' accompanied by roars of laughter on their part. They always had a great sense of the ridiculous, more particularly when at their own expense. They really had the dispositions of happy children, and seemed to bear little or no malice towards those who had occupied and taken away their hunting grounds.

There is one incident which I remember particularly, as showing their kindly and humane disposition. My sister, Kate, a toddler of about two years old, was one day sitting on the edge of the log bridge, which was about an equal distance between the house and the camp, when a pet lamb came behind her and playfully butted her into the stream. We others, frightened out of our wits, gave vent to a succession of piercing screams, which brought some of the lubras running to see what the matter was. Much to our relief, they got her out of the water before she had time to drown, and carried her up to the house, where she was quickly divested of her wet clothing, and was soon none the worse for the ducking.

For the benefit of the young people of the present day, who have, perhaps, never seen any Aboriginals, I should like to describe some of their ways of living. A white man would starve on their diet, which consisted chiefly of fish, caught by spearing, iguana, opossum, kanga-roo, grubs from the roots of wattle trees, and the bulb-like roots of yams and murnongs. Their mia-mias consisted of strips of bark or long branches of trees, supported at an angle against a fallen log or trunk of a tree, away from the weather side. Their clothing in the winter consisted of opossum skins joined together by the sinews of kangaroos and other animals. I never saw the blacks making fire, as, after the white man came about, they could always get it from him, and they generally carried lighted fire-sticks from one camp to another. The men all carried spears and boomerangs, and the women yam sticks. They were all very afraid of the black police, who generally stripped and went in among them with tomahawks, when on a punitive expedition. Like all primitive races, they had a firm belief in witchcraft. A death among them was always attributed to the sorcery of some hostile tribe, and they had a very simple mode of discovering the authors of the trouble. One of the men would hold a yam stick in the middle of a circle, and after some sort of incantation, let it fall. The tribe, in whose direction it pointed, was considered the guilty one, and reprisals would be made forthwith.

There was a mission station somewhere between us and Melbourne, where the blacks were taught English and the tenets of Christianity.[5] One of the lubras, on being asked by my mother, how she liked the mission, caused some amusement by saying: 'Me no like him much. Plenty halleluia, but borak too much damper'. Damper, it will be seen, was greatly appreciated by them, and they were always delighted on receiving gifts of flour with which to make it. If we children happened to be at the camp when the damper was taken out of the hot ashes, the lubras used always to give us most generous slices of it, and nothing pleased them more than to see us enjoying it. They were also very fond of boiled flour, which they used to call 'bubble bubble'.

While on the Plenty, life, socially, was by no means dull. We had pleasant neighbours and, as we were on the route between Melbourne and the Goulburn, the squatters from that district used generally to stay the night, going or coming, as a matter of course. I have known as many as seven or eight travelling squatters arrive at the same time. They were quite content to roll themselves up in their blankets and sleep on the floor. Among some of those whose names I can recall at this day were Messrs. Norman McLeod,[6] Peter Snodgrass, Farquhar McKenzie, and Captain Murchison and his son Roderick.[7] Peter Snodgrass was a very high-spirited young man at that time, and always ready for anything in the way of fun. I remember one night, when sleeping with a crowd on the floor, he caused a great consternation to the others by putting on his spurs! By this simple expedient he secured himself plenty of elbow room and a good night's rest. In later years he entered parliament.[8] His eldest daughter, the late Janet,

Lady Clarke (widow of Sir William), was one of our most popular citizens. Another daughter, the wife of Brigadier General F. G. Hughes, is also well known for her public spirit.[9] Roderick Murchison was a very handsome young man and was a fine horseman. He had bad luck in his later years, his property near Geelong being eaten out by rabbits. He lived the last years of his life in Melbourne (where he died some ten years or so ago), and during that time we used to meet weekly for a game of chess in my home. Murchison's Scrub Exterminator, extensively used by gardeners a few years ago, was his invention.

Being within easy distance of the 'Settlement', as Melbourne was at first generally designated, my mother was able to attend occasional social functions there. We used to stay with my uncle, Mr. Thomas Wills, who for a short time resided in Melbourne, Collins Street, and then in the Heidelberg district, where he had an estate on the Darebin Creek, with a frontage on the Yarra, just a few miles from Melbourne, and conveniently situated on our road from the Plenty. His home, Lucerne, which is mentioned in Rolf Boldrewood's *Old Melbourne Memories*, in the chapter describing the original christening and settlement of Heidelberg, is a large two-storied, white stuccoed house, and may be seen from the Willsmere Road, on the opposite side of the Yarra at Kew.[10]

Lucerne Farm, a sketch by Arthur Wills. Dr G. Buckwell collection

I shall give here some extracts from the *Port Phillip Patriot* and the *Port Phillip Herald* of the year 1840, showing the primitive state of the Melbourne streets at that time, and which are of especial interest to me on account of the names mentioned therein. It appears that the bachelors of the 'Settlement' had given a ball on the 14th January, a short account of which may be of interest to some of my readers, as showing how the early inhabitants amused themselves. A small committee of management had been formed, consisting of Lieut. Vignolles of the military staff, Mr. Smith, presumably the bank-manager of that name, and Mr. Le Souef whose descendants are well known in Australia to-day in connection with their scientific and expert management of some of our zoological gardens.[11] The ball was held in Mr. W. Rucker's newly erected store in Flinders Lane, the ceiling of which was 'covered with the flags of different nations, and the walls tastefully decorated with festoons of evergreen shrubs'.[12] About a hundred and fifty guests were present, and dancing was indulged in till the small hours of the morning. The dances mentioned in the accounts were: quadrilles, waltzes, Spanish and country dances. At about 1.30 a.m., supper was served. It was 'elegantly laid out in a large marquee communicating with the dancing room by a covered passage'. The sound of the popping of champagne corks is especially mentioned as contributing to the general brightness and gaiety! The band left after supper, but the ladies took it in turn to play till dawn. After the ball was over, a 'distressing accident' occurred which was described in next day's paper as follows: 'A party consisting of Mrs. Wills, Mrs. Langhorne, Mrs. Harrison and Captain Fyans[13] were returning from the ball in a carriage belonging to T. Wills, Esq., JP., and when in the act of turning the corner of Bourke Street into Swanston Street, the wheels sunk into a rut so suddenly that the coachman was thrown out, and the horses, startled by the shock, set off at full gallop in the direction of Mr. Wills' stables, close to which they came in contact with a tree with such violence that the carriage was smashed to atoms, and the inmates thrown out and very seriously injured.' It appears, however, that the ladies soon recovered from their shaking, but Captain Fyans who, by the way, was commissioner for crown lands in the Geelong district, was laid up for some weeks afterwards. The coachman was reported as being none the worse for his fall.

Before passing on, I might here say a few words about my uncle, one of the best known colonists of his time. He had been married under rather romantic circumstances. When travelling to England, somewhere about the year 1826, his ship was wrecked on or near the island of Mauritius, and those of the passengers and crew who were saved were hospitably housed and entertained by the inhabitants of

Port Louis. Thomas Wills at that time, a young, handsome widower, was received into the home of Dr. John Richard Barry, Professor of the Colonial College, and, in a short time fell in love with, and married the professor's sister [Mary Ann Barry], who was living with him. After some time they returned to New South Wales, and when Victoria was opened up, came over and settled for some years at Lucerne. I remember his wife as a true 'grande dame' and a splendid hostess.[14] Their daughter, 'Cousin Kate' as we children used to call her, was a beautiful and charming girl in her early teens when I first remember her. She, later on, married Captain Lewis Conran of the 11th Regiment of Foot, Commander of the Forces here, and who was subsequently aide-de-camp to Governor La Trobe, and Sergeant-at-Arms to the first Legislative Council.[15]

There is a very fine specimen of an English oak tree in the grounds of Lucerne–the oldest and largest in the state, I believe. It was planted by Cousin Kate, who brought the acorn, from which it grew, from George's Hall, New South Wales, the home of Mr. David Johnston, a connection of ours. He, by the way, was a younger son of Colonel George Johnston, who was forced into the unenviable position of having to arrest Governor Bligh in 1808.[16] The Lucerne oak flourished so well in the congenial climate and soil, with the added advantage of a small natural pond at it foot, that it soon outstripped its progenitors in size and beauty. Considering that its life dates from the earliest days of the settlement here, I have sometimes thought of suggesting that the shire in which it stands should take on the responsibility of its care and protection, as it would be a pity to let it become damaged in any way.[17] The house, though standing on a rise, was once nearly covered by one of the early floods of the Yarra, some of the furniture actually floating out of the French windows leading on to the balcony.[18] Since then the river has been cleared, and the flood waters never rise high enough to reach the house now. I have very happy school-boy recollections of the luscious peaches in the very fine orchard there! But that has long since disappeared, and the place has been used as a dairy farm for many years now.

My uncle bought a great deal of land in Melbourne and other parts of Victoria at the early sales, and so, knew something of the varying values of property in the first few years. I shall quote the history of one block owned by him, as an example. It was a half-acre block, extending from Bourke Street to Little Collins Street, on the west side of Royal Lane, at the back of the Melbourne Town Hall. He gave £150 for it, and let it at £150 a year, on a twenty-one years' lease. This would appear a pretty fair speculation. But, during the time of the diggings, the lessee, by letting the various primitive buildings she had erected on the block, was making about £7,000 a year out of it!

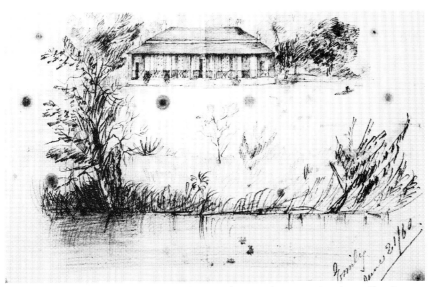

George's Hall NSW, a sketch by Emily Harrison. L. Cooke collection

After my uncle's death in 1872, I, as his trustee, in collaboration with the late Mr. Francis Gibbes, sold it for the sum of £37,000 to Petty, the well-known butcher.[19]

But to return to the subject of life (and its distractions) on the Plenty. My mother, who, while in Sydney, had studied under Wallace, the composer of the opera of *Maritana*,[20] was an accomplished musician, and had brought her piano with her when we came overland. It was, I suppose, one of the few in Port Phillip at that time, and was a source of pleasure, not only to herself and family, but to our numerous visitors.

One thing that counted considerably in the early settlement of the colony was the service of 'assigned' servants, any other kind of labour being practically unobtainable. A great number of these people had been 'sent out' for what, in these days, would be considered comparatively slight offences, so that they were, for the most part, quite trustworthy. At least, I know we never had any trouble with them. They were assigned by the government, under certain conditions, and received a small yearly wage.[21] They all gave good and willing service, both men and women, and I should like to take this opportunity to acknowledge gratefully the large part they played in helping to make life possible in those primitive days. The men generally went by some qualifying sobriquet. For instance, one of our bullock drivers was called 'Long Bill'. He remained with us till my father retired from squatting. 'Bill, the pony' was another, who, as his name implies, was very strong and of a nuggety build. Of the women, I now only remember the name of our nurse, Sarah. She was young and comely when she came to us, and was the kindest nurse any children ever had. Most of this class married in time and settled down in homes of their own, and some did very well afterwards, I am glad to say.

One of the trials of bush life was the danger of bushrangers. In 1842 we were among those who were stuck up by Jepps' gang.[22] Our parents were away at the time, and only the servants were at home. We suddenly heard the galloping of horses coming over the bridge, and, on looking out, saw four or five horsemen, led by Mr. Rider,[23] one of our neighbours, who had been forced into guiding them. They came on calling out, 'Bail up! Bail up!' It was unmistakable what their business was, and, I remember, one of the maids had the presence of mind to run and hide a valuable gun belonging to my father. The bushrangers rounded up all the adults about the place, at the point of the pistol, and made them sit on a form facing the fire in the kitchen, so that it required only one man to keep guard while the others hunted for what valuables they could find. We children were left unmolested and, I think, quite enjoyed the excitement. I remember we especially admired William Foggarty, one of the gang, who was swaggering about in Mr. Henry Norcott's[24] brilliant uniform, with the sword dangling at his side, which he had taken from a neighbouring homestead. Norcott had been in the Austrian Huzzars and had brought his uniform out with him. It was lined with scarlet, with a great deal of gold about it, and so gave the wearer– a tall, well-built man–quite a distinguished air, to our childish eyes, at any rate! I do not think the gang got much from us, as my father never kept any money in the house, but, as they were going off, they shot a goose and requested the cook to have it ready for their dinner next day. But we never saw them again. They next stuck up Dr. Ronald,[25] and after they had left, he hurriedly barricaded the doors and windows as best he could. While he was doing this, someone galloped up and dashed into the yard. The doctor, who was evidently rather excited, did not see, in the gathering dusk, who it was, and taking the horseman for one of the bushrangers looking for his mates, called out loudly, 'Your friends have gone on, Sir.' As misfortune would have it, it happened to be one of the squatters hastening to join his neighbours who were collecting to hunt down the gang. Not knowing the doctor's mistake, he hurried on and overtook what turned out to be the bushrangers. Before he could realize his position, they had seized him and hurried him into the scrub, where they tied him to a sapling while they sat down and had some refreshment, telling him he would be shot when they had finished. Between ourselves, I do not think they ever intended to carry out the threat, but it had a bad effect on his nerves, as the sequel will show. Fortunately the squatters presently appeared, and the gang scampered off, leaving our friend unharmed. But he was no sooner released than he began to run, and was found later on, up to his neck in a swamp.

The squatters followed up the gang and ran them to earth next day at Campbell Hunter's station,[26] near Heidelberg, only a few miles from Melbourne. Here, where my father joined them, they met Snodgrass, Fowler and others who had ridden post haste from town on hearing of the presence of the gang in the neighbourhood. Three of the bushrangers had taken refuge in a hut, but the fourth (Williams), had became isolated in the store nearby. Gourlay managed to arrest the latter, and had tied his hands together behind his back, but had foolishly neglected to take his pistol from him. Suddenly someone called out a warning to Snodgrass to 'look out!' and he turned, just in time to avoid the shot which the man had somehow managed to fire. Then everyone seemed to fire at once, and the man fell apparently dead. I believe Fowler was slightly wounded in the scuffle. The attention of everyone was now directed to the other three. A man, known as 'Hopping Jack,' and Rider, very bravely offered to parley with them, and went to the hut, carrying a white handkerchief. As the men refused to open the door, first 'Hopping Jack,' and then Rider, climbed on to the roof and entered the hut by the chimney. After a long parley, they persuaded the men to surrender, the latter being under the impression that if they did so, without causing bloodshed, the extreme penalty of the law might be avoided. However, they were all condemned to be hanged. Jepps, who had been the second mate of an American ship, was not a brutal man, and it was known that he had threatened to shoot any of his men who should ever molest a woman in any way. On that account, my father and others got up a petition, signed by every woman in the district, to get them off hanging, but without success.[27]

Apropos of bushrangers, a rather amusing incident occurred in the Plenty district some years later, when the land was cut up into farms. Cummerford, a tenant on one of Mr. Thos. Wills' properties there,[28] was riding home from Melbourne one day, when he perceived, a little way ahead, an old friend of ours whom he immediately tried to overtake, calling out in a loud voice, 'Hi! Hi!' and, at the same time waving a huge horse-pistol in his hand. Our friend turned his head, but on seeing the pistol, and thinking he was being hailed by a 'gentleman of the road,' at once put spurs to his horse and galloped off, expecting to be shot in the back at any moment. But, as Cummerford was mounted on one of Mr. Wills' blood mares, he soon overhauled him, still waving the pistol and shouting 'Hi!' He was very concerned, on pulling up, to find that, through his thoughtless action with the pistol, he had caused unnecessary alarm to our unarmed friend.

CHAPTER 3

ON THE AVON

By the year 1842-1843 my father began to find his mistake in settling so near Melbourne. There was no room for increasing stock. And so, it became necessary to move further afield. In the meantime Gippsland had been discovered by Mr. Angus McMillan in 1839, and our friend, Norman McLeod,[1] had occupied some country in what is now called the Bairnsdale district. He described the country in such glowing terms that he persuaded my father to go there, telling him there was still some very good unoccupied land to be had in his neighbourhood. And so we packed up and started on another trek. McLeod, who was with us at the time of our departure, joined the cavalcade and drove the trap, in which we children were travelling. Unfortunately, some months before the move, much to her grief, Addie's pet 'possum had died and been buried; and as she could not bear the idea of leaving him behind, she had surreptitiously dug up the remains, now reduced to hair and bones, put them into a neat brown-paper parcel, and placed it with the other packages in the trap. After we had gone a short distance, McLeod began to sniff suspiciously, and complain of an unpleasant odour. We remained quiet, of course, hoping to avoid discovery. But he finally stopped and made a determined search for the source of such unpleasantness, with the result that poor Addie's pet was ruthlessly thrown out on to the road, to the accompaniment of its owner's heart-broken howls! After the first day's journey McLeod left us and hurried on alone.

The journey to Gippsland proved a most unlucky undertaking. Travelling with stock there was a much more difficult and hazardous

Travelling in the Australian Bush, W. Harvey, from W. Howitt, *A Boy's Adventures in the Wilderness*. State Library of Victoria

affair than on the journey from New South Wales in 1837, where a great deal of the route lay through beautiful open forest land. In the early part, the narrow track, some fifteen feet wide, had been cut out of the thick tea-tree scrub, and further on it was bordered on each side by impenetrable scrub and forest–the timber in Gippsland being about the thickest and tallest in Victoria. It is well known that the giant gums there sometimes reach the height of 400 feet, with a diameter of 23 feet. The drive through this primeval forest must have been very impressive, and the height of the trees would shelter us from the direct rays of the sun during the heat of the day. But this very shade had its disadvantages, in that the track remained muddy and boggy pretty well all the year round. Among some of the most difficult obstacles encountered were the 'hurdie-gurdies'. These were a succession of deep gullies which could only be negotiated by cutting down heavy saplings and attaching them by chains to the drays, to act as brakes. The amount of labour and patience required for this job can easily be imagined. The wild dogs were also troublesome in killing sheep. We had about five hundred head of cattle, and five or six thousand sheep; and, in the end, most of the former were lost in the scrub. The cattle would sometimes stampede through the scrub, and it was impossible for the horsemen to follow them. To add to our troubles, there was a drought that summer, which accounted for the shortage of water on the route. When we reached Western Port, the poor animals, seeing the sea, rushed into it, and many of them were attacked and killed by sharks. When the tide went out, the latter, still feasting, were left in shallow water, and the men went in with axes and killed numbers of them.

At the Tarwin river we met Superintendent C. J. La Trobe, after-wards Governor, with Captain Dana in charge of the black police and Mr. Powlett, at one time Commissioner of crown lands, returning from a tour through Gippsland.[2] To my father's dismay, they advised him strongly to turn back, assuring him that there was not a yard of country left. This advice, though very disconcerting in the face of all we had endured in getting so far, it would have been madness to ignore. So, after some consideration, we turned back.

It was while we were camped near the Tarwin that Long Bill picked up in the dry bed of a creek what he thought was a 'pretty' bit of stone, and showed it to my father. But it was not till some years after, when the latter had become acquainted with the appearance of gold in its natural state, that he realized that he had perhaps missed the opportunity of being one of the first discoverers of gold here.

After having left most of our cattle in the scrubs of Gippsland, we returned to Melbourne, where we remained, George and I attending school for about a year. By that time my father had taken up a fresh run and had a home prepared for us.

In the meantime he had received a letter from Norman McLeod asking him why, in the name of–various things, he had not completed his journey to Gippsland. He explained that he had, with great dif-ficulty, been keeping concealed the whereabouts of some splendid country for him, but of course could do so no longer. He was, naturally highly disappointed that his trouble for an old friend had been in vain. And the old friend very heartily reciprocated!

However, the Gippsland episode was only one example of the bad luck which seemed to dog my father's footsteps through life.

While prospecting for suitable country in the Wimmera he had rather a piquant experience one day. He was on foot, leading his horse, when he suddenly found himself surrounded by about twenty or thirty emus, who made a ring round him at a distance of about twenty yards, and kept on circling round him for some distance as he slowly proceeded. When their evident curiosity was satisfied they made off and began quietly feeding again.

One day, during this quest, Long Bill observed a pair of native companions in the distance, and watched them till they disappeared over a rise. On following them up, he discovered two large lagoons swarming with wild-fowl of every kind, including a great number of swans; hence the name Swanwater which my father gave to the station he took up there. The lagoons, which were about three or four hundred yards apart, always contained water, so that a constant supply for the stock was assured.

The homestead was situated on a rise, within a mile or so of the lagoons, and at the head of a sheoak forest.

Apropos of the word sheoak, I have often wondered why this graceful and quaint looking tree should be so named, because, as far as appearance goes, no tree could be more unlike the oak. But I find, on referring to the late W. R. Guilfoyle's book on Australian botany,[3] that 'the term oak was given to this genus by the earliest settlers because, when worked up, the wood had some resemblance to that of the English oak, and, in fact, was used like it for staves, buckets, kegs, tubs, etc.' But this does not explain the prefix *she*! However, on looking up Professor E. E. Morris' *Austral-English Dictionary*, I find the opinions of several authorities on the subject, but, unfortunately for my peace of mind, none is conclusive. But I shall give a few of them for the benefit of the reader who may be interested. One writer explains that the term sheoak is a corruption of sheac, the name of an American tree, producing the same sort of wood. But, according to another authority, there is no such tree! Again we have shea-oak, a corruption of sheak, the native name for this or a similar tree, in Van Diemen's Land. This would seem to be a likely and reasonable explanation, but according to another authority, there is no such word in the Tasmanian Aboriginal vocabulary! All this only goes to show how quickly the origin of a word can be lost. Another explanation in the same dictionary is to the effect that the prefix *she*

Waterfowl on lagoon, J. Calvert, *Illustrated Australian News* 1869. National Library of Australia

is used in Australia to indicate an inferiority of timber in respect of texture, colour or other character: e.g., she-beech, she-pine. I give it for what it is worth!

The sheoak is of the genus Casuarina, of which the chief kinds found in Australia are the Casuarina torulosa (sheoak), Casuarina stricta (he-oak), and Casuarina tenuissima (marsh-oak). The he-oak is named in contradistinction of she-oak. They are of perfectly distinct species–not as might be thought the male and female of the same species. The appearance of the tree is rather difficult to describe. What might be called the leaves are 'thin, thread-like, articulated branches' which droop 'like the branches of a weeping willow'. It has a delicate, little flower of a reddish-brown color, which gives a pretty effect of autumn tints against the dark green of the rest of the tree. The cones are rather acid and juicy, and I remember that we children used to enjoy chewing them. The timber is very hard, and the blacks used to cut their boomerangs from the trees, at the elbow formed by the junction of the trunk and root.

From the house, we had a good view of the plain, looking towards the Avoca river, and could see horsemen approaching while they were still two or three miles off. In the opposite direction, about two miles away, was an extinct volcano. The crater is now used for the permanent water-supply of the district, I believe. A water course in the plain terminated in Lake Cope Cope, so that the rain was carried into it in the winter time. The run included a section of the lake, and, I remember, we used to visit it at a certain time every year to pick native currants, which abounded there, and which we used for making jam.

The grass at Swanwater was very fine. In summer time it was like hay, and the sheep used to fatten very quickly on it. The cattle station was just where the town of St. Arnaud now stands.

We also had a two mile frontage on the Avon, which ended in a large water hole about fifteen miles north of us. The blacks could never be persuaded to go near it. 'Bunyip quamby[4] longa there!' they used to say in explanation. The Messrs. Donald and Hamilton had a station bordering on it.[5]

The blacks were always very clever and useful in stripping sheets of bark off the trees for roofing. They would cut notches on a stick showing the number of sheets they had cut, and then a dray would be sent out to collect them. The bark of the stringy bark or messmate gums was always used for this purpose.

Sometimes a native rat would get under the roof of the house, and we would send for the blacks to get it out. One of them would spear the rat from the inside and another would lift some of the bark and get the rat out. It was appreciated by them as an article of food.

Besides the game, swan, duck, snipe, teal, etc., with which the lagoons abounded, we used to catch numbers of yabbies in the succession of water holes to which the Avon always became reduced in the summer time. They are a kind of small crayfish, of a brownish color, with long feelers, and, like the latter, turn red on being cooked. We used to fish for them by tying a piece of fresh meat on a string and letting it down just below the water's edge. Presently the yabbie would fasten on to the meat, and then the fisher, with his free hand would quickly push it on the bank before it had time to let go. This was considered great sport by us all, and we used to indulge in it while the sheep-washing was going on in adjacent holes.

We, sometimes, in our wanderings, came across a nest of young dingo pups in the hollow of a log. These were the most engaging and innocent looking creatures to be found in nature, and we should have liked to make pets of them, but were always obliged to destroy them, as they could never be sufficiently civilized to refrain from killing the occupants of the poultry yard. A rather remarkable thing about the wild dog is that, though he howls, growls and whines like any other, he never barks. His howling is one of the gloomy sounds of the bush.

Of the Aborigines and their customs, so much has been written by experts that I am afraid I cannot add to the general information on the subject. Besides which, we were too young to take a scientific interest in their habits and history. We were so used to having them about, that we took them very much for granted, as part of the ordinary scheme of things.

We occasionally witnessed a corroboree. This entertainment was to the blacks what we should call a party, as it was generally attended by the whole tribe. It was always held at night, by the light of big fires. The men used to prepare for it by decorating their bodies with white chalky stripes. During the dance, the lubras would sit together at the side, all cross-legged, with their 'possum skins rolled tightly on their laps, which they beat with their open hands in time with the dance, singing a monotonous sort of chant all the time. The men used to stand together, perhaps in a couple of rows, holding their boomerangs and nullah nullahs in their hands and making a great noise banging them together in regular time. They jumped about in all sorts of grotesque attitudes, shaking their knees in a peculiar way and, at the same time, thumping their sides with their elbows, emitting their breath with a loud puffing noise. The small boys not yet promoted to carrying waddies used to stand in front and beat sticks together. Added to this, occasional boisterous laughs and shrieks would be heard, showing the general excitement and enjoyment. To the spectator it was a weird and fascinating exhibition. But it always had a certain form and meaning, and at the same time showed that the blacks had a strong sense of rhythm, and an idea of singing. My cousin, Tom Wills, at Lexington,[6] was very clever at picking up their songs, which he delivered with a very amusing imitation of their voice and gestures, and could speak their language as fluently as they did themselves, much to their delight.

The blacks were speech-makers on occasion. I have seen one of them, after an absence from the camp, having perhaps visited another tribe, stand up for an hour at a time, relating his adventures and experiences. A friend of mine once told me that he had seen an old lubra, who evidently thought she had a grievance, stand up on a log and scold the rest of the camp loudly for a day and night on end, only ceasing when she fell down in a sort of fit of exhaustion. The others would all go on philosophically with the usual business of the camp, taking no notice of her whatever.

The chief of the tribe[7] in our district went by the name of King David. He had two lubras, in this respect having some slight resemblance to his namesake of Biblical fame! The older lubra had several fine children. One of the boys was named, in honor of my father, 'Piccaninny Captain'. Two others, I remember, were 'Syntax' and 'Anthony'.

'Sulky Jimmie' was one of the blacks who showed by his demeanour, most resentment against the invasion of the whites. He was very fond of one of the babies in the camp, and always slept with it on his chest. This habit saved his life when, early one morning, the camp was attacked by a hostile tribe. A spear was driven through the body of the innocent babe, and he got off with a slight wound!

The blacks were very fond of their dogs. In fact, in most cases they were regarded as more precious than their children, on account of their usefulness in hunting and procuring food for their owners.

In the matter of education, while on the station we were dependent on the good offices of governesses, and it was not always an easy matter to find one who was suitable in every way. It required the possession of no little courage and enterprize for an educated, single woman to leave her native country to come to a new and distant settlement to seek her fortune. As a rule, she had relatives among the settlers with whom she could make a temporary home, and she was always treated with consideration in the squatters' homes where her presence and companionship would probably be a boon to the mistress of the house. Our first governess was a Miss Patterson, who was with us only a short time. All I remember of her was the annoyance she displayed on being asked by one of the blacks (always very child-like in the familiar and intimate questions they would embarrass one with), 'You old man lubra belong to captain?' As she was no longer young, I think she was more incensed at being taken for the '*old* man lubra' than anything else. Our other governess, Miss Annie Mackinnon, remained with us for many years, and was always regarded as a very dear friend of the family. She was a daughter of Hector Mackinnon of Derrichnaig, Island of Mull, and aunt to Hector and Norman Wilson, well known Victorian squatters. She was a woman of strong religious principle, and we owed much to her devotion and careful training in our early years. I shall never forget an episode in which our knowledge of her rigid truthfulness caused us children considerable anxiety. It occurred one evening in the nursery, which had a door opening on to the quadrangle at the back. We were all preparing for bed when a young lubra startled us by rushing in and begging to be saved from her husband who, she said, was going to kill her. Miss MacKinnon had barely time to hide her under a bed before a savage looking young blackfellow pushed his way in without the ceremony of knocking at the door. He was carrying a tomahawk, and he was a most fearsome looking creature as he menacingly demanded: 'Where my lubra? My lubra here?' I remember we all waited in an agony of tense silence for Miss Mackinnon's answer, knowing that prevarication would be fatal. But, to our unbounded relief, she bravely barred his way, saying in indignant tones, 'No! She is not here. And how dare you come in here? Get out at once, you black abomination!' (with a particularly long accent on the last a). This uncompromising reception seemed to disconcert him considerably, for, after a pause, without another word, he slunk out of the door. The situation was saved, but at the expense of great nervous strain to everyone concerned.

I think the lubra waited long enough for her lord's rage to evaporate, and then returned to the camp, in a properly humble mood!

While on the subject of the blacks, I must not forget to mention one of their most striking characteristics, and that is their remarkable powers of orientation. It would seem that the nearer to nature we live the stronger is that power. A blackfellow will never lose his way, even in a fog! There was one remarkable instance of this power which came particularly under my own notice. Soon after we had occupied Swanwater, my uncle, Mr. Horace S. Wills (who had settled near Mt. William in the Grampians in 1840), drove across country from Lexington (some seventy miles), to see us. He arrived one morning soon after day-break, accompanied in the trap by a blind old lubra, who had undertaken to guide him through the trackless bush. A younger lubra, not acquainted with the district, also came to look after her.

Among those who occupied country round about us were the Messrs. Creswick, John Orr, and Foley.[8] The latter, I think, returned to England later. The Hams,[9] too, another well known Victorian family, occupied a part of Swanwater at one time with their stock, while hunting for a station.

Lexington, Ararat. D. Wills Cooke collection

Looking back on those days, we all seem to have been very cheerful and happy. Our parents being naturally hospitable, we had no lack of visitors, and their constant coming and going made the little bit of variety necessary to brighten the ordinary routine of station life.

We were a fairly large family, and all reached maturity without suffering from the usual ailments to which children in town are prone. We were, in our proper order:–Adela (always known as Addie), Colden (myself), George, Kate (afterwards Mrs. Ohlfsen Bagge), Alice (afterwards Mrs. Fred Skinner), Horace, Arthur, and Ernest. An adopted sister, Frances, married Dr. Budd,[10] who was the district doctor for a time, and brother to the head-master of the Diocesan Grammar School, Melbourne.

While we were at Swanwater, my eldest sister, Adela married Henry Norcott,[11] a former friend of the days on the Plenty. He was managing the Raleigh's station which was situated about thirty miles from us, and he generally rode over and spent the week-end with us. He was a very fine horseman, and looked a splendid figure on a horse; besides which, he was very musical and sang well, accompanying himself from memory. His life in the Australian army had no doubt contributed to a natural charm of manner which made him a general favorite. He belonged to a family of fine soldiers, his father being Major-General, Sir Amos Norcott, C.B., K.C.H., etc., and his elder brother Lieut. General, Sir William Norcott, K.C.B. Some years later, he was thrown from his horse and killed, and left my sister with one son, Amos.

While speaking of the various visitors we had at Swanwater, I must not forget to mention good Bishop Perry,[12] whom we all loved. He arrived in the colony early in the year 1848, and he very soon set to work to get into touch with all parts of his scattered diocese, which entailed an immense amount of riding and driving through all sorts of country. I have never heard whether he kept a journal during that time, but if he did so, I should think it would be a most interesting document. In conversation with my mother one day, he said that he did not approve of the title 'My Lord', by which it is usual to address a bishop, and he told her a story showing how the term could be misinterpreted. He had been calling at some house, and heard afterwards that one of the little girls had run in to her mother, in a great state of perturbation, and said: 'Mother! God's in the parlor!' She had evidently heard the person, who admitted him, address him as 'My Lord'. He thought the term should be kept sacred, and would have preferred to be addressed simply as 'Bishop'.

On our journeys to Melbourne we used generally to stay at Ravenswood, then Mr. Fenton's station, but now, I think, part of the estate of the late Dr. Atkinson of Bendigo.[13] We little dreamt that, at some not far distant date, we should be near the same spot under extraordinarily different circumstances, namely, during the rush to the diggings. But, of that, anon.

Owing to the dearth of public houses in the bush, it was the custom for travelling squatters to be up for the night at any homestead where they liked to call in, and, I think there were very few cases where the traveller did not meet with a kind welcome. But I remember hearing of one exception to this rule. It made an impression on me because it happened to our neighbour, Mr. Foley. He was an old gentleman and, being the only magistrate in the district, had always been accustomed to receive every consideration. While on a journey to Melbourne, as evening was approaching, he called at the homestead of one of our rich pastoralists, and asked for the usual shelter for man and beast. To his astonishment and disgust, he was told by the shame-faced manager that he had received strict orders that no one was to be given hospitality under any circumstances whatever, but that, if he liked, he could sleep in the men's hut! Needless to say, Mr. Foley did not accept the kind (?) offer, but rode on some way and camped under a tree for the night.

After we had been at Swanwater for a few years, my father had an accident, the dire result of which affected him to the end of his life, and was the ultimate cause of great monetary loss which would never have occurred if he had kept his health.

He had driven out in a dray, some miles from the head station, to shoot a bullock, reported to be badly injured by a falling tree. On the way out, he had noticed some bronze-wing pigeons and, hoping to have a shot at them on the return journey, he loaded the gun in

Capt. John Harrison 1860s. A.M. Smith collection

readiness before starting back. Driving along, they overtook some
blacks who asked for a lift. In making room for them, he foolishly
took hold of the gun by the muzzle and drew it towards him. The

hammer was lifted by a portion of the tarpaulin covering the carcass and caused the gun to explode, tearing away the flesh of his arm from the wrist to the elbow. Had the bullock driver not applied a tourniquet at once, he would have bled to death in a few minutes. On his arrival home, a doctor was sent for with all speed, seventy miles off. When the latter arrived, he looked at the patient and decided that he was too weak to undergo an operation, in consequence of the shock and loss of blood. For this he charged seventy guineas, and, while journeying to Melbourne, gave out that Captain Harrison was dead. So that when my father, six months afterwards, travelled by the same route, some people received a shock on seeing what they thought must be his ghost! Soon after the accident, Dr. Forsythe, the district doctor arrived, and looked after him so well that he was able to undertake the journey to town in six months' time. The continual lying in bed and want of exercise had, however, caused complications, for which he was operated on in Melbourne, by Doctors Motherwell and O'Mullane.[14] The operation was performed without the aid of any anaesthetic, and he suffered terribly. Either chloroform had not come into general use at that time, or the doctors did not consider him a fit subject for it. But he never recovered his normal health or spirits after that, nor the use of his arm.

With regard to medical services in the bush, the squatters used to take it in turn to house the doctor of the district, so that it would always be known where he was, at any given time. It was most unfortunate that he happened to be absent just at the time of my father's accident.

Though a clever navigator, my father was far from being a good business man, and, instead of managing the station himself, as most of the squatters round about did, he generally employed a superintendent. One, who was with us for some time and whom we all liked very much, was Mr. C. W. Umphleby, father of the late Colonel Umphleby.[15]

During this time, the studies of my brother George and myself were subject to occasional interruption, as we were sometimes called upon to look after sheep during the absence or sickness of a shepherd. This was a job neither of us was particularly keen on, as we found it rather monotonous. But still, the following story will make it clear that we showed quite an amount of zeal in the exercise of our duties. One day we noticed a wether with a lamb, and thinking the latter had been enticed away from its mother, George tried to separate them, with the result that the wether turned on him, knocked him down angrily and jumped on him. I had to go to his rescue, and managed to keep the enraged creature off till he got up–more frightened than hurt–and then we both made for a tree and sat there awaiting events. After a while, much to our surprise, we noticed the lamb taking sustenance from the supposed wether! There had evidently been a mistake in the ear-marking, and George had been trying to separate mother and child. No wonder he was jumped on!

We, of course, like most bush children, were quite at home with horses. We had a mare, by name Zoe, on whose back we had all learnt to ride in turn, and with whom we could do anything we liked. In fact, she was a sort of second mother to us. On one occasion, when George and I wanted to spend a holiday at Lexington, I rode Zoe and he, one of her colts. We made the journey in leisurely fashion, staying with friends on the way. Unfortunately George, who always jumped every obstacle he encountered, ended in staking his mount just before we arrived at our destination. The leg was attended to on our arrival, and ultimately quite recovered, but when our holiday was up we were obliged to leave the colt behind and make the return journey on Zoe alone. At first we tried riding pillion, but were both so ticklish that we fell off several times in our wrigglings, the old mare standing patiently till we picked ourselves up and mounted again. Finally we had to take it turn about to ride and foot it, which made our progress rather slow. But it shows we were pretty strong in the legs, neither of us being more than nine or ten years old at the time, to have got through the seventy miles comfortably.

Towards the end of 1850, my father, feeling quite broken in health, decided to live in Melbourne. He let the station on a five years' lease, with the option of purchase during that time at the then value, to the Whittaker Brothers.[16] This was, of course, a most unbusiness-like arrangement; but he was really too ill at the time to attend to the business himself, and trusted too much to his agents. Soon after, the diggings broke out, and sheep rose in value from 2/6 to 30/- a head. So, naturally, the Whittakers completed the purchase at once. I believe that a short time after, they sold a quarter of the run without stock, for four times as much as the station and stock had cost them.

We were all very sad at the idea of giving up our old home. We boys, especially, felt the change from the freedom of the country and all its distractions to the restraints of the town. But I suppose we should have been obliged to make the change sooner or later, if only for the sake of our education. As a matter of fact, I had already been sent to town as a boarder to the Diocesan Grammar School at the beginning of 1850, so that the break was not so sudden for me.

The Grammar school had been founded by Bishop Perry in 1849, and was carried on in a building which had been erected in Spring Street, in the grounds of St. Peter's church, with money which he had brought from England for that purpose. Mr. Richard Hale Budd,[17] Master of Arts and a Cambridge Blue, was head-master. Before that,

Melbourne Diocesan Grammar School. MCEGS collection

he had established a flourishing private school in Victoria Parade, but, when invited by the bishop to take charge of the new school, he did so, taking his former pupils with him. The former school still served as private residence and boarding school. It consisted of two cottages, still standing, in Victoria Parade, at the corner of Young Street. I am indebted to Miss M. E. Budd, daughter of the late head master, for kindly supplying me with the exact date of my residence there, from the school register, which she still has, in perfect order, written in her father's clear hand.[18]

Of the assistant masters, the one I recall most clearly to mind was Mr. H. H. P. Handfield, who was honorary assistant master, and was afterwards well known as Canon Handfield.[19] Mr. Budd carried on the school for about five years, when, owing to the general rush to the diggings, he began to experience increasing difficulty in securing suitable masters. The domestic staff also dwindled from the same cause. This, in a house with twenty boarders and seventy day pupils, created a problem even more pressing than that of masters. So that, finding his health beginning to suffer seriously from the incessant worry, he reluctantly resigned the position of head-master in 1854.

As there was no one in Australia, at the time, sufficiently qualified to take his place, the school had to be closed, and was not reopened till 1858. In the meantime the government granted the school that fine piece of land on the St. Kilda Road, where it now stands. The late Dr. Bromby[20] came from England to take the head-mastership, and the school was then opened under the name of the Melbourne Grammar School.

Among the boarders during my time, were George and Tom Hepburn, sons of our old friend, Captain Hepburn, of Smeaton.[21] Two
half-brothers of Mr. Budd, Francis and Edward, who had come out
from England to him, were also boarders.[22] The question was recently
raised by 'Prelector' of the *Argus* as to who was the oldest surviving
public school boy in Victoria, and I think it was proved to everyone's
satisfaction that Francis Budd, (my senior by three years) could claim
that distinction. We are both certainly the oldest 'Melburnians' still
living.

The old school building has long since disappeared. But it is a satisfaction to know that its former site is occupied by that beautiful
and majestic structure, the Victorian House of Parliament, where,
not only former boys of the Melbourne Grammar School, but of
every school in the Commonwealth have labored, and are laboring
in the interests and let us hope for the benefit of their country. If it
be true that our minds are affected by our environment, then that
noble building should inspire all who enter there, most certainly to
their highest and best.

To return to the subject of the old school, it is interesting to note
the names of some of the boys of that day. I think that no less than
six Chomleys were there at the same time—all fine high spirited boys,
and all well known citizens in after years.[23] Among others, Robert
Power (late of Power, Rutherford and Co.), Henry Box, Willie Hamilton, and James L. Purves the famous Q.C., later on.[24]

At that time there was plenty of space for playgrounds on the
Eastern Hill, and we boys used to spend a good deal of our time
about the little gully which ran through the ground now known as
the Fitzroy gardens. It was still in its wild state, studded with gum
trees and other forest growth. The gully originally continued its course
below Jolimont into the Yarra. It has since been converted into a
small decorative stream.

I was once for a short time at Mr. Edward Butterfield's school,[25]
in Exhibition Street. Among my contemporaries there, I remember
George and Alex. McCrae,[26] sons of the first Postmaster-General;
Edward Howard, a son of Commissary-General Howard,[27] and who
has recently been writing very interesting and informative articles on
the early days of Melbourne for the *Argus*; and the McPhersons (sons
of a well-known squatter).[28]

My brother George and I were also, for a short time, at Gouge's
school,[29] which was situated near the Melbourne gaol. I do not think
either of these schools had a very long existence. Mr. Butterfield
closed his in 1854, and settled in Brisbane.

But all the schools suffered during the first years of the gold rush,
and it is surprising that any were able to carry on at all. A great many

of the demoninational schools were deserted altogether, both by teachers and scholars.

After resigning from the Grammar School, Mr. Budd accepted a permanent appointment under the Denominational school-board as Inspector of Schools, and did yeoman service in raising the system of education in the colony. Later on, he established a girls' school in Melbourne, which he later transferred to Brighton, where he ended his days after a life of untiring devotion to the cause of education. He died on the 27th March, 1909, at the age of ninety-three, in full command of all his faculties to the last, except for a certain deafness from which he had suffered all his life.[30]

CHAPTER 4

ON THE DIGGINGS

When we first came to Melbourne from Swanwater we occupied a house in Brunswick street (Fitzroy), of which the first block or so constituted, at that date, one of the chief residential quarters of the town. We were there when gold was first discovered in Victoria, and were witnesses of the extraordinary excitement caused by the news in Melbourne.

As may be imagined, my father was not the man to resist the call of such an adventure, and so he determined to join in the general rush. He bought a horse and cart and the usual tent and camping kit, and started off as soon as possible, taking George and me with him. We were joined by a young friend, John Taylor, the step-son of Mr. Butterfield, the schoolmaster.[1]

On our arrival at Ballarat, we took up a claim on the flat, near Black Hill, on a little creek, and set to work. We, at first, tried to dig a hole, but in our unpractised hands, it developed into a sort of funnel, and had to be abandoned. We then took a claim higher up on the hill, and we boys used to put the earth in a bag and run it down to the creek on a small sledge (made from the forked branch of a tree), and wash it in a cradle. The result was, I think, about half an ounce of gold after two weeks' work! Though not very successful, we rather enjoyed the novelty of the life, and the general excitement. There was very little bad behaviour or drinking among the diggers while we were there. Everyone was too intent on the business in hand to indulge in any sort of dissipation.

Every night, at sun-down, there used to be a regular fusilade of shots, as the diggers were in the habit of firing off everything in the way of firearms they possessed, by way of warning to possible thieves of the warm reception awaiting them. We never joined in this business; but we made up our minds to do so when the bottom of a little tin box 2½ inches square, in which we kept our gold, should be quite covered. However, our intention was not carried out, as we did not stay long at Ballarat, but went off soon to a rush at Castlemaine. Unless one struck it rich at once, it was considered waste of time to remain long in one spot. At last we found our way to Bendigo, the richest of all the fields.

But, as the stirring story of the gold fields has been told over and over again, I shall confine myself to relating the incidents which came within my personal experience.

After staying in Bendigo about three months, in which time we each cleared about £100, we went home to Melbourne. But my father and I returned again soon, and pitched our tent at Eaglehawk Gully, three or four miles out of Bendigo. While there, a 'hatter' (a term applied to a man who could not get a mate), who had a claim near us, found a very large nugget. He had only just begun to use his pick when he struck what he thought was a hard stone, but which, to his amazement and delight, turned out to be a nugget worth at least two or three thousand pounds. On receiving an advance of a thousand pounds from one of the banks, he bought himself a horse, and, getting drunk, dashed madly about from one part of the district to another, calling out, 'I'm the – man who found the – nugget!' In about three days' time he was thrown from his horse and killed.

Diggers on the Road to Bendigo, S. T. Gill. La Trobe collection, State Library of Victoria

In contrast to that story was the case of some Canadians. I happened, one day, to be at the store, (which, by the way, consisted of a tent), when a fine stalwart young fellow came in and bought a dozen loaves of bread, which he carried away in a bag. I was so struck with his appearance that I asked the store-keeper who he was, and he explained that the young giant belonged to a party of five Canadians, fine, sober young men, who had been on the fields for some months without experiencing any luck, and who were now living chiefly on bread and water. I could not help feeling sorry for them, and often wondered afterwards, what had become of them.

My father and I used to make a little money by buying gold on commission for the bank,[2] so that, at times we would have a good deal of the bank's cash in the tent; apropos of which, I must relate a rather unpleasant incident. He one day brought to the tent an old friend to whom he had offered such hospitality as we could give. He had found him wandering about without shelter and (as the friend himself explained) without means to pay for any. He was an English university man, who had held a responsible journalistic position in Melbourne, but had lost it through his intemperate habits. As bad luck would have it, my father had to go to Bendigo for the night, and so left me alone with our guest. During the night he seemed very restless, and when I woke up, disturbed by his movements, he would say, 'Harrison! I think there must be thieves about!' But, as we had a couple of rather savage dogs, I knew no stranger could approach the tent without a good deal of noisy protest from them, and so, did not worry, and was quickly fast asleep again. After breakfast which I cooked with the aid of the bushman's friend, a frying pan, next morning, he went off, saying he would have a 'look round', and never came back. My father, on his return a little later, was rather surprised to find that X– had departed so unceremoniously, but was more than disgusted to find that £120 had also disappeared from the tent. We heard afterwards that X– had stopped some days at the Saw Pit Gully pub on the Melbourne road, drinking hard; thus showing that he had had a considerable windfall of some sort! We of course had to make good the money. The episode was one of my first lessons in the ugly possibilities of human nature, and, I must say, it was a considerable shock.

My father lost a splendid chance of laying the foundation of a good auctioneering business while we were there.[3] Most of the men, on leaving the fields, would want to dispose of their mining kits, and new arrivals would be glad of a chance to procure them. So some of the diggers (knowing he had the leisure) came to my father and asked him if he would act as auctioneer for them. To this proposition he consented, and the following Saturday, at 1 o'clock, was fixed for the first sale, and general notice given of it. To my dismay, I found him starting off for Bendigo directly after breakfast that morning, and, when I reminded him of the sale, he said he would be back in plenty of time. However, he had not returned when, by 1 o'clock, a considerable number of diggers had assembled in the vicinity of our tent, with numerous carts containing all sorts of camping and mining paraphernalia for disposal. Two o'clock arrived, three o'clock arrived, and still no sign of the captain! By four o'clock the diggers had begun to bargain among themselves, and by five o'clock, when my father arrived, they had all dispersed. The amusing part of the whole affair was that he was quite annoyed with the diggers for not giving him longer grace.

The laws governing the goldfields soon began to be regarded with great dissatisfaction by the miners. Although the government charged the large amount of 30/- for a licence, there was nothing given in return for the money except the privilege of digging. Naturally, in a place where a population of many thousands had suddenly sprung up, public conveniences were, as might be expected, very inadequate. For instance, a mere tent answered the purpose of a post office, with one lad in charge to distribute letters; and I know we were often kept waiting hours for ours.

The greatest grievance of the diggers was that in connection with licences and the manner of distributing them. Gold was worth £4 an ounce in London, and the amount paid on the fields became reduced

Diggers' Auctioneer, S. T. Gill. La Trobe collection, State Library of Victoria

to £2/10/- at one time, in consequence of the shortness of cash. At first licences had been paid for by half an ounce of gold, valued at 30/-, but a new rule came into force by which they were to be paid for in cash only, so that the men were forced to sell their gold at 50/- an ounce and then pay 30/- cash for the licence, thus incurring great loss.[4]

Further trouble was caused through the waste of time the men experienced in obtaining their licences every month. They would have to walk perhaps some miles to the commissioner's tent, and then wait about for hours, and sometimes even have to return next day, before getting them, on account of the numbers applying at the same time. The fee weighed very heavily on the poor and unsuccessful digger, who was finding it very hard to live in the meantime. In the early days the government actually contemplated raising the fee to £3 a month–this, mind you, for a surface claim which might yield nothing worth speaking of–but wisely abandoned the idea in response to the storm of protest raised at the bare idea.[5]

The troopers used to be sent out to inspect licences, and any man, found digging without one, would be arrested and chained to a tree for want of a lock-up, perhaps all night, till taken before a magistrate, when he would be fined £5.

This sort of thing led, in time, to much friction and bitter feeling between the miners and the officers of the law. Cries of 'Joe! Joe!' used to be the signal, given by the miners to those without licences, on the approach of the police, and thus the deliquents would often have time to get out of the way.

But in my day (1852), the collecting of licences was a very quiet affair compared to what it became later, when a digger-hunt was quite an exciting event, not unmixed with some mirth-provoking incidents, according to the chronicles of the time.

With regard to the diggers themselves, comprising, as they did, men of every class and almost every nationality, a more decent or law-abiding body of men could not have been found anywhere, though, of course, there was the usual smattering of undesirables that will always be found in every assemblage.

With regard to the collection of licences, it is needless to say that no set of sane men, with any sense of justice could put up for long with such tyranny. Many indignation meetings were held, and finally, delegates were elected to go to Melbourne in order to put the various causes of discontent before the government. My father, who felt much sympathy with the diggers, consented to act as one,[6] and so went off and left me alone–a boy of fourteen–to fossick for a living till his return. I used to search for gold in deserted claims, which was rather a dangerous business, as I found one day. After digging a dishful of earth from underneath the earth supports, I crawled back to the entrance of the shaft, where I had a small pool of water for washing. I had scarcely reached the entrance when I heard a thunderous noise behind me, and, on looking back, saw that the earth had fallen in, where I had been lying. Next morning I found that the whole claim had fallen in during the night; so I had a lucky escape!

I led this sort of life for nearly a year, and during that time became very thin. The food, consisting principally of tea without milk, tough meat always fried, pickled onions for vegetables and, at first, damper instead of bread, was not the kind to nourish a growing boy! However, I suppose the life helped to toughen my constitution, or, at any rate, did me very little harm, as I can thankfully say that, with the exception of one painful and prolonged bout of rheumatism a few years ago, I have enjoyed robust health pretty well all my life.

Though, as I have before explained, there was comparatively little crime on the diggings, the following story will show the state of nervousness in which some men existed. One evening, as I was strolling about with one of my dogs, someone in the vicinity suddenly fired off a gun. This so frightened the animal, that he made a dive for the nearest tent, and pushed his way unceremoniously in. There was a most fearful rattling noise, caused by the falling of kerosene tins, billy-cans, etc., which the occupant had evidently placed at the entrance by way of ensuring himself fair warning of intruders; and I could hear him calling out in startled accents, 'Who's there? Who's there? I'll fire! I'll fire!' At which I retired guiltily, feeling sure he would not like the idea of having a witness to his state of unnecessary scare.

One of the greatest miseries endured on the diggings was that caused by the presence of fleas. I used to carry my blankets as far from the tent as possible, and lay them in the sun. The fleas would hop off quickly, but would be back in the tent as soon as I was myself.

It was after being kept awake all night by these pests that I slept till nearly sun-down one day, and was awakened by hearing a familiar voice outside the tent, calling me. It turned out to be our friend, Norman McLeod,[7] who happened to be passing on his way from Mt. Korong where he was running a store, to Melbourne. He was very concerned at my lonely situation and generally run-down appearance, and, as he had a couple of drays with him, he kindly offered me and my belongings a lift home; and I gladly availed myself of the opportunity.

Thus ended my gold-digging experiences.

In 1854, the accumulation of grievances resulted in serious riots on the various goldfields, and the report got about that ten thousand diggers were marching on Melbourne. There was great excitement, and we were all sworn in as special constables to assist in keeping order, if necessary. But the report turned out to be a false alarm!

We all know the sad story of the Eureka Stockade, at Ballarat, so I need not describe it. A very complete account of it was written by my old friend, the late Gyles Turner, in his booklet entitled *Our Own Little Rebellion*.[8] After it was over, an attempt was made to try some of the rebels, but had to be abandoned, as it was found that no jury would convict them.

CHAPTER 5

IN THE CIVIL SERVICE

O n my return to Melbourne, after spending a few months at school again, I entered the Customs about the end of 1853, as Tide-officer in the Bay department. While in this position, I lived at Williamstown. Among my friends there, were William Dempster of the English and Scottish Bank; Captain (afterwards Colonel) Fred. Bull (volunteers) assistant engineer to the council;[1] Henry Lascelles (Customs); and Perry McCrae, of the Bank of Australasia. The latter was a brother of George Gordon McCrae, well known for his superior literary and artistic gifts, and who, though lately attaining the age of ninety, still maintains an active interest in contemporary affairs.[2]

A tide-officer's job[3] was no sinecure in those days, as Hobson's Bay was thick with the ships of all nations, attracted by the rush to the goldfields. Among others, I remember the *Marco Polo* (Captain Forbes), which made the voyage from London in sixty days, instead of the usual ninety.[4] The *Great Britain* too, was the largest vessel afloat at the time, and one of the first steamers of any note to visit us. She employed both steam and sail, and was a noble looking ship. Her captain (Gray) was a big man in appearance, and a tremendous favorite with everyone, so that it came as a great shock to hear of his mysterous disappearance, during one of his voyages. He was supposed to have thrown himself out through one of the port-holes. But I do not think the mystery was ever cleared up.[5]

Altogether, the bay afforded a wonderful sight, which will perhaps never be equalled again in its history. Added to the appearance of the

The Railway Pier, Sandridge, (Port Melbourne). Port of Melbourne
Authority collection

great variety of craft crowded together, was the general feeling of life
and excitement, which filled the air and made one realize the fact that
he was indeed living in stirring times.

Owing to a misunderstanding of the situation here, a great many
ship owners at first lost considerably on their freight. Sixteen shillings
a ton was paid on freight landed in Melbourne, which was, of course,
a tremendous amount, and a subject of congratulation. But they
found, to their cost, that there was the usual catch somewhere! As
all the ships had to anchor in the bay, the owners were obliged to
employ lighters to carry cargo up the Yarra to Melbourne, for which
they were charged 30/- a ton! One tug-boat would take as many as
ten lighters at a time up the river.[6] It will be seen that a number of
people made fortunes without the trouble and fatigue of going to the
diggings.

The captains of ships had a difficult time generally. As a rule, a
fine big clipper ship would no sooner drop anchor in the bay than
a whale-boat would pass slowly under her bows, and the sailors,
without loss of time, would throw a rope over and shin down it into
the boat. For a fair consideration they would forthwith be landed at
St. Kilda, whence they would make their way to the goldfields as
quickly as possible. Deserted ships would thus be held up for months,
unable to get away for want of a crew. I heard of one captain who
made the best of things by striking a bargain with his men, to the
effect that if they stayed on board till the cargo should be discharged,
he would accompany them on the adventure. By this means he made
sure of their services for the return voyage. Some of the ships, after

waiting some months, would be manned by lucky diggers who had made their piles and were returning in triumph to their families.

Sometimes, if a boat were not available at once for landing, the sailors, in their eagerness, would jump overboard and swim ashore, and risk being attacked by the sharks which were fairly numerous.

One of the many interesting incidents that occurred at that time caused considerable amusement in Melbourne. The *Great Britain* had been in quarantine, and on the evening of her release, she came up the bay firing her guns, by way of celebrating the joyful event, I suppose. The other ships in the bay fired their guns in response, and the consequent noise created a scare in the town. The report was actually circulated that the British frigate, *Electra*, had been seen at grips with two Russian ships! A ball was being held at Government House that evening, and the officers attending it all left precipitately, amidst great excitement, for the scene of action.[7]

Of the five years I spent in the 'Bay,' I still have a useful souvenir. It is a case of razors, which was presented to me by a Dutch captain, and which, rather wonderful to relate, I have had in constant use ever since. This fact, I think, speaks well for the quality of steel and workmanship.

There were numbers of Dutch ships in the bay at that time, the captains of which were all of a good type of man, and I got on very well with them always. I can still hear their words, so often hospitably and courteously repeated, 'Officeer, a glass of wine with you!' But I had seen so many lives ruined by the pernicious fashion of shouting which obtained in the colonies in those days, that I had determined to make a rule never to drink anything in the way of spirituous liquors until I reached the age of twenty-one at least, although warned by my friends that it would be a most difficult rule to carry out, without giving offence, especially in my position among sailor men. However, I can honestly say that my excuses were never received in any but the right spirit.

In the year 1858, I was transferred to Melbourne, and remained in the Customs there (with the exception of a year in Geelong), passing through the various grades, till 1888. I was then transferred to the Titles Office, to the position of chief clerk, becoming later on, Registrar-General and Registrar of Titles, which position I held twelve years, till my retirement at the age of sixty.

It was then a new idea to transfer government officers from one department to another, and at first I did not altogether appreciate having to leave the one with which I had been associated so long, and with the work of which I was thoroughly conversant, for another which was entirely new to me. However, I threw myself into the work, and was soon able to effect some reforms, which, as a new-comer, I could see at a glance, would be advantageous.

Through the change from one department to another, I had the advantage of being brought into contact with a fresh lot of men, thus widening my experience, and adding to my knowledge of men in their various spheres.

Portrait of H.C.A. Harrison. L. Cooke collection

Soon after settling in Melbourne, and while in the Customs, I joined the volunteers.[8] But, as my leisure was so fully occupied in other ways, and as there seemed no prospect of war in the immediate future, I resigned after about eighteen months in the artillery. I remember that our adjutant at one time had a serious impediment in his speech, and his orders were very difficult to understand which made things a bit unsatisfactory.

At one time, a volunteer corps was formed from the Customs' staff. The officers were nominated, not according to their knowledge of military affairs, but to their rank in the Customs. One captain, elected in this way, was the best hand at getting his men tied in a knot that I can remember. After a review, one day, on the Melbourne Cricket Ground, where he had been severely hauled over the coals by the colonel, he marched his men down Collins Street, and, when they reached the crossing at Swanston Street, he gave an order which turned them to the right, up Swanston Street. At this, he hastily gave another order, and they turned round and began continuing their way along Collins Street. Finding this further effort unsuccessful, he shouted in desperation: 'D– your eyes, men! I want you to go towards Princes' Bridge!'

CHAPTER 6

ATHLETICS – MAINLY FOOTRACING

Towards the end of the fifties, there was in Victoria a widespread awakening of enthusiasm for almost every kind of sport. Horse-racing, hunting, sculling, swimming, cricket, pedestrianism and, last but not least, football were amongst those I can remember as finding their devoted adherents.

From a school boy, I had always played cricket, and, until we started football, it was certainly my principal form of exercise; and the arrival from England, towards the end of 1856, of my cousin Tom Wills, gave me and many others a special zest for the game, of which he was such a fine exponent. Other forms of sport, however, soon claimed my particular attention.

But I cannot pass from the subject of cricket without special reference to Tom Wills[1] and his play.

Born in New South Wales, he travelled overland with his parents in 1839, at the age of four. He was educated at Rugby School, where he became captain of both the cricket eleven and the football team. On leaving school, he played for Cambridge having, I think, passed a term there, and other clubs. Old Lilywhite's[2] description of him to some onlooker, has passed into history, namely: 'He carries a three pound bat and hits terrific!'

On his arrival here, he was just twenty-one, very handsome and, in figure, the beau-ideal of an athlete. He was one of the first of the very fine cricketers Australia has produced, and, I suppose, that no man in this country has ever been such a popular hero as he was during his cricketing career. Excelsior of the *Australasian*, I think, when writing of him, after his death in 1880, said: 'In his day, he was the best all-round man in Australia, and was a public favorite of the most pronounced type'. His cleverness in knowing when it was safe to take risks was always the cause of much diversion to the onlookers. He was wonderfully quick in detecting the weak points of a batsman, and always had absolute command of his field. As a captain, he was considered 'one of the most astute tacticians that ever led a team to victory, being most fertile in resource, and ever ready for the moves of the enemy.' In another account, Point (*The Leader*) said: 'He was, par excellence, *the* cricketer of Victoria of his time, and we all took a pride in him'.

In one match, I particularly recall, in which he was captaining the Victorian eleven against New South Wales, he sustained a compound fracture of the middle finger of the right hand; notwithstanding which, he came out with the best score in batting and bowling, and won the match!

I should like to add one more extract, from a notice of his death in the *Australasian*, which, I think, puts his style of play, and also his character, in a nutshell. It ran as follows: 'He was, in fact, "the Grace" of Australia, but . . . Tom Wills was as well known for his good nature and kind heart as he was famous for his skill as a player'.

In 1866 he organized and trained a team of Aboriginal cricketers, and was to have taken them to England in 1868,[3] but was unable to get away at the time, and his place was taken by Charles Lawrence, that fine English cricketer,[4] who had been settled some time in New South Wales, and who spent his later years in Melbourne. One of his daughters, by the way, is the wife of Mr. B. H. Friend, I.S.O., the popular ex-chief of the Federal Hansard staff.

The blacks did fairly well in England, but suffered considerably from the climate. Mullagh, the best all-round player of the team, did particularly well, I believe, in a match against the gentlemen of Sussex. He continued to play some years after their return, and made the top score at Melbourne in the second innings of the Victorian eleven against Lord Harris' team which was here in 1878.[5] On the return of the team from England, Wills captained them in the colonial tour which they made before they disbanded.

PEDESTRIANISM

It was quite an accident that I discovered that I was a runner of any account. It occurred in the following way. On being transferred to Melbourne in 1858, I joined the Richmond Cricket Club. 'Gid' Elliot, the famous bowler, was caretaker there, and used to give me practice at the nets occasionally.[6]

Wills and Aboriginal Cricketers at the MCG. MCC collection

One Saturday afternoon in September, 1859, I went down to the ground, expecting to get a game, and found no one there but Elliot, who informed me that all the players, including Wills, Hammersley,[7] another cricketer of English repute, and others, had gone down to the Sir Henry Barkly Hotel, on the corner of Punt Road, near the Yarra, to see a foot-race on the river bank; so I followed on. I found that Prescott, the host of the Sir Henry Barkly,[8] had arranged a race, to be run in heats. I had no intention of entering, as I had never done any running since a school-boy, and besides, was not dressed for the part, being in cricketing flannels and shoes. But Wills and others, who had noticed my pace at football, insisted on my doing so–'just for the fun of the thing.' I found myself in the same heat with Davenport, the professional champion sprint runner, who was dressed in tights, and wore running-shoes. I received four yards' start which was the only one I ever received in my life, and, to my own surprise and, I expect, to his, beat him. I had to run in the final heat against another experienced runner, David Arnott, and won again, easily. *Bell's Life*, the sporting paper, of which William Levey was editor,[9] said of me, when describing the race, 'The winner runs strong and fast, and for 200 yards none but runners of the very first class can live with him'.[10] In November of that year, I took part in a race (150 yards), for a silver cup, for amateur pedestrians only, on the same course. Of nine entries, there were eight starters: Wills (not T. W.), Rogers and myself being at scratch. I won the final heat by five yards, thus establishing my right to the title of champion amateur sprint runner of Victoria.[11]

From that time I ran (always at scratch) at most of the sports meetings that took place in Melbourne, beating all comers, and sometimes giving as much as thirty or more yards' start in the handicap hurdle and steeplechase races.

But the next race of importance was a quarter of a mile for the champion cup, run against Alex. Allan, who claimed to be the professional champion, and was a fine, strapping young fellow.[12] As he was anxious to try conclusions with me, he consented to run for a cup instead of the usual stakes.[13] This race created an immense amount of interest. The course was marked out on the Punt Road, between the Richmond Cricket ground and the Sir Henry Barkly hotel. The way was lined for the last two hundred yards, by a large crowd, many sitting or standing on the fence. I was better prepared in the way of dress this time, wearing running-shoes and socks, drawers to the ankles, and a fairly tight-fitting sleeveless silk jersey. This was the usual costume for amateurs.[14] Shorts had not come in then. Allan, on the other hand, wore nothing but trunks and running-shoes. Before the race, he asked me how I meant to run, and I replied that, as I thought I had the 'foot' of him, I would let him make the pace. And so, the course being cleared, we started off at an easy pace. But I shall let the reporter of *Bell's Life* continue: 'At about 200 yards from the start, the speed was improved, Allan showing a disposition to force the pace, but found Mr. Harrison diligently close! At 300 yards Allan was leading slightly. As he expressed it, he could just see that his opponent was close behind him. He then put on steam to his full extent, and led by three yards. Mr. Harrison also put on some extra power, and the pace became first-rate. When approaching the termination of the fourth hundred, Mr. Harrison threw back his head in a style peculiar to himself (which he invariably does when racing his hardest), and Allan seemed to come back to him. About fifty or sixty yards from the winning post, Mr. Harrison passed his opponent and came in a winner by about four yards. The effect on the spectators, the majority of whom had backed Allan to win for a certainty, was electrical. Having recovered from their momentary astonishment, they greeted the winner with a hearty cheer. . . . The result has proved Mr. Harrison quite equal to any pedestrian, professional or amateur.'

I should like to mention the achievements of some of my contemporaries, and so will give a short account of a steeplechase held on the M.C.C. ground early in 1860.

For this sample, I shall quote from *Bell's Life* of 11 February 1860: 'A quarter of a mile Handicap Steeplechase, described on the card as "The Ladies' Purse", the prizes, a trophy of the value of £20 for the first, and £5 in specie, for the second, over six hurdles and a water jump (16 feet), open to amateurs only. From the novelty of the water-jump, made for the occasion, opposite the grandstand, over which the competitors would have to go twice, this race caused peculiar interest, and the value of the prizes caused a large entry. To prevent the competitors scrambling through the water instead of going over it, a plank was fixed mid-way across the jump. This was about sixty yards from the start, and the winning post was about thirty yards beyond it, so that in addition to six hurdles the water had to be jumped twice–at the start and at the finish.

'Twelve competitors entered, and previous to the race, the stewards announced the following handicaps: Harrison, at scratch; Mount, 10 yards start; Drew, Beardsall, Wills, and Hamilton, 20 yards; Brazenor and Davies, 25; Ryder and Were, 30; and M. Byrne and Hammersley, 40. As soon as the report of the pistol was heard the men bounded

The following pages: Pedestrian Race, *Illustrated Australian News* 1870.
La Trobe collection, State Library of Victoria

off. All eyes were turned to the water jump, over which Brazenor bounded like a deer, taking a decided lead. The ruck followed, and the water was taken in most instances very cleverly. By the time those who had the advantage of a long start had cleared it, Mount and Harrison took it at a flying leap. The hurdles were taken without mishap; at about three hundred yards Brazenor's bolt was spent, and Mount, who had been gradually closing the gap, passed him, followed at a short interval by Harrison. The two foremost men were now racing in earnest, and between the last hurdle and the water jump Harrison took the lead, and cleared the leap about ten yards in advance of Mount, who went over it with Brazenor. The tailing was immense, though, as the competitors arrived at the water, they all essayed it, and, as may be expected, many of them got stuck. After the last jump Harrison relaxed his speed, while, in the hope of overtaking him, Mount continued his, but failed to come nearer than a respectable second, Brazenor third, the rest, nowhere.'

CHAMPIONSHIP RACES WITH L. L. MOUNT

I must now come to my contests with my most formidable opponent, Lambton Mount. He was a son of Dr. Mount of Ballarat, but was a Canadian by birth. He had recently beaten all comers in Ballarat, including Joshua and Whitely both of whom were professional cracks, and was the hero of that district. We were, I think, both about twenty-four at our first contest in 1861.[15]

After my race with Allan, which, as I explained, was taken easily at the start, Mount thought the time in which it was run (53¾ seconds) was my best, and as he had run the same distance in 49½ seconds in his trial runs on a hard, metalled road, challenged me with confidence.[16]

The meeting was arranged to take place on the Melbourne Cricket ground, on the 15th June, 1861. The Melbourne committee, on my behalf, consisted of Messrs. T. Hamilton, Butterworth, Levey, Woolley, R. Wardill; and Messrs. Sherard, Craig, Drury, Kelly and Leonard formed the Ballarat committee on behalf of Mount. Sixty pounds were raised by subscription among our friends for the purchase of a trophy to be given to the winner of two out of three races, namely: (1) 100 yards flat race; (2) a quarter of a mile flat race; (3) a quarter of a mile hurdle race.

It is impossible to describe the keen interest which was taken in this trial of speed. Hundreds of people drove all the way from Ballarat to see it, including scores of diggers, and I remember that Mr. G. Fawcett[17] kindly sent an invitation to the committees and competitors

L.L. Mount

to witness a special performance at the Princess Theatre. I believe there was a double-banked performance of *The White Friars* and *The Beggar's Opera*, in which Rosa Dunn and Julia Matthews were playing.[18] I must confess that my recollections of that evening are rather hazy, but I expect we thoroughly enjoyed it, as the actresses were both great favorites. Julia Matthews was a clever young Australian actress, and she afterwards went to England, where she made a name for herself.

I should like to remark here on the generosity of Australian theatrical managers in entertaining visiting athletes and other sportsmen to Melbourne, one of the most generous of all in that respect being, I think, the lately retired popular and much esteemed actor-manager, Mr. Bland Holt,[19] for whom and his charming wife, all theatre-goers retain a very warm place in their hearts.

In speaking of the theatrical profession, one's memories go back to the time of that great old pioneer, the late actor-manager, the Hon. George Coppin.[20] He was one of the most energetic and public-spirited of men, and his name was associated with many progressive and charitable movements here. An institution that will always be a monument to his memory is the Old Colonists' Home, founded, through his initiative and energy, for the benefit of old colonists or their descendants, who have fallen on evil days. It was a great idea, and has provided many of the more successful colonists with the means of helping (by donating cottages) the less lucky, though equally deserving ones.

With this digression, I must continue the account of my first contest with Mount.

Walter Craig[21] of Ballarat, drove him all the way from Ballarat in his buggy, so that he should not suffer from the fatigue of the very rough and tedious coach journey, and he arrived in Melbourne a couple of days before the race, putting up at the Port Phillip Club hotel.

The day of the contest turned out fairly fine, though the ground was slightly spongy from recent rains. To fill up the intervals of an hour each between our races, some interesting handicaps had been arranged, most of which, I think, were won by J. H. Were. There were several thousand spectators on the ground–a considerable number for those days–and the excitement was great. So sanguine were Mount's backers, that thousands of pounds might have been lost by Ballarat if all the bets offered had been taken up. I was told afterwards that Walter Craig who had brought £10,000 from Ballarat to put on Mount for his friends stood on the steps of the pavilion just before the first race, and called out in a loud voice: 'I'll bet £100 Harrison doesn't win a race!' However, to make a long story short, I won all three. The first 100 yards flat was closely contested, and I won by a yard. Time 10½ secs. The second race, a quarter of a mile flat, considered one of the best contested races ever seen on the ground, I won by two yards. Time 50¼ seconds. In the third race, a quarter of a mile over eight hurdles of 3ft. 6in., I practically ran away from him, winning by about fifty yards. My way of taking hurdles (namely, in my stride) was superior to Mount's; and a day or so after the race he came to my office and got me to give him a lesson; and he afterwards nearly beat me at my own game! The *Ballarat Star* said, when describing my running: 'His head is thrown up highest when his speed is greatest, and in his greatest efforts he wears the appearance of assuming the slowest attitude. He jumps beautifully, gracefully, and without straining,–in this, having a great advantage over his opponent.' A graphic and detailed account of the meeting was also given in *Bell's Life*, the sporting paper of the day [22 June 1861].

Before the contest, Craig had offered Mount £1,000 and expenses if he would go to England and run the championships there; but after the event, he asked Mount to sound me as to whether I would take it on. Naturally, I should have enjoyed pitting my powers against the champions of the old world, but it would have meant my becoming a professional runner, which I had no desire to do, and so I refused. All the same, I appreciated the generosity of the offer, as I am sure it was made from a sheer love of sport. Walter Craig was the owner of Nimble-foot, a famous Melbourne Cup winner, and he took a leading part in all sports of the day. Craig's Hotel at Ballarat, still bears his name.

At the time of his death, it was common property that, a week or so before, when Craig was in his usual health, he had had a dream in which he saw his own horse win the Cup race, and the curious part about the dream was that the jockey was wearing a crepe band on his arm. As it turned out, the horse did win the race, and the jockey wore a crepe band on his arm, because the popular owner had died suddenly, a day or so before the race. But this is by the way.

Mount was naturally disappointed at his defeat, and lost no time in challenging me to another contest–this time to take place on the Copenhagen grounds, Ballarat–much to the disappointment of my Melbourne friends, who could not get away. I at once agreed to give him his revenge, on condition that, in the event of my being defeated, we should have a third and conquering match *within six months' time*, and *at Melbourne*.

The event was fixed for the 19th December, 1861. The conditions of the races were the same, with the exception of the third, which was increased to half a mile, hurdle. This was considered a liberal concession on my part, as Mount had fixed the original distances himself.

Since our last meeting, Mount had been moved to the Bendigo branch of the Oriental Bank, but he was generously given a month's holiday in which to return to Ballarat and train for the event. I managed to keep fit by joining Metzger's gymnasium, a well-known meeting place of the athletes of the day, and among whom was Percy de Jersey Grut,[22] a fine gymnast, and who, about that time, deservedly received much praise for his courageous resistance to a bank robber, in which his athletic strength stood him in good stead.

Metzger's, Johnson's and Tecko's were all popular gymnasiums in my time.[23] The first was in Flinders Lane. The second was also in the Lane, and, more conveniently situated for me, near the Customs House in Market Street. Tecko's was near the East Melbourne Cricket Ground. I attended them all at various times.

I never had any leave in which to prepare for my races, except perhaps, the morning of the race, or the day before, when I had to travel to Ballarat. For this particular event I left Melbourne the day

Activities in the Turn Verein, La Trobe Street, *Australasian Sketcher* 1878

before and, on my arrival at Ballarat, put up at Bath's Hotel (since known as Craig's). There was not so much betting on this match as on the first, as it was expected to be a very close thing.

In the first race, 100 yards straight, Mount was a little ahead of me all the way, but at about fifty yards from the post, as I was making my great effort to pass him, I cannoned against him, there being no division down the course, and he won by about a foot. Time 10½ seconds. Our collision showed the necessity for a division down the course, and one was always provided afterwards. But the absence of one on this occasion was unfortunate for me, as the impetus with which I came against him sent him forward and retarded my course considerably, giving him four or five yards' start, when it was too late for me to recover the lost ground. In the second race, quarter mile flat, for about eighty yards we ran shoulder to shoulder. I then began to gain on him, and continued to increase the gap until, at about forty yards from home, he pulled up, finding it impossible to recover the lost ground. Time 54 seconds. In the third race, half a mile over sixteen hurdles, the distance being one I was unused to, I was advised to make the pace from the start, and for about five hundred yards I kept well ahead of him, but at the second last hurdle from home he overhauled me. After the last hurdle, the crowd, in their excitement, rushed in and fairly surrounded him whilst he ran the last fifty yards, thus blocking me from making any further effort! But I felt I was fairly beaten, having run with bad judgment, and taken it out of myself at the start. And so, when the judges said the race must be run over again, I professed myself satisfied with the result. One can sympathise with the excitement of Mount's partisans when they found him overtaking me, but the interference with the race at the finish was unpardonable.[24]

We had now, each in turn, won the trophy, and it remained for Mount to carry out his promise and run the conquering match, within the stipulated time. But it was not till a year after that, through the negotiations of my old friend, Norman McLeod,[25] who at that time was a stock and station agent in Ballarat, the meeting was at last arranged. Even then I had to consent to run at Ballarat instead of Melbourne. But it was agreed that the trophy (valued at £60) should be subscribed for in Ballarat alone. Hitherto the trophies had been evenly subscribed for by the friends of both sides. Mount, who in the meantime had been moved to the Omeo district, got his usual leave–six weeks this time–and came to Ballarat to prepare for the match. I happened to be then in the Customs at Geelong, and Ted Nicholls, one of the finest runners of that time, who was residing there too, decided to run in the intervening races at our meeting, and we used to take our exercise together on the ground near the Botanical gardens, by way of training for the event. I think he won pretty well all his races on that day.

The match took place on the Copenhagen grounds,[26] Ballarat, on Saturday, the 2nd December, 1862. There were six or seven thousand spectators present, and the excitement was intense. The betting generally, was six to four against Mount. We received a very warm reception on our appearance on the ground, and we both owned to being in good fettle.

The 100 yards race was won by me by about two yards; time 10¼ seconds. My quickest time for this race was 10 seconds. The 440 yards flat race, I won by about ten yards; time 53¾ seconds. I might explain in passing that the 440 yards race has always been considered the most difficult for a sprinter.

By winning the first two races I was entitled to the trophy, and also became again the champion amateur runner of the colony. But, on account of the number of bets, it was arranged from the first that all three events should be run, and so we started for the third race–660 yards, over twelve hurdles of 3ft. 6in.–which proved the most exciting of all. Mount started off ahead of me, but I collared him at about the second last hurdle from home, and we cleared it together, racing shoulder to shoulder to the last hurdle. We then went the last fifty yards at a tremendous bat, amid the most deafening applause, reaching the goal neck and neck, interested backers calling out loudly, 'Dead heat! Dead heat! As fair a dead heat as ever I saw!' and so on. Confusion now prevailed, the crowd pressing in on every side, some claiming me as the winner, and others Mount. Levey, the judge, gave it as a dead heat. A meeting of the committee was convened on the spot. Craig proposed that the race should be run over again, and the proposal was seconded. Woolley moved, as an amendment, that it be not run over again, which was also seconded! Mount then said that he did not think the committee had anything to do with it, but that he was willing to run it again if I was. But I indignantly refused, considering that the whole affair was against all order, and insisted upon abiding by the decision of the judge. Thus ended our last contest.[27]

We had run eleven races in all–Mount having run in a couple of handicaps previously–of which I won eight, Mount two, and one was a draw.

There is always something sad about the word 'last', and one cannot help having a feeling of regret, though mingled with pleasure, on looking back on the days of youthful prowess and enthusiasm. I always enjoyed our contests, and I think Mount did so too; and we were never anything but friendly rivals. He had a fine athletic figure, and was about 5ft. 10in. in height, appearing rather broader across the shoulders than I, whose height was 5ft. 10½in. My weight was about 12 stone, 5 lbs. The natural paleness of my skin at first led the public to suppose that I was not particularly robust, but they soon came to the conclusion that appearances were deceptive–in my case at any rate. Mount and I used to dispose of the surplus gate money, taken at our contests, to various hospitals, he giving his share to the Ballarat, and I dividing mine between the Geelong, Melbourne and Children's hospitals. In recognition of these subscriptions, we were both made life governors of the respective hospitals.

After our first meeting some of my kind friends subscribed among themselves to make me a presentation in honour of the occasion, and at my suggestion, they agreed to divide it between us, so that we should each have a memento as a mark of their appreciation of our athletic attainments. Mount received a handsome gold watch, suitably inscribed, and I a pair of binoculars, which I still have among my treasures.

It is difficult for one of the actors to depict the general interest and enthusiasm which our contests evoked. But there was one instance which I recall with a certain thrill of pleasure because it was so unexpected, and which I appreciated particularly as coming from boys in a spontaneous manner. It occurred some months after my first meeting with Mount. My younger brothers were scholars at the Scotch College, and, with other members of the family, I was attending the annual 'Break-up.' On our arrival at the Athenaeum Hall, we were being escorted to our seats by 'Bobbie' Morrison,[28] the affectionate term by which the brother and assistant of the head master was known, when the boys all began to clap and cheer very heartily. At

Gymnastics and Athletics Meeting at MCC, Calvert, *Illustrated Australian News* 1866. La Trobe collection, State Library of Victoria. Harrison officiated as a judge at this meeting

this I, quite unconscious that the demonstration concerned me in any way, naively remarked to him, 'The Governor must be arriving'. But to my surprise, he replied with a smile, 'Don't you know that it is meant for you?'

It used to be the fashion in those days for amateurs to challenge each other to run, at so much a side, and I was often invited to officiate at these events. I remember one race in which Frank Stephen, the barrister, had challenged Sam Ramsden, the well-known miller, to run 100 yards.[29] The latter for some unknown reason, thinking he would have a better chance in a longer distance, made it 200 yards. He ran the first half well, but being about 18 stone weight, was beaten in the longer distance. Another time, Frank Stephen and Farquharson,[30] the opera singer, had a match, which the former also won. This took place at Mordialloc, so I did not see it.

I continued to run at various sports meetings till the year 1867, when I was defeated by Harris[31] the professional, in the Challenge Cup, on the Melbourne Cricket Ground, having held the championship for eight years. I believe this is still considered a record. The Challenge Cup was presented by the Athletic Sports Committee, for the winner of two out of three specified races, namely: 100 yards, quarter of a mile, and half mile, on three consecutive occasions. I won the first two matches against Harris but lost the third. This was my last race.

My best distance, the quarter mile, run in 50¼ seconds, *on grass*, and *in a circle*, is a world's record, and when Harris won the match at our third meeting, he took 54 seconds, showing I had gone off in my pace by nearly four seconds, and so, I knew it was time to leave off.[32]

But though I ceased to run, my interest in all kinds of sport continued, and I took an active part in the arrangement of various events for many years after.

At first, all meetings used to be carried out by a sports committee, under the auspices of the M.C.C., but in 1866, we formed the Amateur Athletic Club, with the idea of furthering and encouraging all forms of athletics in the colony.

The first provisional committee was composed of: Professor Irving (Head Master of the Hawthorn Grammar School, and afterwards Professor of Classics, English and History at the Melbourne University), the Messrs. M. Byrne, W. J. Hammersley, A. Hardcastle, W. Levey (editor of *Bell's Life*), R. J. Wardill and myself.[33]

All future sports were carried out under the supervision of this club for upwards of twenty-five years, and during that time, such was my enthusiasm, I practically measured all courses and did most of the handicapping for all events on the Melbourne Cricket Ground. In the early days Hammersley, M. Byrne, R. Wardill, etc., were amongst those who worked most energetically in carrying out the various meetings. Levey and Wardill generally acted as judges, and Hammersley as starter. I have with me a programme of a meeting held in the spring of 1881, and under the heading, 'Committee of Management', I find the following names–H. C. A. Harrison, J. Byrne, L. L. Mount, S. C. Lamrock (captain of the M.F.C., at one time), J. P. Tenant, C. Jenvey, W. Slade, E. W. Longdon (M.F.C.). Handicappers–H. C. A. Harrison, L. L. Mount, and W. Slade.

The most difficult of all races to judge is the walking race. It is very hard for a competitor not to break into a run occasionally, for a yard or so, particularly, in a close race, towards the finish; and it requires a very experienced eye to note this kind of slip, especially in a large field. It was the rather foolish custom of some judges to give a man one warning during the race, if his walking were not up to the required standard of fair 'heel and toe'. On one occasion a very ludicrous situation arose in consequence of this. The two judges gave notice to the three starters, who were all at scratch, that *one* warning was all they would get without being disqualified. The consequence was that, at the sound of the pistol, two of them started off, running at full speed, and when I came out of the pavilion where I had retired to change into running dress, I saw the judges running for all they were worth across the ground to intercept them. By this time they had gained at least 100 yards in 150, and naturally the only serious walker, who plodded faithfully along to the end, lost the race (a mile)!

At the present day, interest in foot-racing is not so general as it was, though it is still one of the many kinds of sport indulged in. The more modern game of tennis–'modern' as compared to the older game of which it is a vigorous revival–now takes pride of place (after football and cricket) in public interest. Although it did not become the fashion till I was past middle age, I played a good deal at one time, and learnt enough about it to be able to appreciate the science and skill of others. It certainly is a most fascinating and absorbing game to watch, when in the hands of first class exponents, and I have spent many a delightful hour in watching the play of Norman Brookes, whom Tilden, in his book, rightly places in a class by himself, Gerald Patterson and others, not forgetting Alf. Dunlop, who, with Brookes and the late Anthony Wilding, was one of our first international players.[34] With regard to Wilding, we have had occasion during the recent European upheaval, to mourn the loss of many brave and gallant young athletes–particularly among footballers, of whom I always think very proudly–but I think all Australia was moved to sorrow at the death of that splendid young New Zealander in the early days of the war.

CHAPTER 7

FOOTBALL: 'FATHER OF THE AUSTRALIAN GAME'

Now for a few words about the Australian game of football, for which I still retain my early enthusiasm.

Football always has been, and always will be, to my mind *the* game for strong and vigorous men, for the simple reason that it requires all the best qualities of a first-rate athlete, namely, strength, courage, endurance and self-control. It also requires a sufficient amount of resource and judgment to make it really interesting to the player and yet, at the same time, is quickly and easily learned. It is also much more comprehensible to the general public than cricket for instance, and there are no dull moments for the spectator, the excitement being kept up from start to finish. One has only to hear the continuous roar that proceeds from the vicinity of a big match to know that!

In the pavilion of the M.C.C. we have had many distinguished visitors from other lands, from time to time, to see the game, and they have been practically unanimous in describing the Australian game as being superior to all others as a spectacle for the public. Among others, I may quote Sir Arthur Conan Doyle, who was with us in 1921. In his interesting book, *The Wanderings of a Spiritualist*, he says: 'I have played both Rugby and Soccer, and I have seen the American game at its best, but I consider that the Victorian (meaning Australian) system has some points which make it the best of all–certainly from the spectacular point of view, etc., etc.'[1]

Till the year 1858, no football had been played in the colony. But when T. W. Wills[2] arrived from England, fresh from Rugby school, full of enthusiasm for all kinds of sport, he suggested that we should make a start with it. He very sensibly advised us not to take up Rugby although that had been his own game because he considered it as then played unsuitable for grown men, engaged in making a livelihood, but to work out a game of our own. So a number of us, principally cricketers, got together, and began to play. It was rather a go-as-you-please affair at first, but a set of rules was gradually evolved, which experience taught us to be the best.[3]

The first club formed was the Melbourne captained by Tom Wills. In the same year (1858), clubs were formed in Richmond, South Yarra, Royal Park and Geelong, and in a very short time there was not a suburb of Melbourne, nor a town in Victoria of any importance, without its football club.

In 1865, the Athletic Sports Committee, of which I was a member, gave a great fillip to the game by offering a Challenge Cup to be played for.[4]

The first clubs to enter for it were Melbourne, Geelong, South Yarra, Royal Park, University and Carlton, and we had some famous battles for it (Melbourne being the first winners); and most stirring accounts of them may be read in the newspapers of the day, at the Public Library.

In the early days of football, two goals constituted a game. So that, if neither side succeeded in kicking the required number, the match would be resumed on the following Saturday and continued till one or the other had done so. But, in playing for the Cup, we found this arrangement particularly inconvenient, and so a new rule was made the second season, to the effect that if two goals had not been kicked by one side in the afternoon, the game would be considered drawn. The present system by which the team making the most points wins was not instituted till two or three years after.[5]

On the 8th May, 1866, a meeting of delegates from the leading clubs (Melbourne, South Yarra, Royal Park, Carlton) was held at the Freemasons' Hotel, Swanston St., at which a set of rules was adopted, which formed the basis of those played at the present time.

Before the meeting, some of the delegates asked me to draft a set of rules as they considered I knew more about the game than any of them, which I willingly did.

At the meeting I was voted to the chair, and read the rules as drafted, which were approved and accepted unanimously, without alteration, by the meeting. The delegates were: T. P. Power (Hon Treasurer), B. James, Carlton; R. W. Wardill, Melbourne; George O'Mullane, Hugh Murray, South Yarra; A. E. Clarke, J. W. Chadwick, Royal Park, and myself.

As that meeting may be considered historical in the realm of sport, I shall give the rules then adopted:

1. The distance between the goals shall not be more than 200 yards; and the width of playing space (to be measured equally on each side of a line drawn through the centre of the goals) not more than 150 yards. The goal posts shall be seven yards apart, of unlimited height.

2. The captains on each side shall toss for choice of a goal, the side losing the toss, or a goal, has a kick-off from the centre point between the goals. After a goal is kicked the sides shall change ends.

3. A goal must be kicked fairly between the posts without touching either of them, or any portion of the person of one of the opposite side. In case of the ball being forced (except with the hand or arms) between the goal posts in a scrummage, a goal shall be awarded.

4. Two posts to be called the kick-off posts shall be erected at a distance of 20 yards on each side of the goal posts, and in a straight line with them.

5. In case the ball is kicked behind goal, anyone of the side behind whose goal it is kicked may bring it 20 yards in front of any portion of the space between the kick-off posts, and shall kick it towards the opposite goal.

6. Any player catching the ball directly from the foot or leg may call 'Mark'; he then has a free kick from any spot in a line with his mark and the centre of his opponents' goal posts; no player being allowed to come inside the spot marked, or within five yards in any other direction.

7. Tripping and hacking are strictly prohibited. Pushing with the hands or body is allowed when any player is in rapid motion. Holding is only allowed while a player has the ball in hand, except in the case provided in Rule 6.

8. The ball may be taken in hand at any time, but not carried further than is necessary for a kick, and no player shall run with the ball unless he strikes it against the ground every five or six yards.

9. When a ball goes out of bounds (the same being indicated by a row of posts), it shall be brought back to the point where it crossed the boundary-line, and thrown in at right angles with that line.

10. The ball, while in play, may, under no circumstances, be thrown.

11. In case of deliberate infringement of any of the above rules the captain of the opposite side may claim that one of his party may have a free-kick from the place where the breach of rule was made.

12. Before the commencement of a match each side shall appoint an umpire, and they shall be the sole judges of goals and breaches of rules. The nearest umpire shall be appealed to in case of dispute.

(N.B.–The usual number a side used to be 20. It is now 18.)[6]

Opposite: Football in the Richmond Paddock, *Melbourne Post* 1866. National Library of Australia

The first year of football, I captained the Richmond club; but after that, I joined the Melbourne and succeeded Tom Wills as captain, he having resigned on going to Geelong, where he captained the local club for a season.

On being moved to the Customs in Geelong in 1862, I became captain of that club, succeeding W. Tait. In that club we had some very fine players, such as Ted Nicholls, Tom Hope, Felix Armytage, Jack Warner, Angus O'Dwyer, R. Williams, the Elkingtons, the brothers Timms, Horace and Egbert Wills (after I left), J. Bowden, Buz Robertson, Stodart, Osborne, Adams, Campbell, George G. Smith, etc.

On my return to Melbourne in 1863, I was re-elected captain of the M.F.C., and retained the position till my retirement in 1872. The M.F.C. became very strong and we were the premiers for some years. My vice-captain, for some years was James Byrne (of the firm of Mullally and Byrne), regarded by all as one of the finest and fairest players we ever had. Some others who played for the good old team were: R. W. Wardill, B. Goldsmith, W. J. Hammersley, Jack Bennie, J. Conway, J. B. Thompson, T. Hope, W. Williams, Tom Hepburn (later Inspector of Schools), Chatsworth Tyler, Aitken, T. S. Marshall, Gorman, Charles (generally known as Chubby) Forrester, McCarthy, Neal, Larry Bell, T. and R. Ireland, Woolley, Fleming, Treacey, Shiels, Davidson, the brothers Loughnan, Bob Sillet, Lock, Serrell, Riggall, O'Brien, C. Carr, Bob Simpson (a champion amateur boxer, and son of a well-known squatter), etc.

Of the South Yarra team, some of the best known were: George O'Mullane, Murray Smith, Ogilvy, W. J. Greig, McPherson, Cumming, Billy Freeman, Hugh Murray, etc.

Jack Bennie was known to the public as 'specs.' He always played in glasses, and used to bring half a dozen pairs to the ground every Saturday, and leave them in the care of the umpire, who would hand them out in turn to him as each was broken. They would all be repaired by the next Saturday, only to meet with their inevitable fate again!

Billy Freeman (brother of the late Col. Freeman) was a small man, and was noted for the reckless way in which he would dodge in and out among the players, holding on to the ball. He always had several jerseys torn off his back during the afternoon. But it was all the same to him, for he would simply run into the pavilion and, seizing the first he could find (regardless of the owner's feelings), come out again with renewed vigour.

In the very beginning, one man would perhaps, play with two or three different clubs in a season, so that, in reading accounts of the early games, it is rather confusing to see the same name in the lists

Melbourne Football Club Six, *Leader* 1909, left to right: H.C.A. Harrison, J. Byrne, C. Forrester, B. Goldsmith, J. Bennie, C. Curr. MCC collection

of opposing clubs. That is why I have not given a list of the members of the Carlton Club at that time. It would simply be a repetition of the names in the Melbourne and South Yarra Clubs.[7]

But this anomaly was rectified after a few years.

Another peculiarity which may be noted is the number of captains of one club in the same season. The explanation is that, at first it was not the custom to elect a captain for the whole season. In fact, he was generally elected on the ground just before the play started. I soon saw the many disadvantages of this system, and, at my suggestion, the rule was made to elect one for the whole season.

At first too, we had no umpires, and the captains had to adjudicate in cases of dispute, one of the advantages being the absence of the umpire's whistle!

For years the M.F.C. played in the Richmond paddock, outside the M.C.G. ground. We had no enclosure, and the boundaries were roughly marked by gum trees, from whose boughs the game was often watched by enthusiastic onlookers. Many leading citizens have since told me that they, as boys, spent many happy hours thus perched on high watching the play. But an occasional goal was lost through the ball's collision with a tree on its way![8] In time we were allowed to put up a movable boundary fence. Until that was done the game had always been interfered with by the encroachment of the public.

It took me some years to persuade the M.C.C. to allow us to play on their ground, their objection being that the turf would be spoilt for cricket. But in the end, the committee consented to let us have some trial matches, and found that, instead of ruining the ground, the case was quite the reverse.

The first game on the M.C.C. Ground was that played in 1869 against the Victorian Police Force, captained by Superintendent T. O'Callaghan.[9] They played a good, hard game, but we managed to beat them. The proceeds (about £50) were given to the Children's Hospital. I may say in passing, that Mr. O'Callaghan, though retired, is still well-known for his regular attendance at the city police court in his capacity of Justice of the Peace.

With reference to this match, I went down to inspect the ground next day, and found two or three members of the committee, all with very gloomy faces, who met me with the words, 'Harrison! You have ruined our ground!' Of course I laughed at the idea, but we were not allowed to play on the ground again for some time. But at last, after a Carlton v Melbourne match, which we were allowed to play as a great favor, it was found that the gate money was so much that the committee began to think the risk to the ground was worth while! Then we were permitted to play for half the season, namely, to within six weeks of the cricket season. Now-a-days, a football match may be played with impunity, a few days before the cricket season opens!

After the New Zealand war, we had some good old tussles with the men of the 14th and 40th regiments, which were stationed here for a year or so. The men of the 14th were captained by Captain Noyes, and of the 40th by Lieut. Gordon. We always beat the soldiers, who were pretty rough customers, fresh from campaigning under very hard conditions. They played with their trousers tucked into their heavy boots, and with colored handkerchiefs tied round their heads. They were mostly big, heavy men, and their appearance was pretty awe-inspiring! They had a playful way too, of kicking an opponent in the shins to make him drop the ball. As captain, I once protested that such tactics were against the rules, but the only satisfaction I got was the forceful reply, 'To H– with your rules! We're playing the – Irish rules!' I have bruises on my shins to this day, received in these encounters. Sometimes their captain would fall panting on the ground with the ball under him, and his men would surround him, keeping all intruders off till he had recovered his breath, and woe betide anyone who tried to get through! Every time we beat them, they would say, in their fascinating brogue: 'Wait till Ensign Crosby arrives! He'll show you!'

Opposite: Match on the Melbourne Ground, *Australasian Sketcher* 1883,

This, naturally, made us all think that the Ensign must be a perfect terror, and all looked forward to meeting him. At last he arrived, and he appeared on the field in immaculate white, wearing a belt on which was worked probably by some fair admirer, the words, 'Neck or nothing.' As he was quite slight and boyish looking, our fears were considerably allayed by his apparent want of weight. And, to make a long story short, his career in Australian football lasted about sixteen seconds, as he was carried off the ground, having collided straight off with the redoubtable 'Chubby'! He never played again–here, at any rate.[10]

Towards the end of my football career, fourteen of the M.F.C. played against twenty of the Ballarat club. This was an absurd handicap, but as our secretary, without consulting the committee, had made the arrangement, we had to abide by it. They were a very heavy lot of men, and, as I said before, the odds were ridiculous. However, we did our best, but were beaten by two goals, and some of us felt the result of the effort for some time to come.

Another strenuous game soon after, was that against Carlton, for the season's premiership. For some reason or other it had to be played on a neutral ground, so the South Melbourne was chosen, though not at all suitable, as, at that time, it was not fenced in.

We lost the toss and had to play against a strong gale of wind, and, when I kicked off, the ball was carried over my head about twenty yards behind our goal. However, we hoped to have the benefit of it in the second half, but, to our great disappointment, it had ceased when our turn came to profit by it, and we were defeated by two goals to nothing. Carlton played in their usual brilliant style, but the luck was certainly against us, and, owing to the over-exertion caused by this tremendous effort, I was laid up for about a month after it. That was my last game![11]

Oh happy, glorious days! Is there anything in life to equal the zest of youth? I love to linger over the names of those associated with me in that happy time. Most of them are gone from sight, but they sometimes gather round me in spirit and, together we fight our old battles over again, recalling many an exciting, goal-making kick, or dashing charge. Oh happy, glorious days!

On my retirement in 1872 my old friend and vice-captain, Jim Byrne, became captain and led the club to frequent victory for a season or two.

That year also saw the retirement of Conway,[12] brilliant captain of one of our greatest rivals, the Carlton Club.

Though unable to take further active part in the game, I have ever since maintained a lively interest in it.

In 1884, on receiving a year's leave, after thirty-one years in the

A Football Match, Melbourne v Carlton, *Australasian Sketcher* 1881. La Trobe collection, State Library of Victoria

government service, I took a run Home, and while I was there I tried to get some of the clubs to take up the Australian game. But of that, anon.

I travelled with the Australian Eleven, which was captained by W. L. Murdoch.[13] On the way to Adelaide, Spofforth[14] and I agreed to buy a piano in that city, and have it fixed on deck, with the result that we had many a good dance and concert during the voyage. Before landing we raffled the instrument amongst the passengers, and the cost to all of us only amounted to five shillings each. George Giffen,[15] sad to relate, suffered a great loss, somewhere about the middle of the Indian Ocean. He used to wear two handsome diamond rings, presented to him by the people of South Australia in recognition of his splendid performances in the cricket field. He and I took great interest in getting up sports for the fine lot of children on board, and one day, when playing with them, he picked up a banana skin on the deck and threw it overboard, and, with it his two rings, which unfortunately fitted his finger very loosely. We were all very sorry for him, and did not wonder that he felt his loss acutely. We had a very pleasant voyage but for this accident. A dinghy could have lived in any sea I saw on the way Home.

When in England, as I have said, I tried my best to get the Rugby and Soccer Unions to give the Australian game a trial. As a matter of fact, the British Association game had been founded only six months before ours. Mr. Alcock, the secretary of the Surrey Cricket Club, which played on the Oval, was strongly in favor of supporting my suggestion.[16] He said he had heard so much from returned cricketers in favor of the game that he offered to undertake to get a team of Soccer players to play against a team of Rugby players on the Surrey Oval, the use of which he would give us free of cost, if I could persuade the Rugby authorities to agree. Harry Boyle,[17] the Australian cricketer, and I attended the annual meeting of the Rugby Union, and were received cordially by the members; but they argued that it would be impossible to get a team of Rugby players to practise our game which I offered to teach both teams as all their time would be required to get into form for the coming season. I had formed the hope that some day we should have friendly contests between the British Isles and Australia. It may still happen at some future date, but not in my time.

To continue. The Australian States, including Tasmania, all took up the game, as also did New Zealand for a time. But Rugby had got too strong a hold there for another game to make much headway. Rugby also had (and has) a good following in New South Wales and Queensland. But 'Variety is charming,' and there is plenty of room for both games in Australia. The West Australians are particularly

Playing deck games on RMS *Austral* 1884, J.W. Lindt. La Trobe
collection, State Library of Victoria

keen, and there are some very fine exponents of the game among
them, which was shown by their carrying off the inter-State championship at their Football Carnival in 1921.

The first inter-state match was played in 1877 between the South
Australians and Victorians, and was won by the latter. The South
Australians are now among the best exponents of the game.[18]

In 1877 the Football Association of Victoria was formed, with Mr.
(afterwards Sir) William Clarke as president, R. Robertson and myself
as vice-presidents, H. H. Budd as secretary, and T. P. Power as
treasurer,[19] with nineteen delegates from the subscribing clubs. T. S.
Marshall,[20] who afterwards became secretary, has been a great worker
in the cause of football.

The Association governed the game till 1897, when the Victorian
League superseded it, with the late Mr. Alex. McCracken[21] as president. He was a man of fine character, as well as a keen sportsman,
and football lost a good friend and enthusiastic supporter at his death
a few years ago.

In November, 1905, the first Australian Football conference was
held in Melbourne. I was elected chairman, and the other delegates
were: C. Brownlow,[22] J. Denham, C. M. Hickey, J. Worrall (Victoria); J. J. Simons, T. J. Brett (W.A.); W. H. Harvey, R. F. C.

Sullivan (S.A.); A. E. Nash, M. T. Odgers (N.S.W.); W. H. Gill (Tas.); L. A. Balhausen (Q.); W. H. McKeon (N.Z.); E. L. Wilson (Vic.), secretary.

As a result of the Conference, the Australasian Football Council was established.[23] It held its inaugural meeting in Melbourne in 1906, and has since controlled the game in Australia. Mr. C. M. Hickey, who had been secretary of the Fitzroy Club for about sixteen years, and whose efforts helped to make it one of the leading clubs, was unanimously elected first President, Mr. A. E. Nash (N.S.W.), was elected Vice-President, and Mr. W. Gill (Tas.), Treasurer. The other members of the Council were: Messrs. C. H. Nitschke (Barrier Ranges F.A., N.S.W.); E. Q. McKeon (N.Z.); A. Collison, W. G. Foster (Q'land); W. H. Harvey, R. F. C. Sullivan (S.A.); R. Gibson (North T.F.A.); John Worrall (Vic.); E. Udy (W.A.F.A.); T. J. Brett (Goldfields F.A., W.A.).

At the inaugural meeting, the Council did me the honor of electing me the first Honorary Life Member, 'for special services rendered to Australian Football,' and also gave me the designation of 'Father of the Game.'

In 1908, we celebrated in Melbourne the Jubilee of Australian Football.[24] All the States sent representative teams, and we saw some very brilliant play. The game had made great progress since my day–team work, the keynote of success in every game, having reached pretty well perfection. I have never enjoyed quite such an orgy of football as that week provided! There were matches by day and meetings by night!

The public evinced the greatest interest in all the proceedings, and the attendances were the biggest that had been seen in Melbourne.

I shall never forget the generous manner in which everyone treated me as the 'Father of the Game,' and all the kind things which were said of me at the time–quite disproving the saying: 'A prophet is not without honour save in his own country.' All seemed to realise that it was not given to every man to see the Jubilee of that of which he has been one of the founders, and which had also grown in popularity with the years. And so, I was the subject of most warm-hearted congratulations from every quarter. I can only say that I was not insensible to so much generous appreciation, and, at times felt quite overcome.

At the time of the Jubilee, Mr. C. M. Hickey[25] was President of the Council, and much of the success of the celebration was due to his untiring work and powers of organisation. He is certainly one of those to whom the cause of football is much indebted.

The proceedings culminated in a monster smoke-night, held in the Melbourne Town Hall, on the 28th August, at which the Victorian

At the Football Match, *Australasian Sketcher* 1877. La Trobe collection,
State Library of Victoria

League entertained the visiting representatives and teams. Mr.
McCracken presided, and some very happy and interesting speeches
were made. The late Right Honorable Alfred Deakin, then Prime
Minister of Australia, proposed the toast of the 'Australasian Game
of Football,' and, as might be expected, did full justice to the subject.[26] We were proud to have him–one of the greatest of Australians–with us that night. Being an old footballer (in his boyhood),
he was able to enter into the spirit of the celebration, and I can safely
say that his speech that night was listened to with as much appreciation
and enjoyment as any that he ever made.

One of the finest speeches of the evening was made by Mr. J. J.
Simons. Though quite a young man, he is one of those who have
done much for the advancement of football in Western Australia, and
his keenness and enthusiasm were most inspiring; and we were all

impressed with his idealism and superior powers of oratory. He has always taken a leading part in the work of the Young Australia League in West Australia, and is very interested in the subject of the education and training of youth. He is also a clever organiser, and has several times taken charge of large parties of boys in touring, not only Australia, but America and England.

But to return to the Carnival. It was resolved to hold one every three years in each State in turn. That arrangement necessarily lapsed during the Great War, but has since been resumed.

Before proceeding further, I should like to give a short account of the growth of the game in my birth place, New South Wales. It was first introduced in 1880, by the famous Waratah club, which was originally a powerful Rugby club, but which had among its members some former Victorian players of the Australian game. The New South Wales Football Association was established in 1880 and existed for sixteen years, with Mr. Phil. Shendon as president, and Mr. W. C. Marshall as honorary treasurer. After 1896 the game seems to have languished for a few years. But in 1903 the Victorian Football League sent the Fitzroy and Collingwood clubs to play a premiership match in Sydney, with a view to giving an extra fillip to the game there. There were between twenty and thirty thousand spectators present at the match, showing the strong interest taken in it by the public.[27] Among the enthusiasts, who went from Victoria to witness the match, besides myself, were Messrs. C. M. Hickey, T. Banks (Vic.), R. Ievers (Carlton), J. B. Gleeson (Geelong), E. Copeland and W. Strickland (Collingwood).

I am pleased to say the game has a large following in New South Wales now, especially in the mining districts, which have produced many brilliant and dashing players.

In August, 1911 the Australasian Football Carnival was held in Adelaide, and I was very glad to be present at it. Mr. J. J. Woods (Adelaide) was elected President of the Council, and Mr. C. M. Hickey became Hon. Secretary.

It was a very successful meeting, and the visitors from the other States were most hospitably entertained; and I, for one, thoroughly enjoyed myself.

The cinema was then just beginning its triumphant course, and some very good pictures of the final matches were taken. So that we non-players as well as players had the amusing experience of seeing ourselves on the 'movies' a few hours after taking part in the events recorded.

I regretted exceedingly not being able to attend the Carnival in Perth in 1921, but by that time I was beginning to feel the weight of years, and felt hardly equal to the journey. Even an old footballer, when he has reached the age of eighty-four (my age then), begins to feel that his own fireside is the best place for him! But my heart was with them, all the same, and I know I should have received as kind a welcome there as anywhere. I can only send the West Australian players my congratulations on the splendid progress the game has made there, and express the hope that they will always keep up the present high standard, both in their play and fine sportsman-like spirit.

With this slight sketch of the growth of our game, I would take my leave, and bequeath my fatherly blessing on all true footballers; expressing the hope that they will always do their utmost, not only to excel in the game, but to keep it a clean sport. I feel sure that my love for it and all that it means in the development of a true and honest manliness, will never die, and that my spirit will preside at many a good, rousing game, even after I am gone!

THE "FATHER OF VICTORIAN FOOTBALL."

From *Football*, n.1. 1885

CHAPTER 8

THE MELBOURNE CRICKET CLUB

The task of compiling the history of the M.C.C. has been undertaken by Mr. T. F. Cooke (Public Library), in whose competent and enthusiastic hands the result is sure to be a most interesting, informative, and entertaining book.[1] And so there is no need for me to do more than say a few words about the old club, with which I have been so long associated. An account of the various localities occupied by the club will indicate, to a certain extent, the rapid growth of Melbourne.

In December, 1838, when the town had been in existence but two years, the Melbourne Cricket Club was formed, and its first situation was in Little Collins Street, near William Street. In about eight years' time it was moved to the south side of the Yarra, on the flat between it and Emerald Hill. But in 1854, as the government required the ground for the railway, the club was given a crown grant of the present ground in Yarra Park, where I hope it will remain for all time.

I first joined the club in 1861, when it had a membership of a hundred or so. Its growth has been almost phenomenal, especially since the advent of football as one of its attractions. Its present [1923] membership is: Senior members, 4193; Country members, 1091; Junior members, 483. There is also a waiting list of about 1600.[2]

I was elected to the committee in 1871, and in 1892 became vice-president, which position I still retain.[3]

The Club has practically been one of my life's hobbies, and I have rarely missed a committee meeting in all these years, except through absolute necessity. The work has been a labour of love, for we have always been fortunate in having fine sportsmen on the committee,

MELBOURNE CRICKET CLUB.

MELBOURNE,

28 Sept 186_1_

DEAR SIR,

I have the pleasure to inform you that you have been elected a Member of the Melbourne Cricket Club.

The Entrance Money, £2 2s., and your Subscription for the Season 186_1/2,_ £2 2s., amounting together to £4 4s., you will have the goodness to forward to the Treasurer, Mr. SIDNEY WOOLLEY, 10 Queen-street, at your earliest convenience.

I am,

Dear Sir,

Yours faithfully,

R.W. Wardell

Honorary Secretary.

To _H.C.A. Harrison Esq_

M.C.C. membership certificate of H.C.A. Harrison 1861. L. Cooke collection

with whom it was a pleasure to work, from the days of the secretaryship of my old friend, the late Dick Wardill (hon. sec.), and his late brother Ben[4] (better known to the present generation), to the present day with Hughie Trumble (the popular cricketer)[5] in that position, under the leadership of our present much esteemed president, Sir Leo Cussen.[6] He, by the way, was a few years ago, one of our best footballers, and, I think, rivals me in his enthusiasm for the game.

As I have always been particularly anxious to give the public plenty of shelter and accommodation on the ground, when an extra stand was erected a few years ago on the south side, the committee paid me the compliment of naming it after me.[7]

It will be easily understood that I have spent some of my happiest hours on the pavilion balcony, in company with the best of friends and true lovers of sport, watching some great cricket, football, or other sports. In this way it has been my luck to meet all the most distinguished athletes, either visiting or local, during the space of over sixty years, and I need scarcely say that the experience has been fully enjoyed by me.

The honour of a life membership of the Club has recently been conferred on me by the committee. They had generously offered it many years ago, but, for various reasons, I did not then accept.

Bendemeer, East Melbourne

CHAPTER 9

DISASTROUS EVENTS

Naturally, sport has not occupied all my days, though, till about the age of thirty-six, I certainly devoted the greater part of my leisure to the practice of every kind of exercise then in vogue, including rowing and boxing. Since then I have devoted my energies to the promotion and encouragement of a high standard of sport in the community. This has been my great pleasure, and at the same time, has provided me with an interest outside the ordinary groove of work, which I consider to be a great factor in the matter of health, both of mind and body. I have been lucky in being able to combine work and play without neglecting the former.

When I left the Bay department (after five years) and settled in Melbourne, the town had made tremendous strides, and had quite lost its primitive appearance. Bendemeer,[1] the house which my father had built on Victoria Parade out of the wreck of his squatting undertakings, was already surrounded by many others, and East Melbourne was pretty much what it is now. As for that fine boulevard, Victoria Parade, I think most people will agree with me in regretting that it was not continued to the Victoria Bridge, as Hoddle, the surveyor-general, first intended it to, instead of ending at the street called after him. But, of course, no one ever dreamed that Melbourne would so soon outgrow its original plan.

At the time I am speaking of, the Fitzroy Gardens were beginning to take on the form which has since developed into one of the finest parks any town could possess. Those responsible for the work are deserving of great praise for the choice and arrangement of its various trees, most striking of which are the elms, white poplars, oaks, and Moreton Bay figs. The noble avenue of shady elms, entered at the corner of Clarendon Street and Wellington Parade, is a dream of beauty in the spring and summer time. In contrast is the quaint and picturesque avenue of Lombardy poplars, so seldom seen in this country. I could wish there were a few more and larger specimens of our stately gums, and also some wattles, though perhaps the former require rather too much space to mingle well with other trees in a comparatively circumscribed area. And for wattles, I suppose there are enough varieties in our Botanical gardens to satisfy the most devoted of their admirers! Of the three hundred and more different kinds of acacia (wattle), I believe the Acacia Normalis is one of the most beautiful. I have, in my garden, some splendid specimens of this species, the seeds of which were given to me by the late surveyor-general, Mr. Reed, who is of the same opinion about them. They are very vigorous and quick growers, and the beauty of their feathery foliage is as perfect as the golden fluffiness of their bloom.

Speaking of the Fitzroy Gardens, they are always associated in my mind with the days of my running contests. I used always to make my way backwards and forwards to town, through them, every day, and generally did it at a run by way of exercise, which was practically the only form of training I ever indulged in.

At one time, the spot occupied by these gardens had rather a sinister reputation as a haunt of footpads, and there were many stories of disagreeable adventure connected with them. One, I especially remember, was that in which Mr. Dalmahoy Campbell,[2] the well-known stock and station agent, figured. He was a heavily built man, and was justly regarded as one of the most powerful men in the colony. On this particular occasion, he was riding along quietly when he was set upon by three men. One seized the bridle and the others each caught hold of one of his legs, and tried to pull him off his horse. But, before they had time to do so, he gave the man holding the bridle such a blow with his hunting crop that he fell to the ground, stunned. Campbell then leant over, seized one of the others by the scruff of the neck and slung him across the front of the saddle. By this time, the third man was so frightened that he hurriedly made off! Campbell calmly continued his way till he reached the police station, where he gave his prisoner in charge.

Before I continue my story, I must go back to the year 1851, when we had just settled in Melbourne. It was the year in which three momentous events in the history of Victoria came crowding one after the other.

The first happened on the 6th February (ever since known as Black Thursday). It was one of the hottest days I ever remember, and the discomfort was increased by the stifling smoke which enveloped the town like a black fog, telling of the terrific fires all through the country. We were thankful to be in town, well out of it. I believe that Long Bill, who was still at Swanwater, distinguished himself in his heroic efforts to save some of the wool before the shed was burnt down. The destruction of property, including hundreds of sheep and cattle, was appalling, to say nothing of the great loss of human life which occurred. Victoria has had some bad bush fires since then, but that day will never be forgotten either by the immediate sufferers or their descendants, who still think of the sufferings entailed, with horror.

The second event was the granting of Separation by the British Government to Victoria from New South Wales.

For some years there had been much dissatisfaction with the New South Wales Government, as the affairs of Port Phillip were treated in a very dilatory manner, and frequent petitions had little or no effect. The state of discontent reached such a pitch that there was even a suggestion of having to fight for our rights; and I remember well the consternation of George and myself when, as small boys, my father told us that, in such an event, we should have to take a hand. 'But,' we protested feebly, 'we're too small to fight'. To which he calmly replied, 'That can easily be remedied. You can be stretched!' Our relief on finding such an obviously painful operation unnecessary, can be imagined. My father, who was a fluent and forceful speaker, did his part in arousing an interest in the movement, by stumping the country and addressing meetings.[3]

But politics are not in my province, and I must confine my recollections to events with which I was, to some extent, personally associated, or I shall never have done.

The third event of great importance was the rush to the goldfields of Ballarat and Bendigo, which began about August of this 'Annus Mirabilis.'

I have already described the excitement which prevailed in Melbourne at the time, and my own experiences at the diggings. On my return, what struck me most was the appearance of the extensive canvas town which had spread all over Emerald Hill[4] on the south side of the Yarra.

Naturally, at such a time, no one had time for building, and all newcomers arriving, at one period, at the rate of a thousand a week, were forced to take up their abode in tents. Some of these were quite comfortable, divided into compartments, and furnished with a certain amount of comfort in most cases. The town was divided into streets, so that it was easy to find one's way about.

However, this state of things lasted only a few years, and one of the advantages of the rush was the increase of population to the young country, and the arrival of numbers of artisans, who, after a more or less lucky time at the diggings, settled down here to their various trades and occupations.

Towards the end of the year 1861, our family received a terrible and heart-breaking blow in the news of the brutal murder of my uncle, Horace Wills,[5] and his party, by Queensland blacks. The news created a most painful sensation here, as he was so widely known and respected on account of his high and generous character, public spirit, and untiring energy in all his undertakings.

To his family, the blow was as unexpected as stunning. He had had so much experience with natives, and had had so many hair-breadth escapes from danger in various ways that, to them, he ap-peared to bear a charmed life, and the news seemed not only monstrous but incredible.

After selling Lexington near Mount Ararat[6] in 1851, he had settled on an estate at Point Henry, near Geelong, which he named Belle Vue,[7] on account of the view from there of Corio Bay, which, with the You Yangs in the background, has sometimes been compared with the Bay of Naples, and certainly, on a bright sunny day, with the azure blue of the sky above reflected in the sea below, it is one of the prettiest spots in the spacious Bay of Port Phillip.

Here my uncle interested himself principally in agriculture, doing all in his power to encourage the best methods of farming in the district. He imported valuable stock from England, being the first to introduce Ayrshire cattle, which, for many years were the most popu-lar breed of dairy cattle here. The progeny of his original stock were chief prize winners at shows all over Australia for a long time.

He became a member of the Legislative Council after Separation, and represented South Grant in the Legislative Assembly of the first Victorian Parliament in 1856.

About the end of the year 1859, he took his three younger sons to Europe, where he left them at a well-known school in Bonn. On his return, he immediately began his preparations for taking up a station in the newly opened up colony of Queensland–Moreton Bay, as it was then called–with the idea of settling his sons there on their return from school. He started with 10,000 sheep from Sydney, accompanied by some of his former hands of the Lexington days, who, when they heard of his intention, had asked to be taken on again. After an arduous journey of ten months, through some very rough country, and over the Darling Downs in Queensland, he crossed the boundary of his run on the Nogoa river, the lease of which he had bought from the late P. F. Macdonald, on his fiftieth birthday, a coincidence regarded by his party as a good omen.

Belle Vue, Geelong

The blacks there were very wild and difficult to deal with, but they began coming about the camp, always unarmed, and behaving in a friendly manner. And so it was hoped that by kind treatment they would soon became accustomed to the whites and would learn to behave in a fairly civilized manner. But evidently their cupidity had been awakened by seeing the numerous cases of goods in the camp–the party was said to be the best equipped that had ever reached Queensland–for, after a couple of weeks, on the 17th October, 1861, they suddenly attacked the camp during the afternoon siesta, and murdered everyone in it.[8]

By the position of the bodies, it was seen afterwards that all in the camp had evidently been taken quite off their guard. The body of my uncle was found lying a couple of paces from his tent, and his revolver was lying beside him, with one chamber discharged, showing that he had been felled by several blows as he ran from his tent on hearing the cries of the others.

Fortunately for himself, Tom Wills had been sent back, a day or so before, with a couple of men and a team of bullocks, to get one of the drays which had been left on the road, and so, had a miraculous escape. He returned a couple of days after the event, and, as can be imagined, was overcome with grief and horror.

The men, who had been scattered about the run, were all killed, with the exception of two. One of them had been lying asleep under the shade of some scrub a short distance from the camp, and was awakened by the excited talking of some blacks, which was presently followed by sudden shrieks and the sound of a revolver shot from the camp. He immediately realized what was happening and kept himself closely concealed, and even after he heard the blacks departing, was afraid to move. But at sun-down, another man, who had been shepherding some valuable rams, brought them back to the camp, and then the first man crawled out from his hiding place, and they advanced, in fear and trembling, to the camp together. The sight which met their eyes was so horrifying they did not wait to make a close inspection, but, with one accord, rushed to Mr. Wills' horse, which was still tied under the shade of a brigalow, a species of wattle, near his tent. The one who reached it first, quite beside himself with fear, mounted and galloped off at full speed, deaf to the cries of the other, who was thus left alone in that desolate and eerie place. The rider reached Rainworth, the nearest station, at about 1 o'clock in the morning, with the terrible news, and within twenty-four hours, most of the squatters in the district had mustered and arrived on the scene. They buried the bodies on the spot, that of Mr. Wills being buried in a separate grave, the squatters themselves performing this last office for their friend (he having met many of them since his arrival in the district). The camp was of course a total wreck, the cases had all been broken open, and what had not been taken was lying scattered about–papers, books, and, strangely enough, tea, sugar, flour and tobacco, showing that the blacks had not learnt to appreciate them. But blankets, clothing, and tools of all sorts had been taken. The guns which had always been kept loaded, had been removed from the tent in which they were stacked, but were uninjured. The men never would carry them about, finding them too cumbersome, I suppose.

A few weeks before this occurrence, a troop of black police had been formed for the protection of the squatters, but most of them, at that moment, happened to be at the furthest end of their patrol (two hundred miles off), on a tour with the Governor. The blacks, by their system of spreading news quickly, evidently knew this, and thought it a propitious time to act.

The squatters followed up their tracks, and after a day or so came upon their camp, and killed two or three of them, but, the country being very rough, most of them escaped. However, the black police, on their arrival, followed up the murderers, whose numbers they calculated, by the fires at their camping places, to be about 300 men, women and children, and administered severe punishment, by way of a lesson for the benefit of other settlers. Most of the sheep were recovered, with the exception of two or three hundred, which had been killed.

This was the biggest massacre of whites by the blacks which ever took place in Australia. After it, the conciliatory method was dropped, and no blacks were allowed on any of the Queensland stations for

The Avengers or Settlers Tracking Blacks, W. Hart, *Illustrated Melbourne Post* 1866. National Library of Australia

ten years, on pain of being shot by the troopers. Otherwise the squatters would have found it impossible to keep shepherds.

I shall give the name of those poor martyrs who suffered with my uncle (nineteen persons in all). Their names are worthy of record for their courage in facing the hardships of pioneering work in those days. They were: Patrick Manyon, his wife, daughter Margaret aged ten years, a daughter aged five years, and infant daughter aged a few months; James Scott, cook; Tom Baker, the overseer, his wife, daughter Elizabeth aged 20 years, a son of four years, and infant daughter of seven months, David, an older son; a man, name not given; George, bullock-driver; Little Ned; Henry Watt, an old shepherd; George Elliot, a cricketer, and brother of the bowler; and a man, known as Tom.

Their cruel fate brings to mind the appropriate lines of Kipling in the *Lost Legion*–

> There's a legion that never was listed,
> That carries no colors or crest,
> But, split in a thousand detachments
> Is breaking the road for the rest.

The station, Cullin-la-ringo, was carried on at first by Tom Wills and various managers, and later on by his brothers, Cedric and Horace. They and their younger brother, Egbert, were sent for by their mother soon after the tragedy, and finished their education at the Geelong Grammar School, which had recently been founded.

As the massacre, with its results, was a milestone in the settlement of Queensland, I shall give the letter to the Colonial Secretary, which was drawn up and signed at a meeting of settlers in the neighbourhood of the Comet and Nogoa rivers (head of the Fitzroy river), held at Rainworth, on October, 23rd:

> To the Honourable the Colonial Secretary.
>
> Sir,
>
> We, the undersigned, residents in the Leichhardt District, and now assembled at "Rainworth," beg to represent the necessity which exists for an immediate increase to the number of the Native Police in this neighbourhood. We do not deem it necessary further to refer to the murder of Mr. Wills and his servants, within twenty miles of this station on Thursday last, than to state it was the painful duty of several of us to assist in the burial of that gentleman and eighteen others–his servants and their familes.
>
> We have the honour to be, Sir,
> Your most obedient servants,
> PETER McINTOSH, Weelwandangee.
> ROBERT PATTON, Albinia Downs.
> W. H. RICHARDS, Springsure.
> G. CRAWFORD, Consuelo.
> WM. THOMPSON, Orion Downs.
> J. GREGSON, Rainworth.
> GEORGE N. LIVING, Coogoolvinda.
> ALLAN MACALISTER, Nulalbin.

Some years later, the story told by the blacks, with regard to the murder, was to the effect that it had been committed in revenge for the shooting of two of their tribe for sheep-stealing by the black police, a short time before the arrival of Mr. Wills and his party at Cullin-la-ringo. Their description of the deed was that, early in the afternoon, all the blacks went to the camp. They did not carry their weapons (nulla nullas, tomahawks, etc.), in their hands, but stuck

Elizabeth Wills and Horatio Spencer Wills. D. Wills Cooke collection

them under their opossum hair belts, behind their backs, where they would not be easily noticed. Then they quietly selected their intended victims, and, at a given signal, began their attack simultaneously. Whether or not the reason given was true, the old blacks always remained irreconcilable to the invasion of the whites, and were always ready to kill, given the opportunity. The younger ones were more reasonable, and many of them were very intelligent, and became useful on the stations in later years.

In the same year (1861), and just about the same time, the news was received in Melbourne of the sad and distastrous end of the Burke and Wills expedition.

It was a curious coincidence that two men of the same name, though quite unrelated, should have suffered an equally cruel and undeserved fate in the same year.

I was one of the thousands who walked out to Royal Park to see the expedition start, on the 20th August, 1860. It was most interesting to see the strange cavalcade of camels and horses, of which there were nearly two dozen of each. There were a few Indians in charge of the camels, and the white men were in their working dress, with red jumpers, such as the miners generally wore, and cabbage-tree hats.

It was the best fitted-out exploring expedition, I suppose, that ever started in Australia. There were three or four waggons, loaded with, at least, twelve months' stores. One was made so that it could be used as a flat-bottomed boat, on emergency. Among other useful things they had were rockets and a gong to be used as signals in case any of the party should be lost, and also plenty of firearms. In fact, nothing was omitted that could possibly be wanted under any imaginable circumstances. The whole party looked thoroughly fit and in good spirits, and were evidently looking forward to the adventure.

I recall that the Mayor of Melbourne made a short speech of farewell, and Burke responded.

Everyone knows of the tragic end of the expedition. The choice of Burke as the leader had been considered a mistake by many people, because, though a brave and dashing police officer, he was no bushman, and had not had previous experience in exploration.

The beginning of trouble was the resignation of Landells of his position as second in command, at Menindie on the Darling. This left Burke in an awkward predicament, and he engaged a man called Wright, of whose character he knew very little, to take charge of half the party, and the bulk of the stores, giving him instructions to follow immediately, while he himself hurried on to form a depot at Cooper's Creek, 400 miles off. For some mysterious reason never properly explained, Wright kept his party at Menindie for about three months after Burke's departure. In the meantime, Burke, having formed the depot, and losing patience, decided not to wait for him, but to make a dash for the Gulf of Carpentaria with his now second in command, William Wills who was a very promising young man and the only scientist of the party, Grey and King. He was thus not provided with sufficient stores for his own party in case of unforeseen difficulties and delays, and also left the rest of the party at the depot insufficiently provided for, if Wright should not appear within a reasonable time. The consequence was that Brahe, in charge of the Cooper's Creek depot, after waiting over four months, was obliged to leave and return to Menindie in order to save his own party from starvation.

Of course the dilatoriness of Wright was the immediate cause of the disaster, but it was certainly unwise of Burke to leave the depot before his commissariat was in perfect working order.

As is well known, his party of three (Grey having succumbed on the way) arrived back at the depot in an exhausted and starving state, only seven hours after Brahe had left, and were unable to follow on. By following the instruction, 'Dig,' cut in a tree they found the few stores Brahe had planted.

Before covering up the cache again they left a message explaining their plight and intentions, but quite forgot to leave any outward mark of their having been there. They then tried to make their way to the nearest station (150 miles) in South Australia, but failed, owing to weakness and want of water on the way.

In the meantime Brahe, who had met Wright on the way up, returned to the depot with him, and seeing no signs of interference with the cache, left again for good. The end of these accidents was the death, first of Wills and then of Burke, after much suffering bravely borne. King, left alone, was succoured by the kindly Cooper's Creek blacks till his rescue by the party led by A. Howitt.

In the dash to Carpentaria, everything was most propitious for the explorers. They found water all the way, and the blacks did not molest them at all.

The whole account makes painful reading, and I have only given this resume of the course of events because there was so much discussion at the time, as to where the responsibility for the tragedy lay.

Of the more recent explorers, Ernest Giles was the only one I knew personally, and many an interesting conversation have I had with him concerning exploration. He was a thorough bushman, and also had an exceptionally strong and tough constitution, or he could never have pulled through some of the situations in which he found himself. I have before me a short account of one of his journeys, which he presented to me dated, Kew, 2nd October, 1887, called a *Journal of a Forgotten Expedition*, in which he shows the superiority of the camel over the horse in exploration work.

CHAPTER 10

IN CONCLUSION

On the 10th November, 1864, I married my cousin, Emily Wills, eldest daughter of the late Horace S. Wills. The wedding took place at Point Henry, in the Church School. The children of both the Point Henry and Kensington schools were given a holiday in honor of the event, in which they played quite a large part! They were lined up by their teachers in a double column between gaily decorated arches leading to the church door and strewed the way with flowers, singing a short song of farewell, which they had been especially taught for the occasion, on our departure. The ladies, who had taken so much trouble in arranging this picturesque little ceremony, presented my wife with a beautiful bouquet in the style known as Early Victorian, held in a silver holder of pretty design, which she treasures to this day, in remembrance of our kind friends. I believe the children were afterwards entertained with the usual tea and buns, and a sports meeting was held, in which they took part, and which I hope they all enjoyed, after their exertions of the morning.[1]

I must not forget to say that Norman McLeod (my ever-faithful friend) officiated as best man on that day. His last years were spent in Ballarat, where he married fairly late in life.[2]

It was towards the end of the sixties that my brother, Ernest and I conceived the idea of ascending the Yarra by boat. Others had tried to do so in canoes, but had generally come to grief at the rapids, and so, been discouraged from further effort.

We chose the Christmas holidays for our attempt, in order to have the river at summer level. We hired a small boat from Greenfield's boat house at Princes' Bridge, for the nominal sum of one shilling

Emily Harrison nee Wills.
L. Cooke collection

a day! It was made for one pair of sculls, with a broad beam and iron shod keel. As we were well acquainted with the river as far as Heidelberg, we hired a dray to carry the boat, tent, fishing rods, guns and general dunnage to the bridge there, which we made our starting point. At about a hundred yards from the bridge, I remember, we disturbed a covey of wild duck–the first and the last we saw on that particular trip.

At the first rapid, just above Heidelberg, we landed and unloaded the boat, carried it to the head of the rapid, and then went back for our goods. We found it frightful work forcing our way, with such a pack, through thick scrub and fences, and so, we negotiated all the succeeding rapids by simply stripping, jumping out, and hauling the boat over. On the upper end of the rapid, one of us would get in, ready to pull, while the other pushed her off and jumped in. The banks, most of the way, were covered with pretty flowering shrubs and forest growth, with occasional open patches.

The first night, we camped at the bottom of the garden of Mr. R. D. Ireland,[3] the brilliant Q.C., and spent the evening at the house, where we were hospitably entertained. His two sons, Tom and Dick, who were both in my football team, came down to the tent later, and we put in another hour or so, discussing the game. They were first-class players, and fine young sportsmen, and were naturally very interested in our undertaking.

We carried out the same programme every day, starting off after an early breakfast and continuing till about 5 p.m., when we would begin to look out for an open space for our camp. Immediately on landing, I would catch some shrimps with my landing net, and throw in a line, and we would soon have enough blackfish for our supper and next morning's breakfast. Fixing up the tent was a matter of a very short time, and a few armfuls of bracken, covered with American water-proof cloth, opossum rug and blankets, made a couch fit for a king!

I suppose no sort of life could be healthier or more exhilarating. I know we slept like logs, and our appetites would have satisfied the most anxious mother! I have already discussed the attractions of camping-out, one of the most interesting of which is listening to the weird night sounds of the bush. What could be more intriguing than the loud grunting of the opossum, or more blood-curdling than the wild shrieks of the jennie-bear,[4] to say nothing of the monotonous cry of the mopoke? Though my list does not seem very alluring, for a true bushman these sounds all form part of the secret charm and glamour of the bush. And what could be more pleasant than being awakened at dawn by the twittering of birds, and above all, by the beautiful carolling of numerous magpies?

We continued our strenuous way, passing through Templestowe and Warrandyte. At the latter place, we camped in the Police paddock. I remember that we accepted the invitation of a miner to tea, and enjoyed it, with jam-tins for cups! Our furthest camp that trip was about five miles beyond Warrandyte.

Needless to say the return journey was accomplished much quicker than that up stream. The operation of shooting the rapids was a simple though rather exciting affair. We used to back-water into them, and then float over quite smoothly.

Next Christmas, with unabated zeal, we continued the trip, launching the boat where we left off the previous year, beyond Warrandyte. At that time this place was a mining town. It is a charming spot, especially in September, when the wattle is out, and is, with justice, regarded as one of the beauty spots within easy distance of Melbourne.

Going up, we rowed the boat round the Pound bend,[5] which was three miles in length, and in which distance we had to negotiate no less than ten rapids. The men were then at work on the tunnel, which cuts out the three miles, and is only about one hundred and fifty yards long, with a dam at the upper end. This sharp bend is typical of the many in the tortuous course of the Yarra.

One circumstance of the trip worth particular mention was that, at each rapid we saw a platypus fishing in the middle of the stream.

It would dive and come up at exactly the same spot, the force of the current seeming to have no effect on its position.

We continued our way as far as Castella's bridge, at Yarra Flats, now Yarra Glen. There we had rather an unfortunate accident. On the swampy banks were a good many wild duck, and we landed to do some shooting, while Mr. Isaac Barrow,[6] an old friend, who had joined us for a few days, undertook to continue with the boat. But unfortunately it got entangled in a snag. Luckily we were within sight at the moment, and were able to go to his assistance. I crawled along an overhanging sapling and got into the boat, but the current forced it over and it capsized. I had just time to jump out, but he went under, and by the time he had got safely to the bank, the boat, containing our all–tent, blankets, etc., had floated, bottom up, some distance away. I was very perturbed, as I had left my watch in the pocket of my waistcoat, which I had rolled up and put in the prow of the boat. But fortunately the boat soon became blocked close to the bank, and was rescued without much trouble. Much to my surprise and relief, my waistcoat, with the watch quite unharmed, was still where I had left it. The watch is still going strong to this day!

After some difficulty the tent and blankets, neatly folded up, were captured, gaily floating down stream. Our most serious loss was the tomahawk, but Mr. Bat, of Bat's Hotel, was good enough to supply us with another. A tomahawk is one of the things that are absolutely necessary on a camping-out expedition. I remember that the Yarra banks about there were simply infested with snakes, and we tried to kill as many as we could with the butts of our guns, as they slithered into their holes. We camped near the bridge for a few days and then commenced our homeward way, but not before visiting the famous vineyard of Yering,[7] which was near by. Coming down, it took us about one day to do what we had done in three days going up. We counted the rapids between Yarra Flats and Dight's Falls at Abbotsford, and they amounted to no less than a hundred, in a distance of about, I should say, one hundred and fifty miles. By road to Yarra Flats the distance is only thirty-two miles.

On the return trip we evaded the rapids in the Pound Bend, by carrying the boat over the ridge of hills. Our last camp was in the bend at Willsmere which is on the Kew side of the river, opposite Lucerne, and we rowed the boat back to the sheds at Princes Bridge, having thoroughly enjoyed the experience.

In 1869, my mother received the greatest blow of her life, in the sad death of my brother, Horace, at the age of twenty-one. He had been educated at the Scotch College, and showed great promise as a student, and was altogether of a very fine character.

Some of his contemporaries tried to persuade him to study law, but he had decided, while still a boy, to enter the Ministry. At the time of his death he was acting as tutor to the sons of Mr. Philip Russell of Carngham,[8] and, one morning, according to his usual habit, had gone for a swim in a water-hole used for the purpose of bathing, not far from the house. A little while after, he was found drowned. It was thought that his feet must have become entangled with the weeds when he jumped in, or he may have got cramp. It was a cruel blow to his mother, and she never really recovered from the shock, though she lived another ten years.

After my marriage, we lived in East Melbourne. But after a short time we settled in Kew,[9] which, only a few years before, had been all bush, and where, as school boys, my companions and I had sometimes wandered with our guns, carefully avoiding the blacks, whose whereabouts we could generally guess by the sound of 'chopping out 'possums,' with which I was well acquainted.

When in East Melbourne, I used to ride sometimes, on my old 'bone-shaker' in the evening, to the Saltwater river,[10] where I got some fairly good fishing, bream being the chief catch. But when we came to Kew, I had to confine my attentions to the Yarra, and must confess that the results were not very satisfactory, eels being the principal catch. The blackfish were not as plentiful as formerly, English perch, which had been introduced into the river, having destroyed the spawn of the original fish.

But the fishing I have most enjoyed has been in the Watts, at Healesville and Fernshaw–wading up the beautiful stream, casting the bait, and sometimes, I must confess, with difficulty avoiding entangling it with the brushwood and ferns which line the banks. And the beauty of the brook trout, which abound there!

Fishing is the most restful of all out-door sports, because so absorbing that one becomes lost to the frets and worries of life; so that it is conducive to both physical and mental refreshment. Another point in its favor is that one is not dependent on human companionship for its enjoyment, as with most other sports.

In 1884, after thirty-one years' service in the Customs, I devoted the year's leave which I then obtained, to seeing as much of the world as possible. As I travelled from Melbourne with the Australian eleven, I moved about with them on our arrival, and saw some of the test matches. After visiting France, Italy, Switzerland, Belgium and the Rhine, I returned home via America in company with my old friend, the late J. C. Syme[11] of the *Age*. We visited the chief towns there, and saw most of the geographical wonders, including Niagara Falls.

But the place that charmed me most during my tour was New Zealand, with its wonderful variety and grandeur of scenery in so

On the Watts 1873, J. Gully, *Australian Sketcher* 1873. La Trobe collection, State Library of Victoria

comparatively small a space. I am glad to say that the wonderful Pink and White Terraces had not then been destroyed, for they were unique in their beauty.[12]

My wife and her mother, Mrs. Wills, met me in New Zealand, and we saw most of the sights together, which made it more enjoyable, especially as Syme had continued his way home to Melbourne, via Sydney.

While we were at Rotorua, the Maoris were having a sports meeting, and, when they heard I was there, a deputation of them waited on me, and asked me to preside, and act as judge in some of the events. This, of course I did, with great pleasure. Some of us also spent a short time at a ball they were holding in the evening, and I had the pleasure of a dance with one of the handsome Maori girls.

I also visited the magnificent group of sounds on the west coast of the South Island, each more beautiful than the other! It was a very pleasant excursion. We used to land at each sound and picnic on shore all day, returning to a well-served dinner on board, and devoting the evening to dancing, music, etc.

Before leaving New Zealand, in company with one or two others, I made a pilgrimage to visit Sir George Grey[13] on his island of Kawau presented to him by the Maoris near Auckland. He entertained us in a cordial manner, and showed us his interesting collection–chiefly of Maori curios.

Among other things, he showed me a curious old manuscript which had been sent to him by an Arab, just as he was leaving Cape Colony. It was not written in any language with which he was familiar, and he had never found anyone who could translate it for him. I suggested sending it to the British Museum, as the simplest way of solving the difficulty. However, I see, in reading *The Romance of a Pro-Consul*, by James Milne, that, forty years after Sir George received the manuscript, it was translated by an Assyrian gentleman who happened to be visiting Auckland. But it does not seem to have been of any great value.

It was during Sir George Grey's first Governorship of New Zealand that a tragedy occurred, of which relations of ours were the victims. My father's youngest sister had married Lieutenant Snow, a retired naval officer, and they had settled in New Zealand on the outskirts of Auckland. They were one day found murdered and robbed, and at first the Maoris were suspected of the crime, but it was discovered some time after, that it had been committed by a convict from Van Diemen's Land.

It was while my father was on one of his periodical trips to Melbourne, while we were living at Swanwater, that he came across an account of the dreadful occurrence in an old newspaper. His distress and grief for his sister and her family may be easily imagined. He immediately wrote to Auckland, asking for particulars, expressing the wish that her little girl who, it was said, had escaped should be sent over to his charge. But, in reply, it was explained that the child had been sent for by her father's relatives in Dublin; and so my father felt that his responsibility in the matter ended there.

I finished my tour by a short stay in Tasmania, a charming spot, and an ideal summer resort for Australians.

Two years after my retirement, I decided to work off my superfluous energy by riding to Sydney on my bicycle. The last Test match between the Australians and the English Eleven, captained by Stoddart, was to take place there in February, 1896, and I timed myself to arrive for it, thus travelling in the very hottest season of the year. The journey took me nine and a half days, travelling on an average of sixty-three miles a day. I followed the old Sydney Road, which I had not travelled over since my babyhood, and then under very different circumstances. Instead of a rough track through the bush, there was a hard metalled road a good part of the way, and instead of camping in tents or waggons on the way-side every night, I was able to put up at some quite comfortable inns. Instead of being on my guard against attacks by blacks, all I saw of them were two poor old fellows from a neighbouring mission station, whom I met while sitting on the verandah of a hotel, where I happened to be lunching, about a hundred miles from Sydney, and with whom I had a long and friendly 'yabber'.

I shouted them drinks in memory of old times, and, before I left, they presented me with a dirty scrap of paper, requesting me to write something down at their dictation, in their own language. This I did phonetically, much to their apparent satisfaction. I then, naturally, asked for a translation, which they frankly and gleefully gave:–'Landlord, give Jackie and Tommy another drink!'

I passed through Albury, calling on a few relatives and old friends there, and then on through Germanton,[14] Goulburn, Mossvale, and Picton. It was the first time I had re-visited the place of my birth, and I received the kindest of welcomes from John Antill, (eldest son of the late Major) and all at Jarvisfield.[15] I did not stay longer than a few hours, as I had to hurry on to be in time for the match. Picton is about sixty miles from Sydney, and I felt, on leaving there, that my effort was practically over. But, strange to say, I had my first accident after negotiating the (then) difficult road over Razorback. I ran into a stump and twisted the pedal just before reaching Minto. Fortunately an obliging blacksmith was able to straighten it out for me. The bicycle, by the way, was an Elswick, very strongly and solidly built, with rubber tyres, but had no free wheel at that time. I afterwards had one put on.

I stayed the night at Minto, with my sister, Mrs. Ohlfsen Bagge, who was living there at the time.

On arriving at Strathfield I left the bicycle to be repaired. At about 8 o'clock in the evening, I took a tram into Sydney, and put up at the Hotel Australia, where the cricketers were. I was greeted with surprise by them all, as they had predicted that I should break down before getting half-way, and be obliged to finish the journey by train. Prince Ranjitsinhji[16] added his congratulations to the others and said, 'I should think, Mr. Harrison, that this ride, for a man of your age (62), must be a world's record'. I have no idea as to that, but I appreciated such praise from so famous an athlete and sportsman.

I think I lost about eight pounds weight on the journey, which was not so much considering the continuous exertion in great heat. But I never felt fitter, and could have continued the ride indefinitely.

Since then, I have devoted myself to the hobby of gardening, which gives me sufficient exercise, and provides me with a never-failing interest, as all garden-lovers will understand.

That, varied with reading and an occasional game of chess to say nothing of regular attendances at M.C.C. committee meetings occupies my time. I have also been a justice of the peace for about thirty years, and have only the last two or three years given up regular attendances at the Kew court. I do, however, a fair amount of work in signing declarations, etc., in my own home. I should like to say here, in reference to the periodical discussions as to the advisability of abolishing the system of honorary justices, that I think it would be a mistake to do so, as their work is, on the whole, good, and they save the country a good deal of money by doing work which the ordinary stipendiary magistrate could not possibly have time for. Even in their work on the bench, mistakes in law should be rare, as the clerk of courts is always in attendance to make any difficulty clear.

Of my family of ten children, only four daughters survive. My son, Norman, the only one of my sons to reach manhood, a fine young athlete (a champion hurdle racer, in fact), died in Western Australia, at the age of twenty-five. He was an architect by profession, and had just finished serving his articles at the time of the depression after the collapse of the land boom. As things were not very propitious here, he joined a party of his friends, chief among whom were the sons of the late C. H. Nicolson, P.M., who were going over to Bailey's Reward claim to get mining experience. Unfortunately he contracted dysentery, that dreadful scrouge of nearly all newly opened up country. He had been a member of the Rupertswood Battery organised and supported by the late Sir William Clarke, with Major (now General) Hughes in command, and had won prizes for various events at the Islington Military tournament when the battery went to England.

My daughter, Alma's husband, John Macknight, who was a merchant in Fremantle, W.A., made the supreme sacrifice in France in 1918, at the age of forty-five. Notwithstanding our irreparable loss, we could not have wished him to stay when such a call came, and his memory remains forever precious to us all. He was a son of the late Alexander Macknight, at one time Mayor of North Sydney, well known in Sydney, and, later in Perth as the manager of the Mutual Life Insurance Company of New York.

Let us pray that the nations concerned may all try to be worthy of the tremendous sacrifice of splendid young manhood in that terrible war!

My daughter, Rosalie's husband is James Moore Hickson, who is at present engaged in holding a mission throughout the world 'For the Revival of the Gifts of Healing in the Church.' He has an unusual gift, and, what seems to be still more unusual, the faith to use it.

He was born in Victoria, and is a son of the late Robert Onslow Hickson, and grandson of Captain John Hickson, who brought troops to New Zealand, and fought in the Maori wars. His mother was a daughter of Dr. Watton, who had a station in the Western District in the early days.

Fernshaw on the Woods Point Road, *Illustrated Melbourne Post* 1866.
National Library of Australia

In conclusion, I may explain that I have not thought it necessary for me to expatiate on the obvious blessings enjoyed by the dwellers in this beautiful and hospitable land of Australia. I returned from my journey round the world convinced that this is one of the best countries to live in. The genial climate, making an open-air life possible all the year round, the wide, open spaces, the plentiful supply and comparative cheapness of good food, and the many opportunities, open to a man of energy and determination to make his way or, at any rate, a reasonable living, are a few of the advantages to be found here, which, combined with the high standard of compulsory education, should in time produce a truly fine race, worthy, in every way, of the stock from which it has sprung.

One word more. As with most athletes, I have never been a smoker, though I can easily imagine the pleasurable and sedative effect of the habit; and it is an accepted fact that an occasional pipe can do no possible harm to the feeblest constitution—in an adult. But the incessant cigarette smoking indulged in at the present day by many young boys is, I am sure, most injurious both to their mental and physical health. And so, my parting advice, as an old athlete, to the growing boys of Australia is, 'Avoid cigarette smoking!'

NOTES AND REFERENCES

Colden Harrison was 87 years of age when he wrote his book, elaborating upon a series of articles based on interviews with 'Harrier' of the *Australasian* and published in 1918-1919. He had a collection of cuttings with him when he wrote and eventually we did find his scrapbook. Harrison's fame brought him into contact with many well-known and some of the lesser lights of late nineteenth century Melbourne. The more obvious, such as the famous explorers, we have not included but elsewhere we have tried to provide some information. In such an endeavour, Alexander Sutherland's *Victoria and Its Metropolis*, Garryowen's *Chronicles of Early Melbourne, Bell's Life in Victoria* and *Sporting Chronicle (Bell's L.V.)*, the *Australasian (A'sian)*, and the endeavours of various writers (to whom we are beholden) of the *Australian Dictionary of Biography (ADB)* were our main, but no means our only, sources. The abbreviation PROV indicates the Public Record Office of Victoria, MCC the Melbourne Cricket Club, and MCEGS the Melbourne Church of England Grammar School.

PREFACE
1   *Family Origins*

1 Henry Colden Antill Harrison was commonly called Colden and, for this reason, he is herein referred to by his second name.
2 D. Newsome, *Godliness and Good Learning*, London, 1961, p.216
3 'What the convict system bequeathed to later Australian generations was . . . an intense concern for political and social respectability.' R. Hughes, *The Fatal Shore: A History of the Transportation of Convicts to Australia 1787-1868*, Collins, London, 1987, p.xi

4   R.V. Pockley, *Ancestor Treasure Hunt*, Wentworth Books, Sydney, 1976, pp.25-27; F. Clune, *Bound for Botany Bay*, Angus and Robertson, Sydney, 1965, passim; E. Ford, *ADB*, v.2. Sarah married again after Redfern's death, becoming Sarah Alexander.

5   The records of the midland assizes were lost in the World War II blitz so that it is unlikely that Howe's offence will ever be known with certainty. However a newspaper reference of 1 April 1799 mentions George Happy alias Happy George (Howe's nickname) as being sentenced to death for robbing an Alcester mercer's shop. A letter exists addressed to the Justice of the Assize for the midland Circuit which describes Happy George's crime as 'shop-lifting'. It may be that the adoption of the term 'shop-lifting' to describe the offence made a lighter sentence possible. J.A. Ferguson, *Introduction to the Sydney Gazette facsimile*, vol.16

6   New South Wales *General Standing Orders* in 1802 and the *Sydney Gazette*.

7   S.J. Blair, *Australia's First Printery*, Heritage Australia, Spring, 1985

8   R. Howitt, *Impressions of Australia Felix during four years' residence in that colony: Notes of a voyage round the world*, Australian Poems, London, 1845, pp. 64-65

9   W. Westgarth, *Australia Felix or a Historical and Descriptive Account of the Settlement of Port Phillip*, Edinburgh, 1848, p. 282

10 P. de Serville, *Port Phillip Gentlemen*, OUP, 1980, p. 137

11 A.F. Pike, *ADB* v.2

12 A. Wills, *Autobiography*, 1916, ms., Dr G. Buckwell collection. Arthur Wills was an architect and drew illustrations of the houses to accompany his text.

13 F. Clune, op. cit., p. 141

14 Copies of Horatio Spencer Wills' diary are held by the La Trobe Library, SLV. Original held in L.W. Cooke collection.

15 Ibid., p.1

16 Ibid., 6 Jan. 1851

17 Ibid., 26 April 1847

18 Obituaries quoted by Harrison in ch.6, supported by W.J. Hammersley's assessment of Wills as 'a very peculiar man, rather taciturn, but very good-natured and a very general favourite' in *Sydney Mail* 15 Sept. 1883. Hammersley also described Tom Wills as 'the very model of muscular Christianity'. *A'sian* 8 May 1869

19 See second half of Preface for discussion of the origin of Australian Rules Football and Tom Wills' role in this.

20 H.S. Wills' diary, 26 April 1847 from Lexington. Tom Wills is said to have played cricket on Batman's Hill at the opening of Brickwood's Academy in Sept. 1846, T.F. Cooke, notes for a MCC history, MCC collection.

21 Letter, Tom Wills to his father, H.S. Wills, 18 August 1851, from Bayswater, England, L.W. Cooke collection

22 Letter, Sarah Alexander to her brother, H.S. Wills, 3 April 1853, address London, L.W. Cooke collection. See Preface, 1, note 4.

23 Letter, Horatio Spencer Wills to Tom Wills, 1 May 1853 from Point Henry, Victoria, L.W. Cooke collection

24 *Bell's L.V.* 10 Jan. 1857

25 Letter, Sarah Alexander to H.S. Wills, 10 May 1854 from 12 Dorchester Terrace, L.W. Cooke collection

26 See letters as in Preface, 1, notes 22 and 25.

27 William Roope was Horatio Will's brother-in-law, being married to Kate, the sister of Horatio's wife, Elizabeth McGuire.

28 Letter, Tom Wills to Colden Harrison, 24 Oct. 1861, D. Cooke collection

29 G. Reid, *A Nest of Hornets*, OUP, 1982, pp.126-131.

30 Letter, H.S. Wills to his sons in England, date illegible Jan. 1861, D. Cooke collection

31 C.B. Dutton, Letter, *North Australian* 13 Dec. 1861 p.3, photostat. Dutton was the local squatter who was most sympathetic towards the blacks and his evidence is perhaps more reliable than most of the others. Horatio Wills's attitude to the Aboriginals is difficult to discern. A letter written by him to his sons recounts the story of a battle between some white men and a group of Torres Strait Islanders, describing the blacks as 'prey' and the whites as 'the noble six', 6 July, 1860, D. Cooke collection

32 L.L. Banfield, *Green Pastures and Gold;* the story of Ararat, Canterbury, Vic. Mullaya, 1974, pp.12-13

33 Letter, H.S. Wills written to Tom Wills at Rugby, 1 May 1853, Point Henry, Vic., L. W. Cooke collection

34 Letter, Emily Wills to her brothers, 21 Nov. 1861, D. Cooke collection. Supported by W.J. Hammersley: Tom Wills 'frequently told me that he never trusted the natives, but always carried two six-shooters and often warned "the governor" to do the same, but the old man prided himself on being able to manage the blacks from his experience of them gained in Victoria, and said they would never harm him', *Sydney Mail* 15 Sept. 1883. p.508. Tom was, of course, speaking with the benefit of hindsight.

35 Letter, Elizabeth Wills, 27 Dec. 1861 from Belle Vue, Point Henry, D. Cooke collection. The implication was that the Aboriginal knew only too well why his group was being shot. The numbers killed in retribution differ in the many accounts. Governor Bowen, quoted in Reid, op. cit, p.134, gave an estimated official (and probably conservative) figure of seventy.

36 W.J. Hammersley, *Sydney Mail* 15 Sept. 1883

37 *Rockhampton Daily Record* 8 Nov. 1912

38 D.J. Mulvaney's notes taken from J. Gregson, *Memoirs 1844-1909,* written at Yengo 1906 and added to until 1914, Mitchell Library, MSS 1382. Provocation by the white population existed well before this event, as evidenced by H. Reynolds, *The Other Side of the Frontier*, James Cook Univ. of North Qld., 1981, pp.65-66

39 See, eg., C.E. Sayers, *ADB* v.2, p.606 but also G. Reid, op. cit.; H. Reynolds op. cit.

40 Letter from Emily Wills to her brothers, 21 Nov. 1861, L.W. Cooke collection

41 Horatio's exhortations appear constantly in the correspondence, and Tom's response, 'So go to work "Tom". Remember your poor dear Father's words and work like a man & by God's blessing so I will' was not an isolated example. Letter, Tom Wills to his mother, 17 June, 1862, D. Cooke collection.

42 Letter, T. Wills to mother, 8 June 1862, D. Cooke collection. The uncle was William Roope, see Preface, 1, note 27.

43 Letter, W.F. Ducker to C.S. Wills, 20 Feb.1864; letters, T. Wills to C.S. Wills 2 April 1864; 24 Sept. 1864, D. Cooke collection.

44 Both Tom's mother and sister write to the sons studying in Germany of Tom taking revenge but in the future tense not in the past. Letters from Belle Vue, Geelong 20 and 21 Nov. 1861, D. Cooke collection.

45 Inquest, 3 May 1880, D. Cooke collection

46 Letter, E.S. Wills to Horace Wills, c. May 1880, D. Cooke collection.

47 Obit., *Argus* 23 July 1869

48 *Geelong Advertiser* 18 Sept. 1851; *Melbourne Morning Herald* 9 Aug. 1851

49 Capt. Harrison wrote an open letter in July 1845 to Governor Gipps, D. Kiers, *ADB*, v.4

50 *Port Phillip Patriot* 4 June 1844

51 See Chapter 2 and its Notes and References

52 *Port Phillip Patriot* 4 June 1844

53 *Port Phillip Gazette* 2 August 1845

54 *Melbourne Morning Herald* 26 October 1852

55 See, for instance, *Melbourne Morning Herald* 9 Aug. 1851, 12 Sept. 1851

56 *Geelong Advertiser* 18 Sept. 1851

57 H.C.A. Harrison, *The Story of an Athlete*, ch.4

58 Parl. Papers, 1890, v.1, D3, *Report from the Select Committee upon the Claims of Henry Frencham as Discoverer of the Bendigo Gold-Field*, Minutes of Evidence (of Frederick Fenton) p. 18, (of P. Farrell) p. 11

59 G. Serle, *The Golden Age*, MUP,1977, p. 26

60 Vic. P.P., 1890, op. cit., minutes of evidence by Henry Fencham, p.3

61 F. McKenzie Clark, in F. Cusack (ed.,) *Early Days on Bendigo*, Queensberry Hill Press, 1979, p.76

62 *Melbourne Morning Herald* 22 Dec. 1851

63 *Argus* 12 Sept. 1852

64 *Melbourne Morning Herald* 4 Dec. 1852

65 R.H. Budd was appalled when his brother married Colden's half-sister, Fanny, citing her illegitimacy, her step-mother's notoriety as a bad character, and the constant quarrels between John and Jane Harrison as his reasons. Letter, R.H. Budd to Rev. H. Budd, 10 October 1848, Mitchell Lib. doc. 1049

66 Norman Roderick MacLeod was the son of Archibald MacLeod who
    had brought his family to Australia in 1821. They spent some time in
    Van Diemen's Land, Norfolk Island, Bathurst (1828) Maryvale,
    Liverpool (1834). In the meantime Archibald's brother Donald who
    had also come to Australia in 1821, had been successful as a medical
    man and magistrate and was rewarded with a land grant of 2 000
    acres, which his solicitor took up for him in 1830 at Gundaroo on
    the Yass River, a station which he called Barnsdale, a corruption of
    Bernisdale in the Isle of Skye from which the MacLeods had come.
    At their uncle's property, the sons of Archibald were able to have a
    grazier's apprenticeship and to take part in the overlanding ventures
    originating from this district. Norman was involved in the early
    squatting exploration of the Riverina and of Gippsland. His father
    took up land at what was later to become Bairnsdale. Norman
    became a stock and station agent in Ballarat in the late 1850s
    (MacLeod and Kelly and then MacLeod and Booth) where he died
    on 14 May 1882, leaving a wife and three children. J.D. Adams, *The
    MacLeod Family*, The Gap, 1967; *Ballarat Courier*, obit. 15 May
    1882

Melbourne Cricket Ground, *Australasian Sketcher* 1874

2   The Start of Australian Rules Football and Colden Harrison's Role

1 T.P. Power, *Footballer* 1876, p.7. See also *A'sian* 16 June 1877.
2 N. Gould, *On and Off The Turf in Australia*, E.W. Cole, 1895,
   p.196
3 L. Sandercock and I. Turner, *Up Where Cazaly? The Great
   Australian Game*, Granada, 1981. See also W.F. Mandle, *Games
   People Played: Cricket and Football in England and Victoria in the
   Late Nineteenth Century*, *Historical Studies*, v.15, no 60, 1973,
   pp. 511- 535
4 E. Dunning & K. Sheard, *Barbarians, Gentlemen and Players: A
   Sociological Study of the Development of Rugby Football*, ANU
   Press, Canberra, 1979, chap. 1
5 E. Dunning & K. Sheard, op. cit., chap. 2
6 Ibid, pp.74-76. J.A. Mangan, *Athleticism and the Victorian and
   Edwardian Public School: the Emergence and Consolidation of an
   Educational Ideology*, Cambridge UP, 1981, attributes the great

development in games at public schools beginning in the 1850s mainly to actions taken at Marlborough by G.C. Cotton in an effort to control unruly pupils and by C.J. Vaughan through pupil monitors at Harrow, with E. Thring at Uppingham and H.H. Almond at Loretto providing the ideological support. He suggests that Arnold's role in this has been exaggerated (pp. 16-17), as does D. Newsome in *Godliness and Good Learning*, London, 1961, p. 911

7 E. Dunning in B. Simon & I. Bradley (eds.), *The Victorian Public School: The Emergence and Consolidation of An Educational Ideology*. Cambridge UP, 1981

8 E. Dunning & K. Sheard, op. cit., p. 98

9 Soccer (Association) did not emerge as a national game until 1883. In Ireland the folk football which had been played for centuries was finally codified by the Gaelic Athletic Association in 1884. In 1864 *Bell's L.V.* 25 June, reported 'a sort of Rugby gaining hold in Ireland'; it was described as 'boisterous'.

10 J.B. Thompson (ed.), *The Victorian Cricketer's Guide*, 1860.

11 For a survey of some of these Victorian colonial folk games, A.G. Daws, *The Origins of Australian Rules Football*, unpub. BA honours thesis, Dept. of History, Melbourne Univ., 1954, pp. 9-13

12 E. Dunning & K. Sheard, op. cit, pp.101-102, indicate that this inclination was true as a rough generalization but not accurate about every new English school. Rugby was also initially more popular in England once the split occurred. In 1873, of the 223 football clubs in England playing either Rugby or Association, 132 were playing Rugby, ibid., p.59

13 T.S. Marshall. There are two manuscripts by T.S. Marshall, one a revised version of the other. The first, *Paper on Football*, was written to be given to the annual meeting of the Victorian Football Association on 24 April 1896 and was actually delivered in May 1896; *A'sian* 16 May 1896. It was intended as 'some idea of the early history of the Victorian game' and includes reminiscences by Marshall. The other was entitled *The Rise and Progress of the Australian Game of Football* and follows an almost identical format. References given below refer to both manuscripts and usually quote one of them. Both are held by the Victorian Football League.

14 E. Dunning & K. Sheard, op. cit., pp. 112-113

15 Longstop (W.J. Hammersley), *A'sian* 8 May 1869, p.588

16 Profile, *Bell's L.V.* 2 July 1864. Obit., *A'sian* 17 Dec. 1881, p.779. Surrey cricketer, came to gold-fields, played against the English, went to Sale about 1865 and ran a hotel. Regarded as a 'player' rather than a 'gentleman'.

17 *Bell's L.V.* 31 July 1858, p.3

18 T.S. Marshall, op. cit.

19 *Dr Bromby's Journal* 31 July 1858, MCEGS collection. Although Dr Bromby refers to the St. Kilda Club, there appears no evidence that it was formally constituted as such until early in 1859.

20 Ibid., 5 June. St. Kilda Grammar was a private school, 1856-59, which collapsed from the competition provided by the public schools, G.W. Noble, *Aims, Men or Money? The Establishment of Secondary Education for Boys in South Australia and in the Port Phillip District, 1836-1860*, Ph.D. thesis, Melb. Univ. 1980, p.366

21 *Herald* 7, 23, 30 Aug., 6 Sept.; *Argus* 9, 16 Aug. 1858; *Young Victoria, A Journal of the Scotch College*, no. 6, July 1878, p. 75. Masters for MCEGS were Roderick McKenzie and Frederick John Halden, and for Scotch College James Smith, Thomas H. Smith, Robert Hervey, and Robert Morrison.

22 *Dr Bromby's Journal* 4 Sept.1858. Scotch College numbered 187, MCEGS 113.

23 Robert Hervey, listed in Scotch College Speech Night Programme for 1858; *Scotch College Diamond Jubilee* (booklet), Oct.1911, p.68. His name does not appear in the Rugby School Register for 1842-1874.

24 The Saturdays of 14, 21, and 28 August. See Preface, 2, note 21 above.

25 That membership was initially restricted is indicated when that restriction was dropped. *Argus* 9 May 1859, p.5

26 T.S. Marshall, op. cit. Marshall is writing nearly forty years later and he did not arrive in Melbourne until 1858.

27 The acronym MFB is not explained in the account, but presumably it refers to the MCC Football Club, or Melbourne Football.

28 *Herald* 23 August 1858, p.5: *Argus* 16 May 1859, p.5

29 *Herald* 27 Sept.; *Bell's L.V.* 25 Sept., 1858. Dr Bromby's son Christopher played for St. Kilda and another MCEGS pupil, John Watson, played for Melbourne.

30 *Dr Bromby's Journal*, 25 Sept. 1858. His son, Christopher, played for the St. Kilda side.

31 T.S. Marshall, op. cit. However one has to be careful with this evidence: Fellowes, in fact, was educated at Eton where the football code forbad picking up the ball and running with it.

32 L. Sandercock and I. Turner, op. cit., p. 19, state: 'In August 1858 Wills suggested to the MCC Committee that a game should be devised to keep cricketers fit in winter. He felt the grounds were too hard for rugby and a game should be developed that kept the ball in the air more. The MCC Committee charged him with the task of creating such a game.' This important point is not sourced but probably came from the 1858 correspondence book of the MCC which cannot be located at the time of going to publication.

33 *Herald* 16 May 1859, p.6

34 *Argus* 9 May 1859

35 It may be that the *Herald* had the committee listed incorrectly and that Butterworth, and not Wray, had been elected to the Committee. Bryant was also a member of the victorious 1858-59 Victorian cricket team. Both Wray and Bryant were professionals which may explain why they were not elected to the committee.

36 *Australian Storekeepers and Traders Journal* 30 Nov. 1910, p. 10

37 K. Dunstan, *The Paddock That Grew*, Cassell, 1962, p. 296; T.S. Marshall, op. cit. Bruce later played for the Richmond CC; P. Taylor, *One Hundred Years of Richmond Cricket Club*, 1854-1954, p.122, quoting a *Cricketer's Guide* of the time but giving no date.

38 Minute book and letter book of the MCC held by the Club. T.H. Smith also 1860-1861.

39 Longstop (W.J. Hammersley), *A'sian* 30 May 1868. D.S. Campbell (President MCC): 'In no other country in the world was cricket more supported than in Victoria . . .' *Melbourne Punch* 19 Jan. 1860, p. 212

40 *Bell's L.V.* 26 Sept. 1857

41 Document held by the MCC and copy on display in the Cricket Museum.

42 For example, Wills quoted in P. Taylor, *One Hundred Years of Cricket: the Story of the Richmond Cricket Club, 1854-1954*, from *The Cricketer's Guide* for 1874, edited by T.W. Wills. Original source not sighted. Hammersley recalls only the four, *Sydney Mail* 25 Aug. 1883, p. 363, as does Thompson in *The Australian Cricketer's Guide, 1870-71*, see Preface 2, note 65. T.H. Smith recalls Bruce as being added to the number later, *A'sian* 26 Feb. 1876.

43 *Bell's L.V.* 3 Jan. 1857

44 *Argus* 5 Dec. 1859; *Bell's L.V.* 10 Dec. 1859

45 *Leader* 18 Jan. 1873, Wills wrote: [Hammersley] 'has for the past three years been in the habit of writing me down whenever he thought it would do me an injury, allowing me no opportunity of replying in the columns over which he presides; but really every cricketer knows his name and how very contemptible he is.'

46 'A participant in the three chief matches of this [1858] season' suggested that 'to the best of his belief, had not Mr Wills played in them, not a single dispute would have arisen. As it turned out, there were at least a dozen.'

47 W.J. Hammersley in *Sydney Mail* 25 August, p.363; also described as being 'afflicted with an infirmity of temper' : *A'sian* 11 March 1876, p. 333

48 J.A. Allan, *The Old Model School*, MUP, 1934, p.69; information on Smith acquired by the Hibernian Research Company, Dublin, for the authors in 1987. Ref. D.308/E.O'B.

49 *Dublin University Rugby Football Club 1854-1954*, centenary booklet, pp. 9,17

50 W.W. Rouse Ball & J.A. Venn (eds.) *Admissions, 1801- 1850, Trinity College, Cambridge*, vol. IV, Macmillan 1911. For more on both Thompson and Hammersley, see Preface — Diffusion of the Rules, and on Hammersley, ch.6, note 7

51 D. Newsome, op. cit., p. 56

52 J.R. Whitty, *Early Codes*, in A.H. Fabian and G. Green, *Association Football*, v.1, Caxton, London, 1960, p.143; O. L. Owen, *The*

History of The Rugby Football Union, London. 1955, p.41

53 J.R. Whitty, ibid., pp.141-144; E. Dunning & K. Sheard, op. cit., p.104 *Dictionary of National Biography 1901-1911*, p. 9899: 'Albert Pell is usually credited with introducing into Cambridge University in 1839 the style of football played at Rugby School'.

54 *Herald* 16 May 1859

55 *Argus* 16 May 1859, p.5. Thompson was an *Argus* reporter and it seems reasonable to assume that he wrote the football notes.

56 *Herald* 23 Aug. 1858 p.5

57 W.J. Hammersley, *Sydney Mail* 25 August 1883, p. 363

58 T. Mason, *Association Football and English Society, 1863-1915*, Harvester Press, Sussex, 1980, p.19; E. Dunning & K. Sheard, op. cit., pp. 92-96

59 J.B. Thompson (ed.,) *Victorian Cricketer's Guide, 1859-1860*.

60 T.W. Wills (ed.), *Australian Cricketer's Guide, 1870-1871*, pp. 114-115

61 The first five dealt with the size of the ground, the existence of goal posts and kick off posts either side of the goal posts, beginning the game and the definition of a goal. The ninth rule dealt with returning the ball when out of bounds and the tenth prohibited throwing the ball.
    See page 196 for Rules.

62 When an opposing player had caught the ball and called 'mark'. See below.

63 *Argus* 4 July 1859; *Morning Herald* 4 July 1859

64 Information is taken from the series of articles by J.C. Wainwright in *Bell's Life in Victoria*, June 1864 as republished from the English sporting magazine *Field*, 1863. The Cambridge Rules for 1856 and 1863 are printed in J.R. Whitty, op. cit., pp. 143-146; the earlier 1849 rules no longer extant.

65 J.B. Thompson in T.W. Wills (ed.) *Australian Cricketer's Guide*, 1870-1871, pp. 114-115. Harrison also comments that Wills considered Rugby as unsuitable for grown men engaged in making a living. H.C.A. Harrison, *The Story of an Athlete*, see chapter 7. See also Free Kick, *Bell's L.V.* 21 May 1864

66 E. Dunning and K. Sheard, op. cit.

67 K. Dunstan, Psst! Want to buy a bit of Melbourne?, *Age* 15 July 1986, p. 11

68 Charterhouse and Shrewsbury codes were also primarily non ball-handling allowing catches rewarded by free kicks, but their influence seems to have been negligible.

69 W.J. Hammersley, *Sydney Mail* 25 Aug. 1883, p. 363. See below under the discussion on Harrison as 'father of football'.

70 Free Kick, *Bell's L.V.* 14 May 1864. In this respect the Melbourne Rules resembled the Cambridge Rules of 1856 of which there were only 11.

71 T.S. Marshall, op. cit., *Paper on Football*, 1896, p. 3

72 *Argus* 23 May 1859, p.5; 6 June 1859, p.4; *Bell's L.V.* 14 May 1864: The 1859 rules had been 'simply printed and got up' and distributed to members.

73 Edited by Wm. Fairfax, pp. 90-92

74 *Argus* 16 August 1858, p. 7

75 See, eg., the desirability of playing by the MFC Rules encouraged by the *Argus*, below.

76 Eg., *Ballarat Times* 23 May 1859 quoted his assertion that the 'rules determined upon at meeting of the [MFC] Committee . . . will be strictly adhered to' in matches to be played.

77 *Bell's L.V.* 7 May 1864. MFC general meeting hoped football will 'resume the position it occupied in the list of colonial sports some 2 or 3 years ago.'

78 T.H. Smith, letter, *A'sian* 26 Feb. 1876

79 Sandercock and Turner op. cit, p. 257 suggest that Wills wrote in *Bell's Life* under the pseudonym of Free Kick. This seems unlikely mainly because Free Kick wrote in *Bells* during 1861 and 1862 when Wills was far away in Queensland trying to cope with the family's sheep station, Cullin-la-ringo. Nor is it Wills' style of writing which tends to be confused and flowery in newspapers.

80 J.B. Thompson (ed.), *Victorian Cricketer's Guide*, 1859-1860, p. 111

81 *Argus* 23 May 1859, p. 5. It is difficult to discover what these revisions were; perhaps they were those incorporated into the 1860 rules. See below.

82 *Herald* 8 Aug. 1859, p. 5

83 Phrase used, *Argus* 9 July 1860, p. 4

84 *Argus* 30 May 1859, p. 5; 13 June 1859, p. 4

85 *Argus* 13 June 1859, p. 4

86 *Argus* 11 July 1859, p. 585

87 *Argus* 1 Aug. 1859

88 T.P. Power (ed.), *Footballer* 1875, p. 7

89 Letter, Horatio Wills to his sons in Germany, c. July — Dec. 1860, D. Cooke collection

90 Letter signed G.G.S., Queensland, *A'sian* 2 Sept. 1922, p. 493. George Glencross Smith was an early Geelong player, and a friend of Cedric Wills, one of Tom's younger brothers. Smith also recalled training with Harrison by running around the Botanical Gardens in Geelong. *Argus* 3 Sept. 1960.

91 *Argus* 14 May 1860

92 See, eg., *Herald* 8 Aug. 1859, p. 5

93 Scotch College Speech Night Programme for 1858; J. A. Allan op. cit., p. 69

94 *A'sian* 2 Aug. 1873, p. 140

95 *Herald* 30 Aug. 1858

96 T. Hughes, *Tom Brown At Oxford*, Nelson Classics, pp. 212-213

97 *Dr Bromby's Journal* 6 July 1858

98 *Argus* 16 Aug. 1858, 18 April 1859

99 *Bell's L.V.* 3 April 1858, 30 July 1859

100 *Bell's L.V.* 7 Jan. 1860

101 N. Vance, *The Ideal of Manliness*, in B. Simon & I. Bradley, op. cit.; Scotch College report for 1860: 'While thus using our utmost endeavours for the intellectual, moral and religious training of the

youth committed to our charge, we are careful also not to neglect the physical, encouraging by every means a love for manly and athletic sports and exercises, our earnest aim and endeavour being to educate the whole man.' Quoted in Scotch College Diamond Jubilee booklet, 1911

102 Letter, Free Kick, *Bell's L.V.* 21 May 1864

103 T.P. Power (ed.), *Footballer* 1879, p. 69

104 *Argus* 29 Aug. 1908, p. 17

105 J. Pollard, *Australian Rugby Union: The Game and the Players*, Angus & Robertson, A. B. C. , 1984, pp. 480-481

106 T.P. Power, (ed.), *Footballer* 1881, pp. 63,67

107 J.A. Daly, *Elysian Fields: sport, class and community in colonial South Australia, 1836-1890*, Adelaide, 1982, pp. 63,79

108 T.P. Power (ed.), *Footballer* 1876, p. 126

109 T.P. Power (ed.), *Footballer* 1877, p. 138

110 C.K. Knuckey, *South Australian Football, The Past and The Present, 1860-1965*, p. 25

111 T.P. Power (ed.), *Footballer* 1876, p.17. Probably written by Power himself, using the folksy argot favoured at the time for such recollections.

112 *Argus* 5 Sept. 1859, p. 5

113 Although Colden Harrison is credited by the *Footballer* in 1875 with helping to form the Melbourne Football Club, this specific claim is then denied by first-MFC committee member, T.H. Smith, and conceded by the author of *Footballer's* article. T.P. Power (ed.), *Footballer* 1875 and *A'sian* 26 Feb., 11 March 1876. Such is the potency of print that the *Footballer's* error has been perpetuated by writers on the subject since. *Football*, vol.1. No l. 1885, quotes from *Footballer's* article and also T.S. Marshall, op. cit., R.W.E. Wilmot in *A'sian* 9 Sept. 1926, *Australian Encyclopedia* 1927, etc. It seems likely that Harrison himself would have made both claims if he could have legitimately have done so but he did not.

114 *Bell's L.V.* 28 May 1860

115 *Argus* 4 and 11 June 1860

116 Advertisement by George Marshall in *Bell's L.V.* 28 April, 1860; *Argus* 14 May 1860; *Bell's L.V.* 6 Sept. 1862. Evidence of the shape comes from 'the ball on view at the Great Exhibition of 1851. This ball was made especially by William Gilbert and, dramatically enough, was shown hanging from the cross-bar of a Rugby goal in a stand . . . . On the pillars supporting the roof of the stand proudly appeared the names of the Houses at Rugby School and their crests . . . . Ten years later, at another international exhibition in London, the Gilbert Rugby balls were thought important enough to be awarded a Prize medal and already they were being imported to what at the time, and for many years afterwards, were known as the Colonies. It is worthy of emphasis that even these carefully manufactured balls on exhibition for all the world to see, and doubtless marvel at, still contained animal bladders.' O.L. Owen, *The History of the Rugby Football Union*, London, 1955, p. 33

117 *Bell's L.V.* 31 May 1862.

118 T.S. Marshall wrote in 1896: 'Since the Geelong match, "running with the ball and bouncing it occasionally" had become law.' T. S. Marshall, op. cit. We can find no written confirmation of this between 1862 and 1865; it seems more likely that it became an agreed custom rather than a 'law'.

119 T.S. Marshall, loc. cit.

120 *Bell's L.V.* 28 May 1864. A possible reference to Colden Harrison?

121 The meeting agreed only that the losing side should kick off from the centre after a goal. Tom Wills' motion to have a bar across the goal posts eight feet from the ground as in Rugby was lost on the casting vote of the chairman, *Bell's L.V.* 13 May 1865

122 T.S. Marshall, op. cit., claims this as 1863 but see *Bell's L.V.* 22 July 1865 for account of the same match.

123 *Bell's L.V.* 12 May 1866

124 *A'sian* 28 May 1870. In 1869 an old Etonian football player was so impressed by this new development that he had a copy of the Melbourne Rules sent to England remarking, 'To my mind, nothing could be better worth looking at than the graceful way some of the players handle the ball, bouncing it the whole time and passing through numbers of their opponents, to the great amusement of the spectators, who, I am sure would not take half the interest in the game if there was no dodging allowed.' *A'sian*, May 1869. See also *A'sian* 2 May 1874, p. 555.

125 See *The Story of an Athlete*, ch. 6 and Preface.

126 Wayne Hankin Papers, *Football in Ballarat*, p.24, MCC collection

127 *Australian Storekeepers and Traders Journal* 30 Nov. 1910.

128 *A'sian* 21 July 1877, p. 76

129 VPRO Series 894, Minute Book 1, Board of Education, 1862-65, pp.443, 449; VPRO Series 906, no 10, School Correspondence 541 to 600, Jan. 1864-Dec. 1870 under roll no 569

130 *Bell's L.V.* 29 July 1865

131 *Sydney Mail* 25 Aug. 1883, p. 363

132 *Argus* 1 May 1865

133 MCC minutes 27 Sept. 1869. MCC Annual Reports 1869-1870, 1870-1871.

134 *A'sian* 25 Jan. 1873, p. 108

135 W.J. Hammersley, *Sydney Mail* 15 Sept. 1883, p. 508

136 *Herald* 8 Sept. 1860

137 *Bell's L.V.* May — June 1864

138 *A'sian* 13 July 1867, p. 43: 'reminded old football players who were present of the time when football was first introduced, and when every evening during the winter twenty-a-side could easily be mustered for the fray.'

139 *A'sian* 12 June 1869, p. 748

140 *A'sian* 2 October 1869, p. 429

141 *A'sian* 30 July 1870, letter in response to one accusing him of undue violence; *A'sian* 27 April 1872, p. 525. Harrison's last game was played at Albert Park on 7 Oct. 1871.

142 See, for example, *Australasian Sketcher* 4 October, 1873, p. 123
143 T.P. Power (ed.), *Footballer* 1875, p.12
144 T.P. Power (ed.), *Footballer* 1876, p.18
145 Unidentified newspaper cutting 1926

East Melbourne Cricket Ground, *Australasian Sketcher* 1874

THE STORY OF AN ATHLETE BY H.C.A. HARRISON

Chapter 1   With the Overlanders

1 Henry Colden Antill m. Eliza Wills. He was granted 2 000 acres at Picton, south-west of Sydney, after his retirement from the British Army. Jarvisfield was named after Jane Jarvis, Macquarie's first wife. J.M. Antill, *ADB* v.1

2 The author's mother was Jane Howe, 1816-1880, daughter of George Howe, the NSW Government printer who had been transported for shoplifting. J.V. Byrnes, *ADB* v.1. See also the Preface. Jane actually married Capt. J. Harrison on 12 Feb. 1831 when she was fourteen and he was twenty-eight. H.C.A. Harrison (Colden) was the second of the eight children.

3 Lloyd's register, 1834-36, shows a *Rose* of 69 tons from the Port of Liverpool with John Harrison as Master. Public Record Office, London.

4 The *Friendship* was a two masted schooner of 89 tons, built in Devon in 1824. It was totally wrecked at Norfolk Island on 17 July 1835 after a gale swept the boat away from its moorings and onto a reef. The government denied liability and rejected a claim for compensation. Reg. Syd. no. 8/35, *Historical Records of Australia*, xviii, pp. 496,713-14

5 Capt. Harrison's wife, Jane Howe, was a half sister to Horatio Spencer Wills. Jane Howe was also a half sister to Sarah Redfern (nee Wills) who had been widowed by the convict surgeon-squatter William Redfern's death in 1833. Sarah administered Redfern's estate with her bro. Thomas Wills and friend William Charles Wentworth. Redfern had been associate surgeon to D'Arcy Wentworth, father of William Wentworth. E. Ford, *ADB* v.2

6 Or 'what was called the Major's Line, the well marked track of

Major Mitchell on his exploration journey from the Lachlan to Portland Bay and back over Mt. Macedon and up the Goulburn Valley into NSW. His party being numerous and his drays heavily laden, a deeply cut track was made in the virgin soil and was plainly distinguished for years after.' Reminiscences of Alfred Joyce, written in 1896, G.F. James (ed.), *A Homestead History, Reminiscences & Letters of Alfred Joyce of Plaistow & Norwood, Port Phillip,1843-1864*, 1969, p.104

7 On 11 April 1838, at a camp on the Broken River (near the present town of Benalla), Aboriginals attacked a party of men driving a mob of sheep and cattle overland for the brothers George and William Pitt Faithfull, and seven whites died. Capt. Harrison would have passed through some six weeks earlier. Gipps to Glenelg, 21 July 1838, *Historical Records of Australia*, Series 1, v.19, p.510

8 Capt. John Hepburn had been one of the first overlanders when he brought stock with Joseph Hawdon and John Gardiner to Port Phillip in 1836. A sea captain also, he possibly knew Capt. Harrison and perhaps had advised him of the potential Mitchell's trek revealed. This account reads as if these men all travelled together. However, according to Capt. Hepburn, he and William Coghill had joined together and been overtaken by William Bowman. At the Murray crossing these three men and their parties had caught up with William Hamilton, and at the Goulburn River with Capt. Harrison on 2 March 1838. Thus, to this point, Capt. Harrison had preceeded the others. Hepburn wrote 14 years later that only Alexander Mollison, C.H. Ebden, Capt. Brown and the overlanders mentioned above had crossed the Goulburn with sheep herds to that date. Hepburn's account as published by Bride in 1896 is probably the source of Colden Harrison's information on this part of his life. T.F. Bride, *Letters From Victorian Pioneers*, 1898, C.E. Sayers (ed.), Heinemann, 1969, pp. 68-69

9 Hepburn went on to settle at Daylesford, Bowman at Castlemaine, and the Coghills at Creswick. Hepburn wrote with some sarcasm in 1853: '[Capt.John] Harrison, who was too wise to be advised by me, came nearer the settlement, and took up a country I am not acquainted with, viz. the Plenty.' Ibid.

10 Capt. Harrison wrote 13 July 1844: 'Notwithstanding being one of the oldest squatters on the Plenty, from fortuitous circumstances I have the smallest run and having within the last two days been deprived of every acre of purchased land, a considerable number of my present lambs must die if you decline acceding to my request' [for additional pasturage?]. PROV Series 96, Letter Book Commissioner of Crown Lands (Bourke) 1841-1856. It is suggested that he had in fact about 2 000 ha. (5 000 acres), not a very large amount comparatively.

11 Dr. William Ronald, b. Aberdeen, Scotland, 1808. Medical officer on 3 voyages to Sydney. Married in Launceston 1841. Settled on the east bank Plenty in March 1842, where he built a house called Virtue

Hall on some 4 to 5 000 ha. (12 000 acres). The size of his leased
land progressively dwindled until 1853 when he bought allotment 2
of section 14, parish of Yan Yean, his homestead section of 259 ha.
(640 acres), and remained as the doctor in the district until his death
in 1882. A. Sutherland, *Vic. & Its Metropolis: past and present*,
Melbourne, McCarron Bird, 1888, v.1, p.414; D. Edwards, *Yan
Yean: A History*, Yan Yean School Council,1978, pp.44-45

Richmond Cricket Ground, *Australasian Sketcher* 1874

Chapter 2   On the Plenty

1 John Bear arriv. Port Phillip 1841 in chartered schooner *The Brothers*
and had a run east of the Plenty known as New Leicester or Yan
Yean. As Castle Hill Farm, it was bequeathed in 1851 to his son
Thomas Hutchings Bear who had been managing it. His other son,
John Pinney Bear, was involved in the stock and station agency his
father set up in Bourke Street. The Bears had other squatting
interests later and an interest in the Chateau Tahbilk winery. E.
Heddle Moodie, *Story of a Vineyard: Chateau Tahbilk*, Hawthorn,
1968, passim. Harrison's run abutted Bear's run on the south.

2 Built about 1847, Bear's Castle is the only known pure cob structure
in Victoria. Cob is formed from 'lumps of mixed clay, straw and
water [which] are pitched on course by course while still in the
plastic state . . .. The faces of the walls are pared down as the work
progresses, and when dry they are plastered inside and given some
sort of protective coating on the outside.' About 6.5 square metres in
size, two storeys high and built on stone foundations, the Castle has
round corner turrets (supposedly castellated originally) and windows
with Gothic arches. It was used only as a sheepfold and shepherds'
hut. Bear claimed its erection was due to a shepherd taking seriously
a suggestion he had made in jest. It still exists on a small rise north-
west of Yan Yean Reservoir. M. Lewis, *Victorian Primitive*, Melb.,
Greenhouse, 1977, pp.39,42

3 Yarra Yarra tribe: the name given to the Woiworung Aboriginals
who claimed the land of the Yarra watershed as their territory; also
known as the Wurundjerri and the Port Phillip tribe. N.B. Tindale,
Aboriginal Tribes of Australia, National University Press, Canberra,
1974, pp.208-209.

4 Bendemeer, probably named after 'a river which flows near the ruins of Clilminar' (Persia) in *Lalla Rookh, an Oriental Romance*, published in 1817 by the Irish poet, Thomas Moore. This very popular poem, features Bendemeer in a song about a nightingale and roses on its banks, and concludes:

> Thus bright to my soul, as 't was then to my eyes,
> Is that bower on the banks of the calm BENDEMEER!

5 Wm. Thomas, Assistant Protector of the [local] Aborigines, reported in Jan. 1844 that he had 'with much difficulty . . . established a school on the [Merri] creek, [in what is now the Yarra Bend Park] and that not without a Burden upon myself[;] the small means at my disposal renders it impossible otherwise'. Two years later the Baptist Merri Creek School, or Yarra Aboriginal Mission, was opened in the same vicinity but the Harrisons had departed by then. A. Lemon, *The Northcote Side of the River*, Hargreen, 1983, ch. 2, *A Doomed Race*, for both schools. 'Borak' meant 'to remonstrate against', a possible origin of the word 'barracker'.

6 Norman MacLeod, squatter on the Merri Creek, 1841-42. Best man at H.C.A. Harrison's wedding. See also Preface and index.

7 These squatters, with the exception of Norman MacLeod, were on the way through Whittlesea to their stations on the King Parrot Creek and the Goulburn River, south of what is now Yea. The usual road was via Kilmore and Broadford but 'there was a short cut to Melbourne over a gap in the Plenty Ranges [now the road via Kinglake West] called the "Insolvency Gap" because the squatters in the bad time before the diggings broke out [ie. the financial depression of the early 1840s] had to go by the gap to avoid their creditors on the main road.' C. Fetherstonhaugh, *After Many Days*, Sydney, 1917, p.73

Farquahar McKenzie had come overland with Peter Snodgrass in 1838 and, as superintendent for Capt. John Murchison, taken up the run known as Kerrisdale, and part of this on his own account as Flowerdale in 1840. In 1846 McKenzie became Murchison's son-in-law and Flowerdale was leased by another McKenzie, Capt. Roderick McKenzie. John Murchison was on Kerrisdale until the early 1860s. C. Fetherstonhaugh, op. cit., pp.64-73

8 The 'young blood', Peter Snodgrass, was on his way to his Muddy Creek stations near Yea. His prospective father-in-law, John Cotton of nearby Doogallook, gives the best impression of him at this time, writing in 1846: 'You will have probably heard that my daughter Agnes is likely to be married shortly to a Mr Peter Snodgrass, son of Colonel Snodgrass, who was [briefly acting] Governor of this Colony some years back. Mr P. Snodgrass is well known by most persons in the Colony and every person who does know him speaks well of him. It is said that he was included amongst the wild mob of Goulburn, and that he has dissipated all the money that his father had supplied him with, but he promises to amend, and I have no doubt from the fineness of character and the goodness of his heart,

that he will do so, and, I trust, make a good husband to my daughter.' Evidently love had the right effect and Snodgrass went on to become a rather dull member of the Legislative Council and a pastoralist at Doogallook. G. Mackaness, *The Correspondence of John Cotton, Part 1*; A. Gross, *ADB* v.2

9 Lady Janet Marion Clarke, S. Morrissey, *ADB* v.3; Sutherland, op. cit., v.2, p.467

Major-General Frederick Godfrey Hughes m. Agnes Eva Snodgrass, *Who's Who in the Commonwealth of Australia* 1922

10 'Mr Thomas Wills owned Lucerne close by Alphington . . . He had a strong fancy for the great fodder plant, and was the first proprietor to lay down any considerable breadth of land with it. From it, or as a souvenir of the world-famous lake, the estate was named.' R. Boldrewood (T.A. Browne), *Old Melbourne Memories*, 1884, C.E. Sayers (ed.), Heinemann, 1969, p.161. Neighbour Richard Howitt wrote: 'Mr Thomas Wills, one of the most intelligent gentlemen of the colony, a magistrate, a native of the middle district (Sydney), what we must call an Anglo-Australian. He had bought his estate, the next allotment but one to ours off the Crown on 10 June, 1840; he had paid £3 784 for it. His house and other premises cost as much more. For land clearing he paid in some instances £516 per acre. His estate 176 acres is a valuable one . . .' See also Preface. R. Howitt, *Impressions of Australia Felix*, op. cit., pp.64-65. In 1959, although in a state of disrepair, the house was described as a 'substantial fine building' of early Victorian architecture with 'the refined overall simplicity and the characteristic fine joinery and fireplaces of Colonial architecture . . . the architecture of New South Wales'. Sadly Lucerne was demolished, despite its National Trust classification, to make way for the La Trobe Golf Club car park. (Vic.) *Trust Newsletter*, No. 2, 195.

11 Francis Durell Vignoles, P. de Serville, *Port Phillip Gentlemen*, OUP, Melb., 1980, p.185, (Garryowen) E. Finn, *Chronicles of Early Melbourne, 1835-1852: Historical, Anecdotal & Personal*, Melb. 1888, v.2, p.778.

Smith, James (known as Jemmy), who ran the first Savings Bank with the aid of a boy. 'Mr.Smith was its Comptroller, Secretary, Actuary and Cashier; and no bank in the world ever had a more scrupulous officer. The Savings Bank was a sort of mania with him . . . [and a] depositor was, to his mind, a something almost incapable of wrong-doing.' Garryowen, op. cit., v.1, p.326

William Le Souef was an Assistant Protector of the Aborigines. His son, Albert, was a zoologist and his sons were prominent in the zoological field. A. McEvey, *ADB* v. 5

12 William Frederick Augustus Rucker, German-born son of a French army officer, was a wholesale wine and spirit merchant in Hobart Town who arriv.in Port Phillip in 1837 and became 'the second merchant or wholesale dealer in Melbourne, Batman being the first'. His store was 'in Market Street between Collins and Little Flinders [streets].' Garryowen, op. cit., pp.356,427

13 Mrs Wills: presumably Mary Ann (nee Barry) then married to
    Thomas Wills of Lucerne: see note 10. Mrs Langhorne: probably
    George's wife Mary (nee Cartwright) m. 1837
        Capt. Foster Fyans,1790-1870, soldier who became an important
    figure in early Geelong where he was the first resident police
    magistrate (1837) and the Commissioner of Crown Lands for
    Portland (1840). P.L. Brown, *ADB* v.1. 'A tall, bluff ex-soldier who
    was capable of appropriate kindliness or sternness in varying degrees
    according to circumstances . . .', W.R. Brownhill, *The History of
    Geelong and Corio Bay*, Melb., 1955, pp.62-64:

14 Thomas Wills first m. Celia Reibey in 1822. Ceila's mother was
    Mary, convicted for horse stealing at the age of 13 who then married
    Thomas Reibey, apparently the first settler in NSW outside the
    military cartel to trade substantially; Edward Wills became his
    partner. When both men died in 1811, Mary Reiby took over her
    husband's enterprises. Thomas and Celia Reibey had a dau. Alice.
    From his marriage to Mary Ann Barry, Thomas Wills had two
    children, a son Wm. Henry who drowned before Thos. came to Port
    Phillip, and Catherine Spencer (cousin Kate). Apparently in the early
    1850s the marriage broke down and Thos. Wills went to England
    where he had four illegitimate sons from an alliance with Mary Ann
    Mellard. *Autobiography of Arthur Wills*, ms. private collection.

15 Lewis Conran, P. de Serville, op. cit., p.201. Son of Capt. James
    Samuel Conran. His uncle, Lieut. Gen. Henry Lewis Conran, was a
    colourful bear of a man who was Governor of Jamaica at one time.
    Kate went to England with Lewis Conran when La Trobe left
    Victoria. She died 27 Aug.1884. R. V. Pockley, *Ancestor Treasure
    Hunt*, op. cit., pp.36-37.

16 Col. George Johnston, A.T. Yarwood, *ADB*. v.2. Harrison's
    mother, Jane Harrison nee Howe, and Kate's father, Tom Wills,
    were cousins of David Johnston's wife Selina Willey because Selina
    Willey's mother was a sister of Sarah (m.1 Wills, m. 2 Howe, nee
    Harding). R.V. Pockley, loc. cit., pp.22-23.

17 The oak tree still exists and can be seen on the La Trobe Golf
    Course between the 8th tee and the 12th green.

18 William Westgarth claimed the Yarra rose fifty feet at Heidelberg in
    [Dec.15] 1863. *The Colony of Victoria*, London, 1864, p. 84. 'At
    Dight's Mills near the junction of the Merri Creek and the Yarra, the
    scene could only be compared to a foaming and boiling sea. The
    water rose as high as the third story of the mill.' *Argus* 24 Dec. 1863

19 George Petty 'had bought the Bourke Street (butchering business)
    from that old German gentleman, William Hoffman, who, I believe,
    established it, and later retired to live for many years in affluence on
    that beautiful estate Buddzback, between the west end of Buckley
    Street, Essendon, and Keilor Road.' H.H. Peck, *Memoirs of a
    Stockman*, Melb., 1942, p.56

20 William Vincent Wallace, music teacher, pianist in Sydney 1836-
    1838. *Maritana* was very popular in England and Europe. C.
    MacKerras, *ADB* v.2

21 'The early settlers from New South Wales who came over to Port Phillip at its first settlement had, many of them, assigned servants who were of course taken with them to the new settlement, seeing it was all one colony. These would remain with them till their assignments were completed and were then freed or enlarged on tickets-of-1eave.' G.F. James, *A Homestead History*, op. cit., p.87. Long Bill, see also pp.34, 35, 110. The Port Phillip census of 1841 describes Capt. John Harrison as proprietor of a run with ten persons living there: seven free [Harrison, Jane, Adela, Colden, George, Samuel Jeffrey the superintendent, and one other] and two assigned and one holding ticket-of-1eave. Of this ten, five persons were stockmen, gardeners or engaged in agriculture [leaving Jane, the family and possibly a woman servant?]

22 The gang consisted of an American whaler Daniel Jepp, an expiree convict 'Yanky Jack' or Charles Ellis, and bounty immigrants John Williams and Martin (not William) Fogarty. An affair which seems to have captured the imagination of the colonists. References include C.J. Baker, *Sydney and Melbourne*, London,1845, pp.45-50; R.D. Murray, *A Summer at Port Phillip*, Edinburgh,1843, pp.40-41; W. Westgarth, *Australia Felix*, Edinburgh,1848, p.282; Garryowen, op. cit., v.1, pp.406-409; *Port Phillip Herald* 3 May, 6 May 1842; *Port Phillip Patriot* 2 May, 9 May 1842.

23 George William Ryder had the run Rokeby on the River Plenty between 1840-1842. R.V. Billis and A.S. Kenyon, *Pioneers of Port Phillip*, 2nd ed., Melbourne,1974, p.30. Ryder's Swamp was the original site of the Yan Yean Reservoir and a once favourite haunt of the district Aboriginals, Garryowen, op. cit., p.562. In 1840 Ryder leased portions 5, 6, 11 and 12 Parish of Yan Yean from Thomas Walker, D. Edwards, op. cit., p.44

24 Henry Norcott later married Adela Harrison, Colden's older sister.

25 Dr. Ronald, see ch.1 note 11

26 Campbell Hunter's station was West Lowlands and it was apparently near the Plenty River. P. de Serville, op. cit. p.178; D. Edwards, *The Diamond Valley Story*, Shire of Diamond Valley,1979, pp.95

27 The party consisted of Peter Snodgrass, (ch.2 note 8), Henry Fowler, Oliver Gourlay, James Thompson and Robert Chamberlain. See P. de Serville, op. cit., index. A charge against Gourlay for obstructing justice on another occasion was subsequently dropped. All were squatters and members of the Melbourne Club. ['Hopping Jack' was a horse couper, Mr John Ewart. C. Fetherstonhaugh, op. cit., p.34]. On 28 June 1842 the three condemned men went to the scaffold smoking clay pipes, seated on their own coffins in a cart, and 'about 1000 people all dresssed in their holiday attire' watched the actual hanging. *Port Phillip Gazette* 29 June 1842

28 Doubtless Wm. Commerford, b. Ireland 1814, arriv. 1840, five years later began farming at Kew, 1856 bought 316 acres nr. Lilydale and became dairy farmer. Sutherland, op. cit., v.2, p.407. Thomas Wills leased Lot 56 [Willsmere] to Commerford in 1854 at £200 per year

for 21 years before Wills went back to England. D. Rogers, *A History of Kew*, Lowden, Kilmore, 1973, p.4

South Melbourne Cricket Ground, *Australasian Sketcher* 1874

Chapter 3   On The Avon

1 Norman McLeod took up Numeralla or Lochen, some 16 000 acres on the right bank of the Snowy River from Orbost to the sea. Billis and Kenyon op. cit., p. 261, list him there from July 1847 to June 1850 and from July 1856 to October 1864 but he was probably established before 1847. See also Preface and index.

2 Capt. Henry Edward Pulteney Dana, a close friend of La Trobe's, M.L. Norman, *ADB* v.1; L. Blake, *Capt. Dana & the Native Police*, Neptune Press, Newtown, 1982

Frederick Armand Powlett, P.M. Sales, *ADB* v.2.

La Trobe records meeting Capt. Harrison on 13 March 1845, C.J. La Trobe, *Memoranda of Journeys, Excursions and Absences*, 1839-1854, ms., State Library of Victoria

3 Will. Robt. Guilfoyle, *Australian Botany, especially designed for Australian Schools*, 1878.

4 Quamby = camp

5 William Bogle Hamilton and the Donald brothers, James and John Stirling, arriv. Hobart, barque *Sovereign*, Dec.1838; took up Langi Kal Kal (north of Trawalla Vic.); with younger brother, William Donald, took out licences for Banyenong and Corak runs in 1844 (or 45?). Banyenong homestead was five kilometres north of the present town of Donald, that is, on the east bank of the Richardson River, and Corak adjacent to Lake Buloke. Described as 'pleasant neighbours'. Y. Palmer, *Track of the years: the Story of St. Arnaud*, MUP, 1955 and H. Anderson, *The Flowers of the Field: A History of the Ripon Shire*, Hill of Content, Melb., 1969, p.176 and index.

6 Lexington, see this ch. note 8, and ch.9 notes 6 and 7

7 The tribe would have been the Jaara (Lewuru) whose territory encompassed the area of the upper Loddon and Avoca rivers, east to about Castlemaine, west to St. Arnaud and Lake Buloke, north to about Boort and south to Daylesford and the Dividing Range and the eastern headwaters of the Wimmera River. There were about fourteen small bands which divided this area between them. N.B. Tindale, op. cit., pp.204-205

8 Horatio Spencer Wills squatted at Mt. William, 1840-1841, and held
   Lexington, La Rose and Mokepille stations from 1842 to 1852, Billis
   and Kenyon op. cit., p.161. See Preface and ch.9. L.L. Banfield,
   Like the Ark; The Story of Ararat, op. cit., C.E. Sayers, *ADB* v.2
   Henry, Charles and John Creswick settled a run where the
   Richardson River joins the Avon River; Charles and John later
   divided this into the Banyena and York Plains stations. James (not
   John) Orr took up the Yawong Springs run in 1846: the town of St.
   Arnaud developed from the New Bendigo goldfield which would
   have been on the southern corner of this run, according to
   Y. Palmer, op. cit., p.43. Henry Foley with Alexander Cameron,
   first occupied the Coonooer run which was directly north of
   the Yawong run.
9 Thomas, Jabez J. and Theophilis Job were the sons of the Rev. John
   Ham, founder of the Collins St. Baptist Church. Arr. 1842, the sons
   rented a farm on the Plenty River (which is probably where they
   knew the Harrisons), but after being burnt out, they went looking
   for land in the Mallee where they settled just south of Swan Hill to
   be ruined by drought. Not surprisingly they turned to other
   pursuits, publishing a squatting map of Victoria in 1847, and Ham's
   Illustrated Australian Magazine in 1850 which did not survive the
   'general scramble for the precious treasure' — gold. Another brother,
   Cornelius Job, was joined by Theo. as land auctioneers and estate
   agents. Billis and Kenyon, op. cit., p.78; C.P. Billot, *Melbourne: An
   Annotated Bibliography to 1850*, Geelong, Rippleside Press, 1970,
   p.163; Sutherland, op. cit., p.565; I.F. McLaren, *ADB* v.4
10 Dr. Henry Budd, 1820?-1856, a surgeon who came to Victoria in the
   1840s from Mauritius. He married Frances in 1848. Brother to
   Richard Hale Frances, the headmaster of the Melb. Diocesan School
   who did not approve of the match, citing the alleged immorality and
   convict forebears of her 'foster' mother, Jane Harrison, but also that
   she was Capt. John Harrison's illegitimate daughter. Letter Ralph
   Biddington, 14 Feb. 1986; R.H. Budd to Rev. Henry Budd, 10 Oct.
   1848, Mitchell Library Doc. 1049
11 Henry Norcott, see ch.2 note 24
12 Dr. Charles Perry, first Anglican Bishop of Melbourne, 1848-1876,
   A.de Q. Robin, *Charles Perry, Bishop of Melbourne*, Univ. of W.A.,
   1967
13 Stuart Gibson and Frederick Fenton took up the Mount Alexander
   run in June 1849 and Bendigo was later sited on its subdivision called
   Ravenswood. Frederick Fenton held the run for about 16 years.
   When gold was found on the run about the beginning of October
   1851, Fenton allegedly told Capt. Harrison of its discovery, *Report
   of the Select Committee on the Claims of Henry Frencham*, Vic. Parl.
   Papers,1890, Mins. of Evidence, pp.18-21. Hugh Leigh Atkinson 'a
   successful Sandhurst doctor and mining investor', F. Cusack,
   Bendigo: a History, Heinemann, Melb.,1973, p.20

14 Dr. Arthur O'Mullane, arriv. Port Phillip *William Metcalfe*; 1839?, founding member of the Port Phillip Medical Association, owned one of the first two-storied houses erected in Melb., on the east side of Queen Street between Collins St. and Flinders Lane; 'a general favourite with his patients through his suavity and skill'. Garryowen, op. cit., index. Dr. James B. Motherwell: 'a warm-hearted Irishman, of large practice, and many friends', E. Daniel & A. Potts, *A Yankee Merchant in Goldrush Australia*, Heinemann, Melb., 1970

15 Charles Washington Umphleby, 1827?-1892, came to Vic. 1842, pastoral pursuits Ararat district, joined John Goodman mercantile business in Melb., later managing director of the Victoria Ice Company, retired to property Rosedale, Gippsland; father of Lieut.-Colonel Charles Edward Earnest Umphleby, 1857-1900, commanded the permanent artillery at Queenscliff and killed in the Boer War, also of T. & H. Umphleby. *A'sian* 27 Feb.1892., p.407

16 Whittaker bros.: John Beard and James Jr., sons of James Whittaker. Swanwater taken up March 1855, according to Billis and Kenyon, op. cit., p.159

17 Richard Hale Budd, arr. Port Phillip Sept. 1840, Melb. Diocesan Grammar School, 1849-1854; Inspector and Secretary, Denominational School Board, 1854-1874. Also held squatting leases, A. M. Badcock, L. J. Blake, *ADB* v.3. See also this chap, note 30

18 The Melbourne Diocesan School register was donated to the La Trobe Library SLV by Mary Elizabeth Budd, and is preserved in the Library's manuscript collection. Mary allegedly was a rather crabby music teacher who idealized her father. Letter, R. Biddington, op. cit. The register shows that Colden Harrison began at the school on 8 March 1850 and left the following Christmas.

19 Henry Hewett Paulet Handfield worked with Richard Budd for three years, whilst preparing for ordination into the ministry under the personal supervision of Bishop Perry with whom he had come to the colony in 1848. 'An incumbent of St. Peter's from 1853-1900, he exercised a considerable influence on Melbourne's leading social circle, was well-liked, and was a popular preacher'. A.de Q. Robin, op. cit., p.214-215; B.R. Marshall, *ADB* v.4

20 Rev. Dr. John Edward Bromby, from Hull, arriv. 1858 with his ten children to be principal of the Melbourne Church of England Grammar School, 1858-1875. Sutherland, op. cit., v.2, p.463; M. Clark, *ADB* v.2

21 Capt. John Hepburn, see chap.1 notes 8 and 9. Although Harrison had not followed Hepburn's advice on where to take up land when they met overlanding, Hepburn's Journal shows that they had 'remained on friendly terms for many years'. L.M. Quinlan, *Here My Home*, OUP,1967, p.112

22 Henry Francis Hasting and Edward Waldron Vincent Budd, half-brothers from Richard Budd's father's third marriage, who came to Australia to live under Richard's care. Henry became a squatter in

the Riverina and Edward died [aged 18?] in 1853, annotations by
Budd in Melbourne Diocesan School register, op. cit.

23 The sons of Mrs Mary Elisabeth Chomley, widow of the Rev.
Francis Chomley, arriv. in 1849 to join her bro. Charles Griffith and
her sis. Mrs W.P. Greene. Allegedly Irish blue-bloods, P. de
Serville, op. cit., p.174, *Cyclopedia of Vic.* op cit.,v.1, p.188.
Consisted of Hussey Malone who became Chief Commissioner of
Police, William, Henry bank manager, Arthur Wolf crown
prosecutor, George Hanna squatter nr. Avoca, and Charles Albert.
Melbourne Diocesan School Register, op. cit.

24 Powers (Robert and Herbert), Rutherford (Gideon) and Co. was a
stock agency in Collins St. Robert Power was a well-known
sportsman in his time. An enthusiastic amateur rider, he was a
founder of the Victorian Racing Club and served on its committee
for many years.

Henry Box, son of Henry Box of Little Collins Street. Presumably
bro. of John Burnett, William Draper, and Charles Valette Box.

Wm.S. Hamilton, son of William Hamilton of Glenaroua,
Sugarloaf Creek, north-west of Broadford, became a 'landed
proprietor' accord. to the register. Father, an overlander. J.A.
Maher, *The Tale of a Century; Kilmore 1837-1937*, 1938, p.13

James Liddell Purves, M.L.A., M. Aveling, *ADB* v.5; 'celebrated
leading barrister and wit of the 'eighties and nineties' Peck, op. cit.,
p.114

25 Edward Butterfield's school was, according to Garryowen, op. cit.,
p.638, 'a tolerably efficient establishment . . . . The teacher was an
able though not over personally popular individual, and the
speculation not proving as payable as anticipated, he abandoned the
business . . . .' In fact Butterfield took over a school begun by Wm.
Brickwood, moved it from Swanston Street to Flinders Lane and
then into larger premises in Stephen street [now Exhibition St.]. At
the time of the gold rushes he went to Queensland where he rose to
become the chief clerk in the Department of Public Instruction in
Queensland [a position more responsible than the title suggests].
G.W. Noble, *Aims, Men or Money? The Establishment of Secondary
Education for Boys in South Australia and in the Port Phillip District
of New South Wales*, 1836-1860, unpub. Ph.D. thesis, Melb.
Univ.,1980, pp.353-354

26 Alexander McCrae was the brother of Andrew Murison McCrae. See
ch.5, note 2

27 Edward Cussen Ormond Howard, *Jottings of Old Times* in *Argus*,
Feb.- April, 1923. From 1854-1878 Bank of Australasia, then
Commercial Bank of Australia until retirement in 1905. An early
native of Melbourne, (born 1837), he developed an interest in
Melbourne's history. Biog. in Ms. 000608, Box 61/9 a, Royal
Historical Society of Victoria.

28 John and Helen MacPherson whose sons included John Alexander,
M.Leg. Ass. 1864-1878 and briefly Premier of Victoria,1869-1870;

William who ran the family station Nerrin-Nerrin in the Western
District; and James, solicitor. D. Fitzpatrick, *ADB* v.5

29 George Gouge conducted a school 'near his private residence in La
Trobe Street nor far from Swanston Street . . . The playground was
opposite Mr. Gouge's residence and, being mostly open country in
that direction, there was no lack of space for recreation purposes.
The collapse of the school took place in the early fifties, when Mr.
Gouge retired from business.' Harrison is described as 'a regular dab
at marbles' and 'the champion runner of the school'. E.O. Howard,
Argus 8 Oct. 1921

30 Richard Budd established the Educational Institute for Ladies in
Russell Street but the advent of the Presbyterian Ladies College drew
away some of his pupils and he moved in 1885 to Rooding, his home
in Cochrane Street, Brighton, where the school was known
colloquially as "Mr. Budd's". The school had considerable status in
that it was large, well-organised, prepared girls for Matriculation,
and was presumed to benefit from the classical training and
experience of Richard Budd. In his latter years much of the school
was run by his two unmarried daughters, Mary and Emma. Noble,
op. cit., p.403

Civil Service Cricket Ground, *Australasian Sketcher* 1874

Chapter 4   On the Diggings

1 See ch.3 note 25

2 Harrison advertised as general commission agent and gold broker,
Argus 25 Aug.1852

3 Harrison advertised as an auctioneer, *Argus* 31 Oct. 1853; *Bendigo
Correspondent* 29 Oct.1853

4 This new rule was introduced just before 1 Jan. 1852. The diggers
may well have been under a misapprehension: the London price was
for fine gold. 'Gold recovered from mines is more properly referred
to as gold bullion. It is an alloy with a percentage of silver or copper
which varies from field to field, and its value varies accordingly. In
addition the alluvial gold produced and sold on the field in 1851
necessarily contained a significant percentage of granules of iron
pyrites and other impurities.' H.J. Stacpoole, *Gold At Ballarat: The
Ballarat East Goldfield : Its Discovery and Development*, Lowden,
Kilmore, 1971, fn. p.56

5 On 1 Dec. Vic. Govt. announced that 'the licence fee was to be
   doubled from 1 Jan. 1852. The roar of protest was such that the
   decision was revoked within a fortnight.' G. Serle, *The Golden Age:
   a history of the colony of Victoria 1851-1861*, MUP, Melb., 1977,
   p.25
6 See Preface for the part played by Capt. John Harrison
7 N. MacLeod at Mt. Korong. See also Preface and index.
8 Henry Gyles Turner, *Our Own Little Rebellion—the Story of the
   Eureka Stockade*, Melb.,1913

Carlton Cricket Ground, *Australasian Sketcher* 1874

Chapter 5   *In the Civil Service*

1 From 1860 William Dempster was the second manager of the
   Williamstown branch of the English, Scottish and Australian
   Chartered Bank, in 1854 the first bank to open at Williamstown,
   W.P. Evans, *Port of Many Prows*, Hawthorn, 1969, p.44
      Fred Bull, son of architect and Williamstown borough surveyor
   Wm. Bull?, ibid., p.114
2 Farquhar Peregrine Gordon McCrae, fourth son of Alexander and
   Georgiana McCrae. George Gordon was the eldest son; his
   reminiscences of life at Arthurs Seat in the 1840s appear in *Vict. Hist.
   Mag.* v.1, 1911, pp.17-26
3 A tide-officer (waiter) was a customs officer who awaited the arrival
   of ships (formerly coming in with the tide) and boarded them to
   prevent the evasion of custom-house regulations. *Shorter Oxford
   English Dictionary*, 1936. H.C.A. Harrison was appointed 2 June
   1853.
4 'The 185-foot long, 1,625-ton *Marco Polo* was built by James Smith
   at St. John, New Brunswick, in 1850. Flush decks and square
   superstructure combined with an extremely fine underwater form
   enabled this ugly duckling of the clipper fleet to carry large cargoes
   at high speeds . . .. With a crew of thirty and a similar number of
   passage workers, and more than nine hundred passengers, she sailed
   [from Liverpool] on 4 July 1852 and embarked at Port Phillip Pilot
   sixty-eight days later.' Capt. J. Noble, *Port Phillip Panorama; a
   Maritime History*, Hawthorn, Melb., 1975, p.137. She made regular
   voyages to Melbourne until 1871. 'Great risks were taken by some
   skippers on the Australian run in their craze for speed. The most

notorious of them, [James Nicol] "Bully" Forbes of the *Marco Polo*, proclaimed his slogan as "Hell or Melbourne", and on his record run in 1852 he showed his passengers hell enough.' G. Serle, op. cit., p.58; J. Lovey, *Tall Ships and Sailormen*, A Marine History Publication, n.d., p.7

5   J.J. Shillinglaw, John Gray : a reminiscence, *A'sian* 4 Jan. 1873, p.8. *The Great Britain*, now partially restored, is a tourist attraction in Bristol. 'In the Shetlands there is still a suspicion — lacking solid foundation — that [Capt. John Gray] was murdered by a steward who knew him to be secretly carrying home a large quantity of gold in his cabin.' J. O'Callaghan, *The Saga of the SS Great Britain*, Rupert Hart-Davis, London, 1971, p.126; B. Greenhill, Exuberance Renewed: Restoration of the SS *Great Britain, Country Life*, 23 Feb. 1984

6   'Horses were being used to help tow ships up the River Yarra, a tow-path having been cut through the tea-tree on the eastern bank. Sometimes there was only five feet of water on the bar and shipping had to wait for a sufficient depth. If these delays became too lengthy cargoes were transferred into lighters and towed upstream. In addition to the delay this transhipment added about ten pence to the freight.' *Melbourne Advertiser* 23 April 1838 quoted in J. Noble, op. cit., p.55

7   *Argus* 8 Sept. 1854; 9 Sept.1854

8   Under the provisions of the Volunteer Act of 1854, a force of some 2 000 volunteers was easily raised to train to defend the Colony. There were 10 companies in Melbourne and suburbs and an artillery company at Portland, Brighton and Williamstown. C. Daley, *The Early Defence of Melbourne, Vic. Hist. Mag.* v.22, 1947, pp.11-13

St. Kilda Cricket Ground, *Australasian Sketcher* 1874

Chapter 6   Athletics — Mainly Footracing

1   Thomas Wentworth Wills, 1835-1880, son of Horatio Spencer Wills and Elizabeth McGuire, Harrison's cousin and brother-in-law. See Preface.

2   Frederick William Lillywhite, known primarily for perservering with round-arm bowling in England which helped to make it respectable, and for fathering three sons all of whom have a place in cricketing history. According to W. J. Hammersley, Lilywhite actually said of

Wills,' You've got no style, but can keep the bat straight and give a bowler a d—d smack when he least expects it.' Wills was pointed out to Hammersley by an unnamed professional as 'that young fellow from Rugby who plays with a 4 lb. bat and hits terrific.' *A'sian* 8 May 1869, p.588

3 The prowess of Aboriginal cricketers at Edenhope led to Tom Wills' appointment as their coach, in anticipation of a match to be held in Melbourne and duly held against the MCC on Boxing Day, 1866. The *Illustrated Melbourne Post* 24 Jan., p.6 reported: 'they have been thoroughly acquainted with the various points of the game [which] was made manifestedly evident by the manner in which they conducted themselves in the field'. Despite this and a large and generally supportive crowd of 8 000, the MCC won by nine wickets. Wills, perhaps wisely, did not go on the trip to England which was preceded by suggestions of exploitation and financial mismanagement and involved the Aboriginal cricketers in an exhausting schedule. They did play at Lord's, the opposition including an earl, a viscount, a lieutenant-colonel and a captain. D.J. Mulvaney, *Cricket Walkabout*, MUP, Melbourne, 1967

4 Charles Lawrence had come to Australia with the first English team in 1862 and stayed to become Australia's first paid cricket coach; he is considered to have effected a marked improvement in Australian cricket standards. J. Pollard, *Australian Cricket: the Game and the Players*, Sydney, 1982, p.621

5 Johnny Mullagh was the star of the Aboriginal side. He returned to Harrow which named its sports ground after him and later erected a memorial to him. D.J. Mulvaney, *ADB* v.5

6 Gideon Elliott, a fast round-arm bowler from Surrey who set the record for Victorian first class bowling, taking 9 wickets for 2 runs (in 19 overs) against Tasmania in 1858. Obit. *A'sian* 2 Aug. 1873, p.140. His brother was one of the party killed in Qld., see ch.9. J. Pollard, op. cit., p.336

7 William Josiah Hammersley, b.1826 in England and played a few times with the Surrey and Marylebone CC Elevens. Middlepace bowler and good slip-field. He came to Victoria in 1856 and played in the 2nd intercolonial match between Vic. and NSW in Jan. 1857. He played first class cricket until 1862 when he joined *Bell's Life* in Victoria and then became the sporting editor of the *Australasian* until 1882. For this weekly he wrote on cricket under the nom de plume of Longstop but he was interested in all sports and was frequently a starter at athletics meetings. M. Maria Wilson, 1 s., 2 dau. Died Fitzroy in 1886. *Sydney Mail* 18 Aug.-15 Dec., 1883; obit. *A'sian* 20 Nov. 1886, p.981.

8 William Prescott was the host of the Henry Barkly Hotel from 1861 until his license was cancelled in 1863. The Hotel was on the site of the present Riverside Inn, that is, east of Punt Road and on the north bank of the Yarra. A.Wishart, *Hotels in Richmond*, 1975, typescript, Richmond His. Soc.

·9 William Levey, S. Mellor, in G.C. Levey, *ADB* v.5. Bell's Life in
Victoria and Sporting Chronicle, a colonial copy of an English
sporting weekly, began 1857, absorbed into the *Australasian* in 1868.

10 *Bell's L.V.* 17 Sept.1859. Harrison's recollection does not entirely
agree with Bell's description of the race which reports that
Devenport agreed to concede a win to Harrison after Devenport ran
in front of Harrison and a collision 'caused both men to stop'. This
was a handicap race. Also *Herald* 12 Sept., 13 Sept.

11 According to *Bell's L.V.* 26 Nov.1859, T.W. Wills did compete in
the second heat off scratch but was defeated. Harrison ultimately
defeated the winner of this heat, White, and of the third heat, Zoe
Wills, to whom he gave starts of two yards and four yards
respectively. Of course Harrison's account could be the accurate one.

12 Alexander Allan, came from Glasgow and worked as a storekeeper
on the gold-diggings at Burnt Creek. Evidently a professional runner
as *Bell's* refers to him as 'Allan' in contrast to 'Mr Harrison'. *Bell's
L.V.* 2 June, 1860

13 Amateurs could run for trophies but not for money.

14 *Bell's L.V.* 2 June, 1860: 'Mr Harrison who on previous occasions
had run in trousers, at the suggestion of his friends, and with the
desire not to throw away a chance, was for the first time attired in
drawers. Though not a model for the Apollo Belvidere (sic) in his
upper works, he is as nearly perfection as is possible to conceive
from the waist downwards. His seeming want of bulk across
the shoulders, is, perhaps, an advantage to him in his pedestrian
exploits . . .'

15 Lambton Le Breton Mount, b. Montreal 1839, arriv. 1853, gold-
diggings, surveyor, clerk Union Bank at Ballarat, cashier Oriental
Bank Ballarat; 1864 tried to settle in NW Australia but defeated by
drought, then sheep-farmer 1867-68, ret. Victoria and went into
business, m. 1874 Frances Glynn, 2 dau. 1 s., *Men of the Time in
Australia, Victorian Series*, 2nd. edition, 1882, McCarron, Bird &
Co., Melbourne, comp. by H. M. Humphries, p. cxii.; *Bell's L.V.*
22 June, 1861.
    Joe Whiteley, b. 1836 Oldham England, arriv. Victoria May 1857.
Bell's L.V. 16 Jan. 1858

16 This information follows that provided by *Bell's L.V.* 15 June 1861;
Bell's L.V. 16 Jan. 1858

17 Son of water-colour artist George Rowe, G. Fawcett Rowe began as
a scene painter at the Cairncross Theatre in Bendigo and moved on
to become an actor adept at mimicry, and theatrical manager,
Lorgnette, 7 Sept. 1889, p.5. He became a dramatist, and did several
adaptations of Dickens' novels for the stage. E. Irvin, *Dictionary of
the Australian Theatre*, 1788-1914, Sydney, Hale & Iremonger, 1985,
pp. 249-250

18 'Slender in person, with an expressive face, a sympathetic voice,
much grace of movement, a quick intelligence, and that ready
apprehension of the dramatic aspects of a character which constitutes

such an important item in the outfit of an actress, Miss Dunn possessed unusual requisites for taking what is known as the "juvenile lead" in companies with which she was associated during her professional career . . . .' *Cylopedia of Victoria*, 1905, v.3, p.6

Julia Matthews, 1842-1874, an Australian soprano whose auburn curls and charming voice is said to have captured the heart of explorerer R. O' H. Burke; she appeared at Convent Garden. *Cyclopedia of Victoria*, op. cit., p.13; J. Gittings, *ADB* v.5

19 Joseph Thomas Holt, 1831-1942, professional actor whose forte was comedy. Took up producing in 1880; the sceneshifters became the hardest worked members in his melodramas which were noted for spectacular effects such as real animals, motor cars. D. Shoesmith, *ADB* v.4; *Age* 11 Nov. 1933, p.6; Irvin, op. cit., pp.133-134

20 George Coppin, 1819-1906, comedian, theatrical manager, politician, bank director, and philanthropist. *A'sian* 17 March 1906, p.638; S. O'Neill, *ADB* v.3, Irvin, op. cit., pp.75-76, A. Bagot, *Coppin The Great*, Melb. 1965. In 1869 he formed the Old Colonists' Association in honour of the pioneers and, with a Government grant of land in North Fitzroy, encouraged the financing of cottages for cheap rental to 'reputable elderly citizens'.

21 Walter Craig, see also pp.78,82. From Northumberland, Craig arriv. in Vic. in 1852, began a horse stud in 1856 and bought Bath's Hotel, Lydiard St., in 1857. It was soon the head-quarters of the turf world especially during meetings at Dowling Forest. Craig was a member of the Ballarat Turf Club and a steward for the VRC. The Hotel became Craig's, then the Royal. Obit., *A'sian* 20 Aug. 1870, p.233

22 Percy Jersey de Grut, 1845-1926, educ. MCEGS, and provided the Jersey de Grut Science prizes at the School. A keen yachtsman. Bank manager, English, Scottish and Australian Chartered Bank. In 1864 as a ledger-keeper at the E.S.& A Bank, cnr. Geo. & Gertrude Sts., Fitzroy, De Grut tackled 2 of 4 armed robbers, felling one with a brass candlestick. The other 3 subsequently caught: two were hanged, and two sentenced to 15 years' imprisonment. *Dr. Bromby's Journal* op. cit., 15 June 1864, p.26; *Argus* 13 April 1926, p.11

23 Melbourne gymnasiums appear to have begun in May 1860 when the Melbourne Deutscher Turn-Verein (gymnastic association) opened at 78 Russell Street. Ernst Metzger was the Turn-Verein's first instructor and for most of the next thirty years he taught gymnastics to the boys of the Melbourne and Geelong public schools. The Turn-Verein was situated in Russell Street, then Exhibition St., La Trobe St. and Fitzroy. It closed in 1914. Obit. *Scotch Collegian*, July 1904, vol.1, no.1, p.64.

Gustave von Techow moved from the Turn-Verein to set up his National Gymnasium in late 1864 on the n.w. corner of Queen and Little Lonsdale St., later sited between 1869 and 1906 next to the old East Melbourne Cricket ground which is now part of the Jolimont railway yards. Von Techow allegedly was a Prussian army officer who had fled the country after refusing to fire on a crowd. With a

sound knowledge of the German system followed by his experience at the Turn-Verein, he was sought for advice in 1865 when the Board of Education in Melbourne instituted courses in gymnastics and military drill for its teachers, hundreds of whom he trained.
R. Crawford, *Pelops*, Journal of the School of Physical Education and Leisure Studies, Phillip I.T, Bundoora, Vic., v.1, no.1, Jan. 1980

Johann Lars Jonssen, a 'robust, bearded Swede', became the proprietor of a Melbourne gymnasium on the corner of Russell St. and Flinders Lane in the 1860s and 1870s after a stint as the gymnastic instructor to the denominational school board from 1857 to 1859. He was teaching gymnastics, calisthenics, and Indian club-swinging at St. Patrick's College in the early '70s. *Age* 7 April, and subsequent letters, May to August, 1934 for all three gymnasts.

24 Additional detail on these races can be found in *Bell's L.V.* 21 Dec. 1861; *Argus* 18 Dec.1861 described it as 'a gala day'.

25 Norman McLeod, see Preface and index.

26 The Copenhagen Ground was at the Turf Hotel, Ballarat. R.J. Ross, *Pedestrianism and athleticism in England and Australia in the nineteenth century: a case study in the development of sport*, unpub. thesis, Univ. of Q., 1984, p.58

27 *Bell's L.V.* 6 Dec. 1862

28 Robert Morrison, vice-principal, 1869-1904. E.L. French under Alexander Morrison, *ADB* v.5. Played in first football match against Melbourne Grammar.
A. and E. Harrison began at Scotch College in 1865.

29 Francis John Stephen, Melbourne solicitor, who unsuccessfully sought to enter the City Council and Leg. Ass. 'As expert in his conveyancing on legs as on parchment'; Garryowen, op. cit., passim.
Samuel Ramsden, proprietor of Carlton Flour Mill who also established Melbourne's first paper mill on the present site of the APM mill. D. Rogers, *A History of Kew*, op. cit., p.78

30 Robert Farquharson Smith, an American bass who arrived in Melbourne in 1856 and was more popular with audiences than with his managers. H. Love, *The Golden Age of Australian Opera*, Sydney, 1981, p.21. He ran near Mordialloc Hotel against Stephen who won. *Bell's L.V.* 24 May 1863

31 John Gregory Harris born 9 May 1846(4?) in Collins St. *A'sian* 1 Aug. 1868; 12 March 1870 p.332. First professional run against Houlahan of Sydney on 1 Aug. 1868

32 Adolphe Nicole's choronograph, able to time athletics, was invented in 1862 but was doubtless too new to be used on Harrison's performances. Earlier timing clocks were not reliable enough to record athletic times accurately, and no allowance was made for wind assistance. Harrison's career spanned Sept. 1859 to April 1867. In that time he ran in 54 footraces of which he lost fifteen. His best time for 100 yards was 10 secs, for 440 50.5 sec., for 880 yards 2 mins. 12 secs . He won the Challenge Cup in 1865 and 1866 but was defeated by Harris in 1867. *A'sian* 4 May 1867, p.556 A chronology

of Australian pedestrianism until 1879 can be found in J.M. Heaton, *Australian Dictionary of Dates and Men of the Time*, 1879, Sydney, p.205. See also R.J. Ross op. cit.

33   Professor M.H. Irving, Vice-chancellor Melbourne University, 1887-1889, was a keen sportsman, founding amateur rowing in Victoria and an excellent rifle shot. G.C. Fendley, *ADB* v.4

W.J. Hammersley, see Preface and ch.6 note 7

R.J. Wardill, L.R. Cranfield, *ADB* v.6

34   Sir Norman Everard Brookes, 1877-1968, W.H. Frederick, *ADB* v.7. Norman Brookes, Anthony Wilding and Alfred Dunlop all played international tennis until the advent of the first World War. Brookes and Wilding in particular were a contrast — Brookes reserved, small and wiry but with an idiosyncratic approach to his tennis, Wilding outgoing, tall and well-built with a careful and orthodox tennis style. Dunlop was older than both and came from New Zealand like Wilding; he was an expert doubles player. The three played as an Australasian team in Davis Cup tennis. Brookes was President of the Lawn Tennis Association of Australia 1926-1955, and was knighted in 1939. 'Big' Bill Tilden's childhood tennis hero was Brookes, 'an idol who lived up to expectation' when Tilden played with him. Tilden greatly admired Brookes' miraculous touch, and ability to dissect and use tennis strategies skilfully. W.J. Tilden, *The Art of Lawn Tennis*, Methuen, 1920, p.170-171

Gerald Patterson, 1895-1967, outstanding at Wimbledon after World War 1, he played in 46 Davis Cup rubbers for Australia between 1919 and 1928. M. Brady (comp.), *Encyclopaedia of Lawn Tennis*, A.S. Barnes, N.Y., 1969, p. 57

Chapter 7   Football

1   A.C. Doyle, *The Wanderings of a Spiritualist*, Hodder and Stoughton, London, 1921, pp.92-93. Doyle wrote on viewing 'a cup final' in October 1920: 'There is no offside, and you get a free kick if you catch the ball. Otherwise you can run as in ordinary Rugby, though there is a law about bouncing the ball as you run, which might, as it seemed to me, be cut out without harming the game. This bouncing rule was put in by Mr. Harrison who drew up the original rules, for the chivalrous reason that he was himself the fastest runner in the Colony, and he did not wish to give himself any advantage. There is not so much manhandling in the Victorian game, and to that extent, it is less dramatic, but it is extraordinarily open and fast with none of the packed scrums which become so wearisome, and with linesmen who throw in the ball the instant it goes out. There were several points in which the players seemed better than our best — one was the accurate passsing by low drop kicking, very much quicker and faster than passing by hand. Another was the great accuracy of the place kicking and of the screw kicking when a runner would kick at right angles to his course. There were

four long quarters, and yet the men were in such condition that they were going hard at the end. They are all, I understand, semi-professionals. Altogether it was a very fine display, and the crowd was much excited. It was suggestive that the instant the last whistle blew, a troop of mounted police cantered over the ground and escorted the referees to the safety of the pavilion.

2 Thomas Wills, see ch.6 and Preface.

3 See Preface for a detailed discussion of the origin of the game.

4 This Committee was short-1ived, handing over its funds and responsibilities to the Victorian Cricket Association in 1867. *A'sian* 16 Nov. 1867

5 Scoring with points was officially introduced in 1897 but during the 1890s they were noted without being included in the score.

6 In 1898 the League was still playing 20 men a side with four followers and a rover but the Association had reduced the number to 18. *A'sian* 18 June 1898, p.1361

7 For some reminiscences and information on the very early footballers see T.P. Power (ed.), *The Footballer* 1876; *Leader* 7 May 1898, p.8; *Leader* 15 Aug. 1908, p.36; *Leader* 22 Aug. 1909; *A'sian* 20 Oct., 27 Oct., 3 Nov.1923, pp.842, 896, 951

8 Richmond paddock: 'Melbourne had its ground outside the cricket ground which some time later had a reversible grandstand which worked on a pivot, enabling it thus to be used both in connection with summer and winter games. One side of the football area was roped off along the gumtrees, the outside galvanised fence of the cricket ground being another boundary, and unfortunately players often dashed into it. For about 60 yards from the goal, the ground consisted of hard gravel, and many players carried lasting momentoes from it on their faces and arms.' Elm Grove, quoted in *Age* 16 Dec. 1933. The grandstand was built in 1877 and burnt down in 1884. It consisted of a two storey building, the ground floor being occcupied by ladies rooms, a skittle alley, a large luncheon room and two refreshment bars. The sitting accommodation was above this and reached from the lawn in front by three broad stairways. The lower storey had a series of brickwork arches, resting on bluestone foundations, and the iron roof was supported by a series of brickwork pillars. It is difficult to discern how the stand was reversible but several descriptions refer to this novel feature. Presumably the seating accommodation was the reversible part. *A'sian* 6 Sept. 1884, p. 448

9 T. O'Callaghan, 1845-1931, chief commissioner of police, career detailed *Cyclopedia of Vic.* op. cit., v.1, p.188

10 These matches against the 14th (Buckinghamshire) Regiment of Foot regiment, nicknamed 'the Rugged and Tough', under Captain Noyes were played in 1867-69. Capt. Noyes was a Rugby [style not School] player, accord. to *Argus* 8 July 1867. Lieut. C.S. Gordon, educ. Marlborough College, good cricketer, *A'sian* 16 Jan. 1869. The soldiers became legendary for their violent style of play, *A'sian* 2

October 1869, p.429. The match in which Charles Forrester 'fixed' Crosby was played on 13 June 1868, *A'sian* 20 June 1868, p. 780

11 This game was played on Albert Park on 7 Oct. 1871. The spectators heavily supporting Carlton encroached onto the game, *A'sian* 14 Oct. 1871. Harrison was persuaded to retire following 'doctor's advice', *A'sian* 27 April, 1872, p.515

12 John (Jack) Conway, 1843-1909, b. Fyansford, educ. MCEGS, rep. Vic. against Eng., Dec.1861 and played first class cricket 1862-75, capt. Carlton football team 1868-1871. Mainly remembered for his initiative, management and promotion of the Australian cricket eleven which toured Aus. & NZ in Nov. 1877 followed by the first tour of England in 1878. 'Conway was as strong as a house (sic). Forty-three in the chest, with thighs, calves, biceps and forearms to match, he was a formidable opponent to shoulder in a football field, and in the old days when he captained Carlton in their great matches with Melbourne it was something to be remembered when that grand and fearless footballer, the great old skipper of the reds, H.C.A. Harrison — lithe, sinewy, well conditioned, strong and hard as nails — sprang with panther-like bound against the Herculean captain of the blues, solid as a rock, waiting for the charge. The impact was so tremendous that the very ground seemed to tremble with the shock.' They don't write them like that any more! *A'sian* 28 Aug. 1909, p.535; *The Wisden Book of Obituaries*, Macdonald, London, 1986, p.180

13 William Lloyd Murdoch, 1854-1911, famous Australian batsman who captained Australian test teams to England in 1880, 1882, 1884 and 1890. J. Pollard, op. cit., p.731

14 Frederick Robert Spofforth,1853-1926, fast bowler known as the Demon. 'Irresistible as an avalanche', Spofforth bowled 11 overs for 2 runs and 4 wickets in the 1882 match; the Australian victory evoked the *Sporting Times'* epitaph for English cricket and 'the ashes' as the symbol of cricket supremacy between the two countries. J. Pollard, loc. cit., p.943

15 George Giffen,1859-1927, all-rounder who played in 31 Tests. J. Pollard, ibid., p.430. Scored 271 out of 562 and took 9 for 96 and 7 for 70 for S.A. against Vic. at Adelaide in Jan.1891. First Aust. bowler to take all 10 wickets in first class cricket in Aus.

16 British Association football founded in 1863. Charles Alcock, b. 1842, helped to form the Wanderers F. C. in 1864. A journalist, specialising in cricket and football, for the *Sportsman and the Field*. He was first elected to the F.A. Committee in 1866 and became hon. sec. in 1870. In 1868 initiated the *Football Annual*. D. 1907. N.L. Jackson, *Association Football*, George Newnes, London, 1897, pp.143-145

17 Henry Frederick Boyle, medium pace bowler who 'virtually invented the silly mid-on position.' J. Pollard, op. cit., p.178

18 Carlton v. Waratah at Sydney 23 & 25 June 1877 — 2 games, one under Rugby Union Rules won by Waratah 2-0, one under Victorian

Melbourne Football Club team, 1877

code won by Carlton 6-0. Melbourne v. S.A. Natives at Adelaide 13
Aug. 1877, won by Melbourne 5-0, followed by St. Kilda v.
Adelaide 18 Aug. won by St. Kilda 5-2, and St. Kilda v. S.A.
Natives on 20 Aug. won by St. Kilda 7-2. *A'sian* 13 Oct. 1877,
p.461

19 Sir William Clarke, S. Morrissey, *ADB* v.3
    Capt. Robert Robertson, President of the Carlton Football Club,
    1874-85
    Henry Hale Budd (Melbourne), 1844-1905, son of R.H. Budd (see
    ch.3 notes 17 and 30). Cricketer and solicitor. Letter, R. Biddington
    op. cit.
    Thomas P. Power (Carlton), editor of the *Footballer* 1875-1881,
    the publishing of which the Association took over in 1879. B.1845,
    educ. Scotch College.

20 Theophilus Smith Marshall, arriv. Vic. 1858, played cricket and
    football from 1863 with Royal Park; 1866-69 mined in N.Z., then
    taught in north-eastern Vic.until 1880, hon. secretary of the
    Victorian Football Association 1885-1896, former Carlton vice
    president. Quoted in G.P. Dowling, *The North Story*, Hawthorn,
    1973, Appendix 1, pp.339-340; Sutherland, op. cit., v.2, p.525; T.S.
    Marshall, *The Rise and Progress of the Australian Game of Football*,
    1896, ms.

21 Alexander McCracken, partner of R. McCracken & Co. brewers,
    president VFL 1897-1915, educ. Scotch College, Essendon Football
    Club, president Royal Agric. Soc. of Vic., and racing man. L.
    Sandercock & I. Turner, *Up Where Cazaly*, op. cit., p.179

22 First Australian Football Conference Nov. 1905, *Leader* 16 Nov.
    1905 p.18. Charles Brownlow, for years secretary of the Geelong
    Club, and after whom the famous Medal was named.

23 Inaugural meeting Australasian Football Council Nov. 1906, *Leader*
    10 Nov. 1906, p.16, *A'sian* 17 Nov. 1906, p.1168

24 9-28 Aug. 1908
25 Con. M. Hickey, 1866-1937, b. Timor West, joined Public Service
    1884, transferred Melbourne 1887 [Pensions Department]. Played
    Fitzroy 1887-1894 as 'a solid half-back', rep. Vic. 1893. Secretary
    Fitzroy Football club,1893-1910, founder member VFL, vice-
    president, chairman Permit and Umpire Committee, president
    National Football Council 1906-1909, secretary from 1911. *Football:
    Official Journal of the Victorian Football League*, 10 June & 10 Aug.
    1931 vol.1, VFL Annual Report for 1938, p.22
26 Deakin's speech, *Argus* 29 Aug. 1908, p. 17; *A'sian* 5 Sept. 1908,
    p.16
27 *Leader* (30 May 1903, p.16) reported 18 000 spectators watched this
    match which, if accurate, was a considerable crowd given the
    population of Sydney at the time. See also *A'sian* 30 May, 1903
    p.1205

Chapter 8   *The Melbourne Cricket Club*

1 Thomas Fleming Cooke, 1879- ?, Chief Librarian of Victoria, vice-
   president of Carlton Football and Cricket Clubs, and responsible for
   the Jubilee History of the Carlton Cricket Club in 1914. R. Ramsay,
   Fellows All—The Chronicles of the Bread and Cheese Club, Melb.,
   1943. Cooke's history was never completed although his minutely
   written notes are held by the MCC. The history of the Melbourne
   Cricket Club was eventually written by Keith Dunstan and entitled
   The Paddock That Grew, Cassell, Melb., 1962.
2 The original membership list of the MCC is dated 16 Nov. 1838. In
   1861 on its 21st birthday, the MCC had 154 financial members.
3 Until H.C.A. Harrison died on 2 Sept. 1929, 37 years.
4 Richard Wilson Wardill, 1835-1873, was hon. sec. to the MCC until
   1864. He played in 10 first-class matches, scored the initial century
   in first-class cricket (110 for Vic. v NSW at Melb. in 1867-1868). His
   brother, Benjamin Johnson ('Major') Wardill, 1842-1917, also
   secretary MCC 1879 when it had 572 members until he retired in
   1911 when it had 5 353 members. Took Aust. teams to Eng. in 1886,
   1899 and 1902. A first-class cricketer and fine rifle shot. J. Pollard,
   op. cit., p.1066; L.R. Cranfield, *ADB* v. 6
5 Hugh Trumble, 1867-1938. All-rounder known for being Australia's
   highest wicket-taker in Tests against England. Retired from cricket in
   1911. Medium-paced bowler, he had taken 929 wickets at an average
   of 18.44. Capt. Australian side 1901-1902, secretary MCC 1911-
   1938. J. Pollard, loc. cit., p.1006
6 Sir Leo Finn Bernard Cussen, 1859-1933, barrister and solicitor who
   specialised in engineering cases as he had first trained as a civil
   engineer, Supreme Court judge, 1906, president MCC 1907-1933. K.
   Dunstan, op. cit., p.133

7 The stand was built in 1908 and demolished in 1936. The Victorian Football League Headquarters were opened in 'Harrison House' on the corner of Spring St. and Flinders Lane on 19 March 1930 until the League moved to a new building in Jolimont in 1972. It moved again in 1982.

Chapter 9   Disastrous Events

1 Bendemeer, see chap.2 note 4
2 Dalmahoy Campbell, 1811-1867, b. Isle of Skye, arriv. NSW 1821, station near Wellington 1833, overlanded Adelaide 1838, general manager Boyd's Royal Bank stations, Melb. 1845 stock and station agent with Will. Morris Harper. Sutherland, op. cit. v.2, p.466. 'A noted personality in Melbourne life in the gold times and quite a social leader in the new colony. Strong both physically and mentally, and of course a Scot, he resided at Essendon upon a property of some 100 acres between Pascoe Vale Road and the Moonee Ponds Creek, about a quarter of a mile north of the Moonee Valley Racecourse', H.H. Peck, op. cit., p. 15. 'In his day he was a City Councillor, an expert in judging the qualities of fat cattle, and testing samples of whisky . . . ', Garryowen, op. cit., p.748
3 Separation meeting — for Capt. Harrison's participation, see Preface.
4 Emerald Hill = South Melbourne
5 Horatio Spencer Wills, see Preface and ch.3 note 8
6 H.C.A. Harrison's original footnote: 'Mount Ararat was on part of the run at Lexington, and was so named by my uncle, because it was the first place on which he settled after his long journey from New South Wales, not because of its resemblance to the original (on which the "Ark" of Scripture rested), as I have seen it stated somewhere.' L.L. Banfield writes that on a circuit dinner, 'Sir Redmond Barry asked about the settlement of the district and was informed that Horatio Spencer Wills had named Mount Ararat, because like the ark he rested there after his patriarchal journey with his family, his flocks and herds from New South Wales in 1840. His Honour then inquired if it had occurred to anyone to design a coat of arms for the rapidly growing town, and he suggested that it should incorporate the ark, the dove and the olive branch. The idea won immediate approval, and Sir Redmond was asked for a motto. Without a moment's hesitation he gave it: "Gaudium adfero" — 'I Bring Joy.' *Like the Ark, The Story of Ararat*, Cheshire, Melbourne, 1956, p.186
7 Horatio Wills sold Lexington and Mokepille, some 120 000 acres on 23 Dec. 1852. Belle Vue was built during 1853 on land originally bought by his brother T. Wills [now part of Leopold]. Point Henry is a peninsula about 3 km. long and a 0.8 km. broad which separated the Outer Geelong Harbour from the Inner. Belle Vue was burnt down in March 1979. *Investigator* [Geelong His. Soc. mag.], pp.86-88

8 For discussion of the Cullinlaringo deaths, see the Preface. Early in
   1860 Horace Wills met John MacDonald who told him 'that his
   brother Peter, who had gone with the diggers during the great gold
   rush, . . . had been out exploring far back from Keppel Bay and had
   discovered some fine country referring particularly to one beautiful
   place as he stated called "Cullinlaringo", a name given to it by his
   brother and which means "Cullin" — "sought", "laringo" — "and
   found"'. Letter, Horace Wills to his sons in Germany, from Belle
   Vue, Geelong, 12 July 1860, written after his visit to Cullinlaringo
   and explaining his decision to see it.

Chapter 10   In Conclusion

1 Colden Harrison's wife Emily was the sister of his good friend and
   cousin Tom and daughter of Horatio Spencer Wills, Harrison's
   mother's step-brother. The marriage took place at Point Henry three
   years after the Cullinlaringo deaths, at the schoolhouse church the
   Wills attended. The Wills family still retained Belle Vue there.
   Geelong Advertiser, 15 Nov. 1864. The children of the marriage are
   discussed on the last pages of Harrison's autobiography. Tom Wills
   wrote from Belle Vue to Cedric Wills on 14 Nov.1864: 'On
   Thursday last, the 10th, Emmy and Colden were married. There was
   a grand arch made at the last gate down the lane for them to pass
   under. The church was covered in sentiments [?] made out of
   flowers. The ladies of the Point presented Emmy upon her arrival at
   the church with a silver bouquet holder containing artificial flowers.
   George Smith ate so much of the lunch that he got tremendously
   sick. Uncle Thomas was present and lots of others . . .' , D. Cooke,
   private collection.
2 Norman MacLeod, see also Preface and index.
3 Richard Davies Ireland, 1816-1877, J.B. Woods, *ADB* v.4. Arriv.
   Vic. 1852 and defended Eureka Stockade men. Leg. Ass. 1857-1867,
   twice Attorney-General and once Solicitor-general. Described as
   'thick, sound, robust, round-headed as he is, the glance of his eyes is
   irresistible . . . His whole head and strong-built frame tell that he is
   ready to settle at once with anybody, either with the tongue or with
   the fist. His eloquence savours pretty strongly of Daniel O'Connell
   and is flavoured with colonial pepper; hence Mr. Ireland will always
   exercise a potent spell over a jury.' Raffaello Carboni, *The Eureka
   Stockade*, 1855, MUP, 1963, p.148
4 Jennie-bear = koala. Jenny — used as a prefix to denote a female
   animal, as in jenny-ass, and especially in names of birds.
5 The Pound Bend is upstream from Eltham at Warrandyte; it was an
   Aboriginal Reserve in 1841. By building a tunnel 639 feet (195 m.)
   long, 13 feet (4 m.) wide and 14 feet (4.3 m.) deep across the almost
   circular river bend and thereby short-circuiting some 5 km. of river,
   the Evelyn Tunnel Goldmining Company had hoped to expose the

river bed into which a gold reef ran. In 1870 when the diversion was to go ahead, the river refused to co-operate and even when the water was induced to use the tunnel, the remaining mud thwarted further attempts to recover any substantial amounts of gold. The tunnel was the ambitious scheme of David Mitchell, the father of Dame Nellie Melba. G. Keogh, *History of Doncaster and Templestowe*, City of Doncaster and Templestowe, 1975, p.38

6 Isaac Le Pipre Barrow Jnr, educ. MCEGS, took party to the source of the Yarra in 1873, surveyor. Or possibly father of same name who worked in the Customs Dept. Letter, C. Ramsay-Sharpe, 26 June 1986.

7 Yering was originally a cattle station taken up in 1837 by Wm. Ryrie who planted a vineyard of one acre, the first in the colony. Donald Ryrie wrote: 'By searching among old books and papers, I find my brothers William and James arrived at Yering with cattle on the 24 Sept. 1837, the latter remaining there. In May 1838 William left Arnprior [their father's residence] on the Shoalhaven River NSW . . . and we reached Yering on the 6 of August. We bought from Arnprior cuttings and rooted vines of sweetwater and black cluster. The first wine was made from black cluster, and it was capital, sound and well-flavoured. Under date 19 July 1845 this wine was bottled. In August of the same year 296 additional vine cuttings were planted out. In 1850 we left Yering for View-hill on the opposite of the side of the Yarra, having given possession to the purchasers, Messrs De Castella and De Meuron.' Quoted in a letter from James Dawson, *A'sian* 6 August, 1870, p.185. In 1856 Paul de Castella substantially extended the Yering vineyard, importing in 1859 10 000 vines, half of which were Sauvignon; they proved to be the making of the vineyard's reputation. Sutherland, op cit., v.2, p.407

8 Philip Russell, arr. Port Phillip, 1843, M.L.C., 1869-1875, held Carngham from 1843 to 1867, P.L. Bown, *ADB* v.6

9 34 Walpole Street, house no longer in existence.

10 Saltwater River = Maribyrnong River

11 From 1879 Joseph Cowen Syme was a junior partner in the *Age* until he quarrelled with the senior partner, his uncle David, and the partnership was dissolved in 1891. C.E. Sayers, *David Syme, A Life*, Cheshire, Melbourne, 1965, pp.130-137

12 Described as 'a fanlike staircase whose terraces covered more than 7 acres and glittered in the most delicate shades of pink, white and turquoise. The formation was the work of a geyser above it, which for untold years had played upon the mountain slope, creating rippling falls, and then with its volcanic touch, transforming these into symmetrical terraces which required only the glint of sunshine or moonlight to bring out the unique tracery and colour of their beauty.' The terraces were destroyed by the volcanic eruption of Mt. Tarawera in 1886. A.H. McLintock (ed.), *An Encyclopaedia of New Zealand*, v.1, Wellington, 1966, p. 476

13 Sir George Grey, lieutenant-governor and then governor of N.Z. 1845-1853, 1861 — 1868, ibid., pp.877-880
14 Germantown = Holbrook
15 Antill and Jarvisfield, see ch.1 note 1
16 Ranjitsinhji, Kumar Shri; 1872-1923, Indian born (later the Maharajah of Nawanagar) played for England. The match was actually in Feb./March 1897 and "Ranji" scored a century. P. Bailey, P. Thorn and P. Wynne-Thomas, *Who's Who of Cricketers*, Newnes, Middlesex, 1984, p.837

THE LAWS OF THE MELBOURNE FOOTBALL CLUB.
AS PLAYED IN RICHMOND PADDOCK, 1859.

1. The distance between the Goals and the Goal Posts shall be decided by the Captains of the sides playing.
2. The Captains on each side shall toss for choice of Goal; the side losing the toss has the kick off from the centre point between the Goals.
3. A Goal must be kicked fairly between the posts without touching either of them, or any portion of the person of one of the opposite side. In case of the Ball being forced between the Goal Posts in a scrimmage, Goal shall be awarded.
4. The game shall be played within a space of not more than 200 yards wide, the same to be measured equally on each side of a line drawn through the centres of the two Goals; and two posts to be called the "kick-off" posts shall be erected at a distance of 20 yards on each side of the Goal Posts at both ends, and in a straight line with them.
5. In case the ball is kicked behind Goal, any one of the side behind whose goal it is kicked may bring it 20 yards in front of any portion of the space between the "kick-off" posts, and shall kick it as nearly as possible in a line with the opposite Goal.
6. Any player catching the ball *directly* from the foot may call "mark." He then has a free kick; no player from the opposite side being allowed to come *inside* the spot marked.
7. Tripping, holding, and hacking are strictly prohibited. Pushing with the hands or body is allowed when any player is in rapid motion, or in possession of the Ball, except in the case provided for in Rule 6.
8. The Ball may at any time be taken in hand, but not carried further than is necessary for a kick.
9. When a Ball goes out of bounds (the same being indicated by a row of posts) it shall be brought back to the point where it crossed the boundary-line, and thrown in at right angles with that line.
10. The Ball, while *in play*, may under no circumstances be thrown.
12. In case of deliberate infringement of any of the above Rules by either side, the Captain of the opposite side may claim that any one of his party may have a free kick from the place where the breach of Rule was made; the two Captains in all cases, save where Umpires are appointed, to be the sole Judges of Infringements.

Published in the Australian Cricketer's Guide for 1858-1859.
State Library of NSW

Index